The World of Science

The World of Science

p

This is a Parragon book
This edition published in 2003

Parragon
Queen Street House
4 Queen Street
Bath BA1 1HE, UK

Copyright © Parragon 1999

This edition by Design Principals, Warminster

ISBN 1-40541-633-5

Printed in China

Contents

Section 7
Science Projects 205

Plants and animals

Chemistry

Air and flight

Water

Sound

Light

Energy and forces

Electricity and magnetism

Introduction

WHEN DID SCIENCE BEGIN? Perhaps when early humans, more than a million years ago, picked up rocks and chipped them to form stone tools. Someone tried several different kinds of rocks. She or he noticed that a particular type of rock produced a cleaner, sharper edge than the other types. This was one of the first trial-and-error series of experiments. Gradually other kinds of rocks were tested and found to be even better. Materials scientists do the same today, formulating the latest metal alloys and tailor-made composites for special purposes.

Stone-age tools more than 10,000 years old show excellent crafting skills and an early knowledge of materials science.

Scientific method

Science is supposed to progress in a sensible, rational, step-by-step way known as the scientific method. We have an idea, a theory or an hypothesis. This must be in such a form that it makes predictions. We design experiments and tests to check the predictions. During the experiments we study, observe, measure and assess. We examine and analyze the results. If they fit the predictions, they support the original theory. After double- and triple-checking the experiments and results, we can move to the next stage.

A map showing the revolutionary ideas of Nicolaus Copernicus from the 1540s, that the Earth and other planets go around the Sun.

In this way we gradually build up a vast and interlinked body of knowledge and understanding, that stretches from the tiniest particles of matter, to the entire contents of the Universe.

Real science

The reality, however, is rather different. Science is not always logical and sensible, moving forwards in small, tried-and-tested stages. People have sudden insights and flashes of inspiration that can cause a scientific revolution. For example, Isaac Newton supposedly had his ideas about gravity when an apple fell nearby, perhaps even on his head. This simple event led to his theory of universal gravitation. It was so important that it formed a new foundation for the physical sciences for more than three and a half centuries. Then Albert Einstein brought yet another huge advance in the early 20th century, with his theory of special relativity, followed by his theory of general relativity.

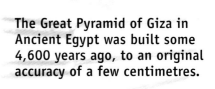

The Great Pyramid of Giza in Ancient Egypt was built some 4,600 years ago, to an original accuracy of a few centimetres.

Fields of science

There are many branches or fields of science. In general, they fall into three broad groups. These are physical, chemical and biological.

The physical sciences deal with matter, energy, movement and the structure of the Universe. It is also concerned with machinery and technology.

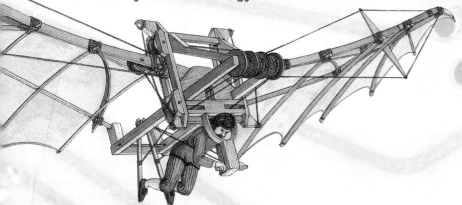

Leonardo da Vinci's idea for a flying machine (from about 1500) was never built, and in any case, it would have been far too heavy to fly. But it showed great scientific foresight and ambition.

The Industrial Revolution, which began in Britain in the mid 18th century, harnessed the power of machines for mining, processing, factory production and transport. Steam-powered railway locomotives began to puff across the countryside.

The brilliance of Albert Einstein (1879-1955) produced enormous changes in science. His ideas about gravity, time, space, particles and forces were fitted into the new framework of relativity theory.

Chemical sciences include the study of substances or chemicals (the chemical elements), what they are made of, and how they differ from each other in their many properties and features. Another very important area of chemistry is how substances or chemicals change when they combine or react together.

The biological sciences cover life and living things in all their forms, from microscopic germs to giant redwood trees and blue whales. It studies how they survive, move about, feed, breed and interact with their surroundings or environment.

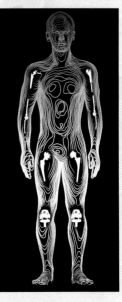

Biology, technology, materials science, engineering and design meet in the production of titanium-and-plastic body parts such as artificial joints.

Combined sciences

Traditionally, these three main branches of science were very separate. Today, they are usually found together. To make an artificial part or prosthesis for the body, such as a joint, requires all three branches to come together. The joint must withstand physical stresses and strains, chemical exposure to body salts and fluids, and biological contact with the body's microscopic cells.

The sections in this book reflect the main branches of science, but also highlight the links and connections between them. The pages begin with the basic building-blocks of matter, atoms, and the forces that hold them together. They move to an ever-larger scale, ending with a look at the whole Universe and the nature of space and time.

Why do science?

Why is science carried out at all? To increase knowledge and understanding – although this

The re-useable space shuttles have launched hundreds of satellites and carried out thousands of experiments in the "zero gravity" of space.

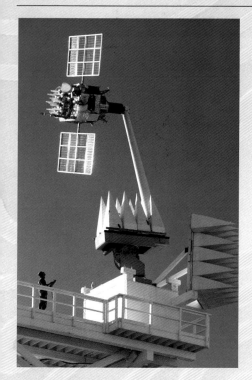

The world shrinks daily as information transfer becomes faster and easier, using the science of telecommunications.

may not seem to be especially relevant to daily life. However science has brought enormous changes to our modern world. We have hi-tech gadgets such as CD players, mobile phones, cars, planes, computers and the Internet. Most people live longer, more comfortable, healthier lives than ever before.

Yet our planet is at greater risk than ever before. Pollution darkens the skies and soaks into the soil and water. Our natural resources such as petroleum (crude oil) have almost been used up. Famine and disease are widespread in some regions. Playing with nature's genes could unleash a new breed of medicine-resistant super-bugs. However, these are not the results of science itself, but of the way that science is used and applied.

In 1986 the nuclear reactor at Chernobyl, in the Ukraine, exploded and spread harmful radioactivity over millions of square kilometres.

Wealth and comfort in the industrialized world relies on land and resources which are often sited in less developed regions. Also the natural world suffers great damage.

Global warming, acid rain and ozone loss are just three of the major threats to our world environment.

1

Matter and Chemicals

All substances, matter and chemicals – from a pin-head to a star – are made of atoms. The atoms join or bond together to form molecules. Atoms and molecules can separate and then join together in new combinations. This is chemical change. Matter exists in three main states: solids, liquids and gases.

Atoms

BIG THINGS ARE MADE of smaller things. For example, a log cabin is made of dozens of logs. A log is made of millions of tiny fibres of wood. A fibre of wood is made of even tinier fibres of a substance called lignin. And lignin is made from groups of very tiny things indeed – atoms. Take apart any object, from a skyscraper to a pinhead, and you eventually find that it is made of these tiny particles, called atoms, which are far too small for us to see. All objects, items, materials, substances, chemicals and other forms of matter consist of atoms.

One kind of atom

Another kind of atom

Join or bond between atoms

Different kinds of atoms

Atoms are not all the same. There are about 112 different kinds. These different kinds of atoms are known as the chemical elements, and they are shown on the following pages. The names of some chemical elements are familiar, such as aluminium, iron and calcium. The names of other chemical elements are less well known, such as xenon, yttrium and zirconium. The atoms of the different chemical elements are all different from each other. So aluminium atoms are different from iron atoms, both kinds are different from calcium atoms, and so on. But all the atoms of one chemical element are exactly the same as each other. A lump of pure iron contains billions of iron atoms. Every one is identical to all the others. And they are all identical to every other iron atom, anywhere in the Universe.

Science discovery

Since ancient times, some scientific thinkers suspected that everything consisted of tiny particles. Democritus (about 470-400 BC) of Ancient Greece suggested the world and everything in it were made of particles, which were so small that they were invisible to our eyes. He believed that these particles were unimaginably hard, lasted for ever, and were always moving about. Parts of the modern theory of atoms are similar to the ideas of Democritus.

Atoms joined together
Sometimes atoms are on their own. At other times they join together with other atoms, to form groups of linked atoms called molecules. These are often shown as "ball-and-stick" diagrams or models.

Even elephants are atoms
Every piece and scrap of substance or matter is made of atoms. That includes the ground beneath your feet, trees, cars, houses, computers, compact discs, water and the invisible air all around us. All living things are atoms too, including birds, flowers, microscopic germs, huge trees, tigers, elephants – and your own body.

See also: Inside atoms page 18, Elements page 20, Molecules page 22

Science discovery

John Dalton (1766-1844) was a science teacher who also kept detailed records of the weather. He suggested that every chemical element consisted of tiny particles, atoms, which were identical to each other but different from the atoms of other chemical elements. He also gave names and symbols to about 30 chemical elements. However he thought that atoms were solid spheres, like metal balls, which could never be destroyed. Also, some substances which Dalton believed were elements are now known to be combinations of elements, or compounds.

Dalton's element symbols

- ⊙ Hydrogen
- ◑ Azote
- ◍ Carbon
- ○ Oxygen
- ⊘ Phosphorus
- ⊕ Sulphur
- ⟁ Mangesia
- ≋ Lime
- ⦀ Soda
- ⦀ Potash
- ⊕ Strontian
- ✿ Barytes
- Ⓘ Iron
- Ⓩ Zinc
- Ⓒ Copper
- Ⓛ Lead
- Ⓢ Silver
- ⊛ Gold
- Ⓟ Platina
- ⊛ Mercury

Atoms across the Universe

Everything in our world, including planet Earth itself, is made of atoms. And everything outside the world is made of atoms too. Space is not perfectly empty. It has bits and pieces of gases and dust floating about in it, and these are made of atoms. Objects in space, such as planets, stars and comets, are made of atoms. So are our own satellites, rockets and spacecraft. Most of the matter or substance in the Universe is inside stars, like our Sun. The main chemical element in stars is called hydrogen. So hydrogen is the commonest substance in the whole Universe. For every 100 atoms in the Universe, 93 are hydrogen atoms and only seven are of other elements.

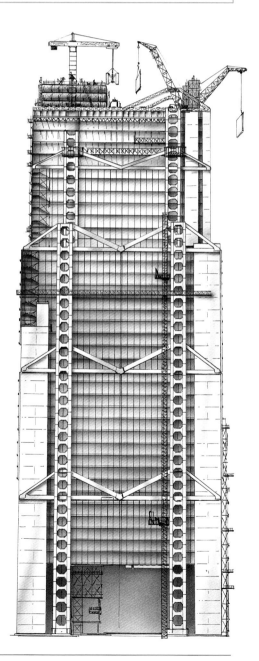

HOW BIG ARE ATOMS?

- ▶ Very, very small! An average atom is 0.000,000,001 metre (one millionth of 1 millimetre) across.

- ▶ Blow up a balloon. It seems to contain nothing and weigh almost nothing. But it contains about 100 billion billion (100,000,000,000,000,000,000) atoms of the gases which make up air.

- ▶ A tiny grain of sand contains so many atoms, that if each one were the size of a pinhead, the grain would be about 2 kilometres across.

Building blocks

A skyscraper is made of many smaller building units fixed together, such as steel girders, beams and panels. A house is made of smaller building units, such as bricks. Atoms are similar, but far smaller. They are "building blocks of matter".

Inside atoms

ATOMS ARE THE MAIN BUILDING BLOCKS of matter. The smallest particle of a chemical element which still has all the features and properties of that particular element, is one atom. But atoms are not the tiniest particles of all. They are made of even smaller pieces, called sub-atomic particles. There are three main kinds of sub-atomic particles. These are protons, neutrons and electrons. In every atom of every chemical element, each kind of particle is the same. So the electrons in an atom of iron are exactly the same as the electrons in an atom of sulphur. The protons in carbon atoms are the same as the protons in aluminium atoms. And the neutrons in an atom of titanium are the same as the neutrons in an atom of oxygen. What makes these chemical elements different is how many sub-atomic particles they have in each atom.

Energy in atoms
Sub-atomic particles in atoms can be split or broken apart from each other. This releases massive amounts of energy in a split second – the atomic bomb.

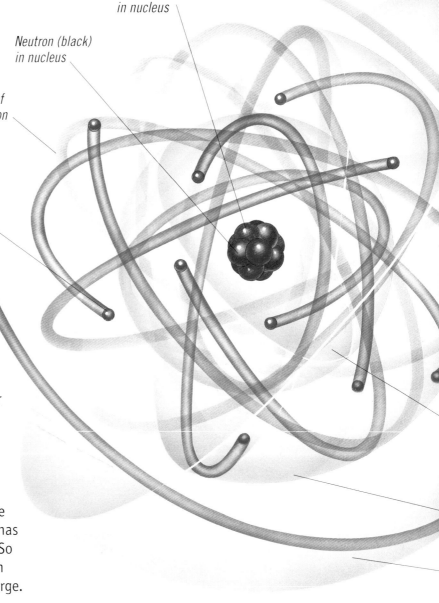

Proton (red)
in nucleus

Neutron (black)
in nucleus

Path of
electron

Electron in middle shell

Electron in outer shell

An atom

An atom has a central part called the nucleus. This contains the sub-atomic particles named protons and neutrons. Each proton has electrical charge, almost like a tiny electrical battery, but not both positive and negative – only positive. Neutrons are the same size as protons but they have no electrical charge. Electrons are much smaller than protons and neutrons. They are not in the nucleus. They whizz around it, in layers known as shells. Electrons in the outer shells have more energy than those in the inner shells. Each electron also has an electric charge, which is negative – opposite to the charge of a proton. Usually an atom has the same number of protons and electrons. So the positives and negatives are equal, which means the whole atom has no electrical charge.

See also: Atoms page 14, Elements page 18, Electricity page 78

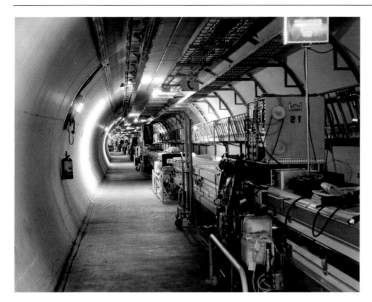

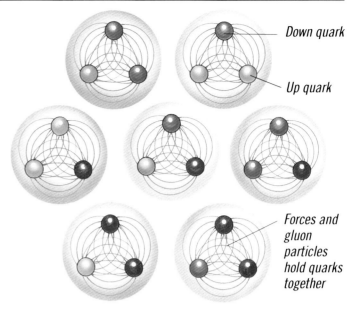

Down quark

Up quark

Forces and gluon particles hold quarks together

How do we know?

Studying the smallest particles inside atoms requires the most massive scientific equipment in the world. These "atom-smashers", known as accelerators, are housed in immense buildings or underground tunnels many kilometres long. The accelerator gives huge amounts of energy to atoms and their particles, by making them travel incredibly fast. Then the atoms and particles are made to collide or hit each other, to study the pieces that result.

The smallest particles?

There are many other sub-atomic particles besides protons, neutrons and electrons. They include muons, gluons, gravitons and dozens of others. And even particles such as protons and neutrons are not the smallest of all. They are made of even tinier pieces – quarks. There are six kinds of quarks, with the odd names of up, down, strange, charmed, bottom and top. For example, a proton is two up quarks and one down quark. Quarks, along with a group of particles called leptons, which includes electrons, are probably the smallest pieces of matter. They are fundamental or elementary particles.

Science discovery

During the 18th century, scientists developed their theories about atoms as the smallest particles, which lasted for ever and could not be split up. But more research in the late 19th century led to the idea that atoms were not the smallest particles. By 1911, Ernest Rutherford had carried out experiments in Manchester, England, which showed that atoms had even smaller particles inside. He suggested that there was a small, heavy nucleus at the centre of an atom, with much smaller, lighter particles called electrons orbiting around it (shown on the right). The electrons could circle at random around the nucleus. In 1913, Neils Bohr improved this idea by suggesting that electrons had to stay at certain distances from the nucleus, in layers called shells (shown on the left). This is the idea still accepted today.

Ernest Rutherford (1871-1937)

Nucleus

Electron

Rutherford's "Solar System" version of the atom

Inner electron shell

Middle electron shell

Outer electron shell

Elements

AN ELEMENT IS A SUBSTANCE OR CHEMICAL whose atoms are all exactly the same, with the same number of electrons, protons and neutrons. There are about 112 different elements, as shown in the chart on the following pages. Each element has certain physical properties, such as its colour, shininess and hardness. Other physical properties include the temperature at which it melts (turns from a solid to a liquid) or boils (changes from a liquid to a gas), density (mass in a certain volume), and how well it carries or conducts electricity. An element also has chemical properties. These include the way that it joins or combines with atoms of other elements, in chemical reactions, and how easily it undergoes such reactions.

Different forms of an element – ①
Some elements can exist in different physical forms. One is carbon. If its atoms are squashed near together, it forms one of the hardest substances in the world – diamond. But it also forms other substances (see right).

A useful element

Silicon is an element. Pure silicon is a dark, slightly shiny, brown-grey substance. It has the curious property of carrying or conducting electricity – but not particularly well. So it is called a semiconductor. Silicon can be made as crystals which are cut or sliced into thin layers, wafers, smaller than a fingernail. These are known as silicon chips. Then microscopic electrical devices are formed on the chips, using various methods such as acid chemicals or high-powered rays. The results are microchips (integrated circuits). These are found in hundreds of kinds of machines and devices, from computers and music systems, to planes and satellites.

Valuable elements
Silver is a beautiful, lustrous (semi-shiny) element. It is easy to shape and polish, and resists corrosion. These features have made it valuable since ancient times, for jewellery, decorative objects such as silver plates, and coins. It is also an excellent carrier of electricity and is used in electrical devices.

Saving elements
Aluminium is an element which is a shiny, silvery metal. It is familiar as the metal which makes drinks cans. Aluminium is found naturally in the Earth's rocks. Extracting and purifying it cost huge amounts of time, energy and money. Using aluminium several times, by recycling cans, saves more than nine-tenths of this energy and money.

See also: Crystals page 30, Metals page 40, Computers page 106

Science discovery

Antoine Lavoisier (1743-1794) was a map-maker and invented a new method of lighting streets with gas lamps. He also took over a tax-collecting business, which gave him money to pursue his main interest, chemistry. Lavoisier carried out hundreds of careful and accurate experiments on different elements and other substances. He devised the idea of conservation of matter, which means chemicals and substances are not usually created or destroyed, but changed into different forms. In 1787 he introduced the system of giving each chemical element its own symbol, as shown on the next pages.

Elements at high speed

Very fast-moving jet planes, such as the Lockheed SR-71 Blackbird, get incredibly hot as they push their way through the air. So their outer coverings contain elements which can withstand great heat. One of these is titanium, mixed with iron and other elements to form heat-resisting steel.

Different forms of an element – ② and ③

If atoms of carbon are spaced farther apart than in a diamond (see left), and linked more loosely, they form a very different substance. They make the soft, black lumps that we call coal. A third form of the element carbon is the soft, black, slippery powder known as graphite.

Yellow element

Pure sulphur forms brittle yellow lumps, sulphur crystals, or a yellow powder known as amorphous ("shapeless") sulphur. These pure forms of sulphur are found around volcanoes and hot springs. Sulphur is extremely important in the chemical industry, used to make matches, fireworks, paper, pesticides and medicines.

Glowing elements

The bright flashing lights of advertising signs are sometimes called "neon lights". Indeed, the element neon is used in some of them. When high-power electricity is passed through a tube containing neon gas, this glows fiery red. Similar gases give off other colours. Argon in a tube glows deep blue-green, while krypton glows brilliant green. These elements all belong to a group called the inert or noble gases. These gases are found in tiny quantities in normal air. They have no colour, taste or smell in their natural form. They are called inert (inactive) because their atoms hardly ever join or link with the atoms of other elements.

Table of elements

One of the basic sets of information in all of science is the list of pure chemical substances, called elements. The list can be drawn as a large chart known as the periodic table of chemical elements. There are 112 elements so far discovered. Of these, about 90 are natural, occurring on and in planet Earth, or among the planets and stars in space. The other elements have been made, or synthesised, in chemistry and physics laboratories. The periodic table groups the elements according to their similarities and differences. These are physical, both in the way their atoms are made up of smaller particles, and in the physical features of an element, such as its weight and density. They are also chemical, in the way that an element reacts or combines chemically with others.

Element names

Each element has its own name, such as boron, lithium or zinc. Some names are taken from ancient Latin, Greek or other languages. Other elements are named after their discoverers or generally famous scientists. Arsenic, a very poisonous element, gets its name from *arsenikon*, the old Greek name for the yellow mineral "orpiment", which is rich in arsenic. The chemical symbol for each element is one or two letters, usually taken from a shortened version of the full name. It is an international symbol, recognised by scientists all over the world. The atomic number of an element (see opposite) is the number of the particles called protons inside the nucleus of each atom of the element. This number of protons is the same as the number of electrons whizzing around the nucleus of the atom.

Science discovery
The periodic table of chemical elements was proposed in 1868 by Dmitri Medeleev (also spelled Mendelayef) (1834-1907). He wrote down the features and properties of each element on a card, then tried arranging the cards in different patterns. The best arrangement showed how the elements in each column (downwards) have very similar properties.

The lightest element
Hydrogen is the lightest of all the elements, because its atoms have the simplest structure, with fewest sub-atomic particles – only two per atom. The nucleus of a hydrogen atom is just one proton. The rest of the atom is just one electron, going around the proton.

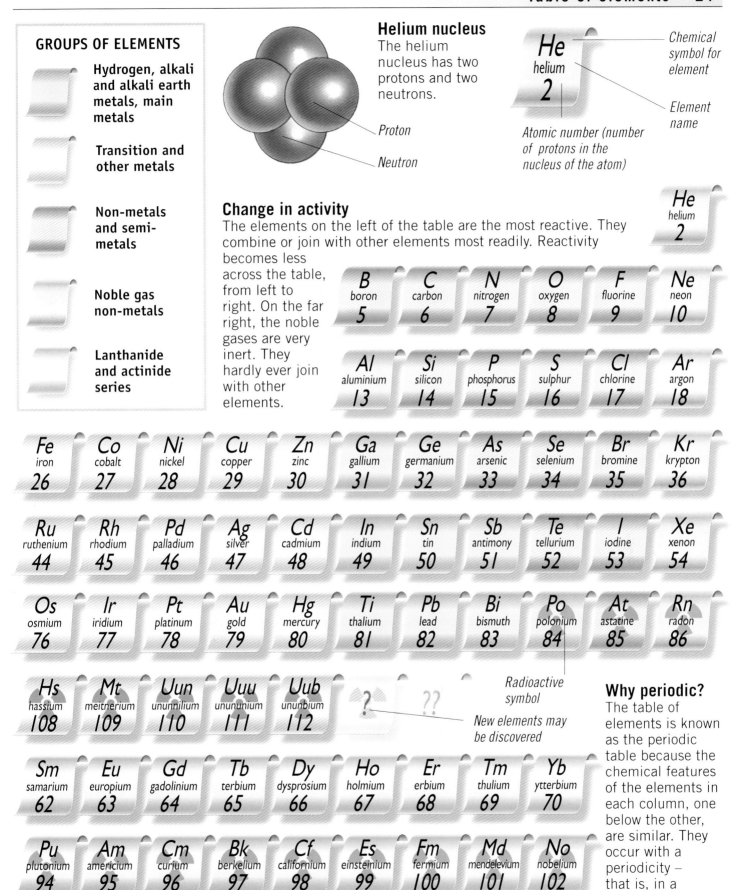

GROUPS OF ELEMENTS

Hydrogen, alkali and alkali earth metals, main metals

Transition and other metals

Non-metals and semi-metals

Noble gas non-metals

Lanthanide and actinide series

Helium nucleus
The helium nucleus has two protons and two neutrons.

Proton

Neutron

He
helium
2

Chemical symbol for element

Element name

Atomic number (number of protons in the nucleus of the atom)

Change in activity
The elements on the left of the table are the most reactive. They combine or join with other elements most readily. Reactivity becomes less across the table, from left to right. On the far right, the noble gases are very inert. They hardly ever join with other elements.

He
helium
2

B boron 5	C carbon 6	N nitrogen 7	O oxygen 8	F fluorine 9	Ne neon 10
Al aluminium 13	Si silicon 14	P phosphorus 15	S sulphur 16	Cl chlorine 17	Ar argon 18

Fe iron 26	Co cobalt 27	Ni nickel 28	Cu copper 29	Zn zinc 30	Ga gallium 31	Ge germanium 32	As arsenic 33	Se selenium 34	Br bromine 35	Kr krypton 36
Ru ruthenium 44	Rh rhodium 45	Pd palladium 46	Ag silver 47	Cd cadmium 48	In indium 49	Sn tin 50	Sb antimony 51	Te tellurium 52	I iodine 53	Xe xenon 54
Os osmium 76	Ir iridium 77	Pt platinum 78	Au gold 79	Hg mercury 80	Ti thalium 81	Pb lead 82	Bi bismuth 83	Po polonium 84	At astatine 85	Rn radon 86
Hs hassium 108	Mt meitnerium 109	Uun ununnilium 110	Uuu unununium 111	Uub ununbium 112						

?

??

Radioactive symbol

New elements may be discovered

Sm samarium 62	Eu europium 63	Gd gadolinium 64	Tb terbium 65	Dy dysprosium 66	Ho holmium 67	Er erbium 68	Tm thulium 69	Yb ytterbium 70
Pu plutonium 94	Am americium 95	Cm curium 96	Bk berkelium 97	Cf californium 98	Es einsteinium 99	Fm fermium 100	Md mendelevium 101	No nobelium 102

Why periodic?
The table of elements is known as the periodic table because the chemical features of the elements in each column, one below the other, are similar. They occur with a periodicity – that is, in a regular cycle.

Molecules

ATOMS ARE THE MAIN BUILDING BLOCKS of matter. But usually, they do not exist alone, each atom on its own. Atoms are generally joined to other atoms. When one atom joins with, or bonds to, one or more other atoms, the result is a molecule. Some molecules are made of atoms of the same element joined to each other. For example, the oxygen in the air around us is not in the form of oxygen atoms, each drifting about on its own. It is in the form of oxygen molecules. Each oxygen molecule is two oxygen atoms joined together, written as O_2. Molecules made of the atoms of different elements joined together are known as compounds.

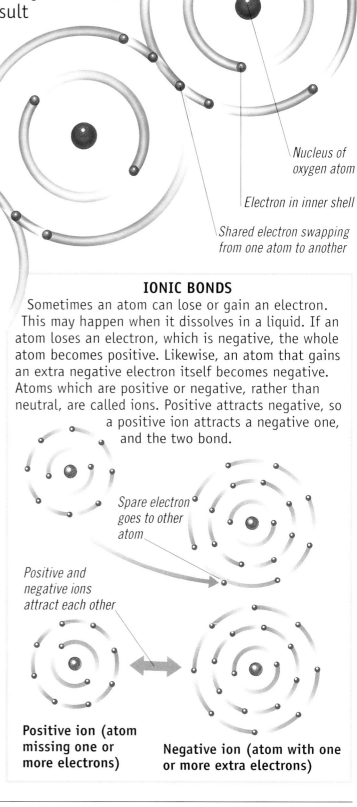

Nucleus of oxygen atom

Electron in inner shell

Shared electron swapping from one atom to another

Electron in outer shell

Ozone
When three atoms of the element oxygen covalently bond to each other, the result is a tri-atomic molecule of oxygen, written as O_3. This is better known as ozone.

Bonds between atoms
There are several ways that atoms can join together, or bond. One is the ionic bond, on the right. Another is the covalent bond, above, when atoms share one or more electrons. This happens because the various layers or shells of electrons in an atom can accommodate, or hold, up to a certain amount of electrons. The innermost shell holds up to two, and the next shell holds up to eight. If the outermost shell is not quite full of electrons, it can sometimes "borrow" an electron from another atom, and hold onto it part of the time. Likewise, if the outer shell of an atom has just one electron, it can donate this spare electron to another atom, but still hold onto it for part of the time. Two atoms which share one or more electrons like this have a covalent link or bond.

IONIC BONDS
Sometimes an atom can lose or gain an electron. This may happen when it dissolves in a liquid. If an atom loses an electron, which is negative, the whole atom becomes positive. Likewise, an atom that gains an extra negative electron itself becomes negative. Atoms which are positive or negative, rather than neutral, are called ions. Positive attracts negative, so a positive ion attracts a negative one, and the two bond.

Spare electron goes to other atom

Positive and negative ions attract each other

Positive ion (atom missing one or more electrons)

Negative ion (atom with one or more extra electrons)

See also: Inside atoms page 16, Dissolving page 34, Crystals page 30

Changing molecules

Burning is a chemical change. It happens when molecules break apart to release their atoms. Then the atoms join or bond together in new combinations. As a result, substances or chemicals alter into different substances or chemicals. When something burns, its molecules combine with molecules of oxygen, and give off light and heat.

Common molecules

These are tiny grains of common or table salt, seen under the microscope. (The colours are added by computer.) Each grain contains billions of molecules. Each molecule is made of two atoms. One is sodium, Na. The other is chlorine, Cl. These two atoms are joined by a covalent bond to make sodium chloride, NaCl. The millions of molecules of common salt fit together into a regular framework and form a particular shape called a crystal, as shown on later pages.

Partly formed crystals

Crystal face or facet

A supply of molecules

Molecules of oxygen and other gases float around in the air. They are so small, and so far apart, that we cannot see them. But we know they are there, because we breathe in air, to get oxygen into our bodies. Oxygen is a vital part of the chemical changes inside the body, which break down food to get the energy from it for the body's life processes. In water, we cannot breathe oxygen. So divers must take their own supply of oxygen, in tanks.

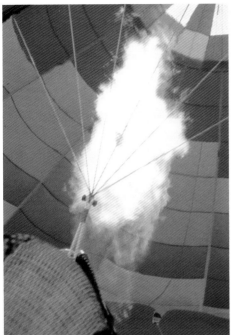

Changing places

At a huge event, people may wander about, to see who is there and what is happening. If they meet a group of people they like, they might sit together, stay a while and talk, then move on again. Likewise, atoms also move about. They link at certain times, by the process of chemical change, into molecules. Then they separate and continue their wanderings. Sooner or later, as a result of more chemical change, they join or bond with other atoms – and so on.

More about molecules

SOME MOLECULES ARE SMALL. They contain only a few atoms, like common salt, with one atom of sodium and one of chlorine. Other molecules are gigantic. They contain thousands of atoms. Of course, atoms are so minute that even a molecule containing a million of them is still far too small for us to see. But when giant molecules group together, into stacks or piles or bundles, containing millions of them, they become large enough to see. One very important group of molecules is the carbohydrates. Their molecules always contain atoms of the elements carbon (C), hydrogen (H) and oxygen (O). The sugars we eat, in the form of sweets, candy and chocolate, are carbohydrates. The hard outer casing (exoskeleton) of an insect such as a beetle is made of chitin – also a form of carbohydrate.

The molecule of life

One of the most important of all molecules is DNA, de-oxyribonucleic acid. It is shaped like a long ladder with rungs, which has been twisted along its length like a corkscrew. This shape is called a double-helix. The rungs of the DNA ladder are smaller subunits of the main DNA molecule, called nucleotides. There are four kinds of them. The pattern of the nucleotides contains information, in the form of a chemical code. This is genetic information for living things, such as how our own bodies develop, grow, move about and digest food.

Polymers

A polymer is a very large molecule made of many smaller, identical units. These smaller parts are monomers. They may be strung together like links in a chain or piled up like bricks in a wall. Lots of sugar molecules joined like this form the polymer starch, found in bread.

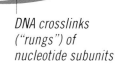

DNA crosslinks ("rungs") of nucleotide subunits

Science discovery

Genes carry the information about how living things grow and carry out their life processes. In the 1940s scientists suspected that they were in the form of chemical molecules. The actual molecules were found to be DNA, de-oxyribonucleic acid. But what was the exact shape of DNA? In 1953 two scientists in Cambridge, England, worked out that the DNA molecule was a double helix. They were Francis Crick and James Watson.

James Watson (1928-)   **Francis Crick (1916-)**

See also: Atoms page 14, Molecules page 22, Crystals page 30

**DNA
double
helix**

*DNA backbone
("ladder") of
sugar subunits*

Hairy molecules

Animal fur, and the hair on our own bodies, is made mainly from a substance called keratin. This is in the form of very long, fibre-like molecules. Keratin is a polymer, made of many smaller, simpler subunits joined together in repeating fashion. It also forms our fingernails, and the claws, horns, hooves and feathers of animals.

Lots of different shapes

You can get an idea of types of molecules, by looking at types of buildings and the rooms they contain. A house is small and has only a few rooms. It is like a small molecule, such as sulphuric acid, H_2SO_4. A skyscraper is like a giant polymer molecule with hundreds of rooms or subunits, all the same shape and size.

Artificial molecules

Many kinds of molecules are not found in nature. They are made, or synthesized, in chemical laboratories and factories. They include the molecules in artificial fibres such as nylon, which is used for very strong ropes, and also rayon, viscose and acrylic. Most kinds of plastics are also artificial polymer molecules.

Solids, liquids and gases

MATTER IS ANY PHYSICAL SUBSTANCE OR OBJECT that exists in the three dimensions of space. It can be as huge as a planet or a star, or as small as one atom – or even as tiny as the sub-atomic particles inside an atom. Whatever its size, matter also exists in one of three main forms. These are solid, liquid and gas. They are called the three states of matter. A housebrick, lump of wood or sheet of steel are solid. The petrol for a car's engine or the oil for cooking food are liquid. A cylinder of oxygen in a hospital or an "empty" room contain gases. Each form of matter has its own features and properties. But the atoms and molecules in matter do not change for each different state. What changes is the way that the atoms or molecules can move about, or the way they are forced to stay still.

Changing states

The same matter or substance can change state, from solid to liquid, or from liquid to gas. These processes are called melting and boiling, and are shown on the next page. Another change of state happens when substances burn, or combust. In a vehicle engine, liquid petrol sprays into the cylinders inside the engine, along with air containing oxygen. The petrol catches fire and burns rapidly, combining with the oxygen in a mini-explosion. The result is not another liquid but a variety of gases. These leave the engine as exhaust fumes.

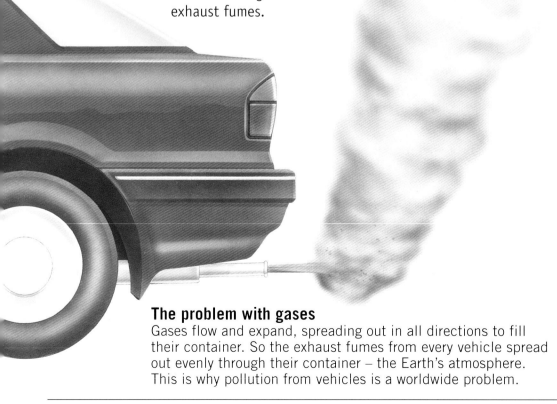

See-through solid

The glaze on a shiny vase is solid. Most solids are opaque. You cannot see through them. But clear glass, glazes and varnishes are see-through, or transparent. The glaze protects the beautiful colours and patterns of the paints beneath and allows them to show through.

The problem with gases

Gases flow and expand, spreading out in all directions to fill their container. So the exhaust fumes from every vehicle spread out evenly through their container – the Earth's atmosphere. This is why pollution from vehicles is a worldwide problem.

See also: Atoms page 14, Melting and boiling page 28, Water page 32

THE FOURTH STATE

▸ The three main states of matter – solid, liquid and gas – have been known since ancient times.
▸ In the 1920s, a fourth state of matter was discovered. This is known as plasma.
▸ Plasma exists only at incredibly high temperatures, in nuclear power experiments, or inside stars.
▸ Small amounts of plasma also form in flashes of lightning.
▸ Plasma is like gas. But some atoms lose electrons and become positive, while the electrons move off freely.
▸ Charged particles such as these are called ions. So plasma is like a gas made of ions.

Swimming in the dry

Children enjoy messing about in a "ball pool". They can lie, roll, wade and swim. It's similar to splashing about in a real swimming pool of water, but without getting wet. The small, lightweight, hollow balls of the ball pool are like giant versions of the tiny atoms or molecules in a real liquid. They are free to move about. They flow when pushed around or poured out of a bucket. Also, like a real liquid, the balls cannot be forced nearer together or compressed.

Solid water

Solid water is called ice. In a solid, the molecules can move very little. They are held in a rigid framework or pattern by bonds between them. So a solid stays in the same shape, unless subject to powerful forces, such as twisting or crushing.

Liquid water

Liquid water is called – water! In a liquid, the molecules can move about fairly easily. This is why liquids flow and take up the shape of the container they are in. But the molecules in a liquid cannot be squashed nearer together or pulled farther apart, so liquids cannot be compressed or expanded by force.

Gaseous water

This is called water vapour. It floats in the air. In a gas, the molecules can move about very easily. This is why gases flow and take up the shape of the container they are in. But the molecules in a gas can also be squashed nearer together or moved farther apart. So a gas can be compressed into a smaller volume, or expand to fill its container.

Melting and boiling

MATTER CAN CHANGE IN STATE, from solid to liquid, or liquid to gas, or back again. This usually happens when heat energy is added to the matter. The heat gives extra energy to the atoms and molecules, which makes them move around more. When a solid is heated, eventually its atoms or molecules have enough energy to break free from their rigid framework. They begin to move around more freely, and the solid turns into a liquid. This is called melting. Each substance has its own particular temperature at which it melts. This is known as its melting point. Similarly, when a liquid is heated, at a certain temperature it becomes a gas. This temperature is called its boiling point. For pure water at normal temperature and pressure, the melting point is 0°C and the boiling point is 100°C.

Boiling hot
Each liquid has its own boiling point. Some cooking oils boil and begin to burn at more than 200°C. which is far hotter than boiling water at 100°C.

Under pressure
When a gas turns into a liquid, this is called condensation. This can be carried out by taking heat away from the gas, which is known as cooling. Or it can be carried out by compressing the gas – squeezing it to make it take up less space. The atoms and molecules of the gas squash closer together and change state into a liquid. They also receive heat so they become warmer. Huge ocean tankers carry natural gas compressed into liquid form, called LPG, liquid petroleum gas. This saves vast amounts of space.

Molten rock
"Solid as rock" is not always very solid. Even rocks melt if they become hot enough. Deep below the Earth's surface, the temperatures and pressures are so great that rocks are melted, or molten. They are known as magma. When they ooze or spurt out of a volcano, glowing and flowing, they are called lava.

Science discovery
Robert Boyle (1627-1691) was a chemist who did many practical experiments. He showed that for a gas which is kept at a constant temperature, then the pressure that the gas is under is proportional to its volume. So squash a gas into half its volume, and its pressure doubles. This is Boyle's law.

See also: Molecules page 22, Water page 32, Heat and cold page 58

Water-skating

Skating on ice is really skating on a very thin film of water. The blade of an ice skate has an upside-down U shape. Its two thin edges rest on the ice with great pressure. Increasing the pressure of a substance makes its temperature rise. So the ice melts into water for a split second as the skate goes over it. When the skate has passed, the ice then freezes again.

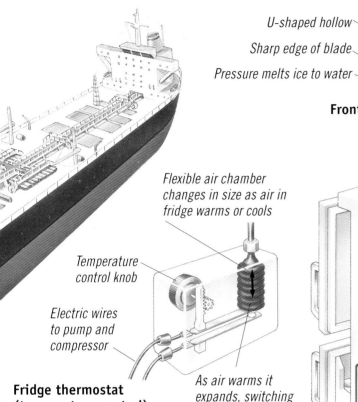

U-shaped hollow
Sharp edge of blade
Pressure melts ice to water

Front view of ice skate blade

Only one edge of the blade touches the ice

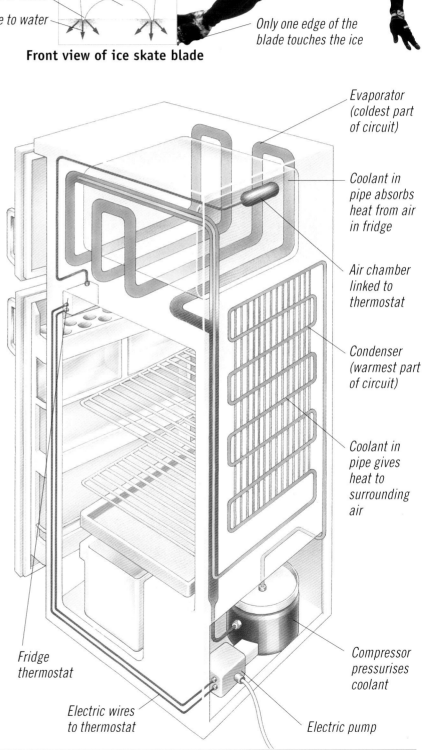

Flexible air chamber changes in size as air in fridge warms or cools

Temperature control knob

Electric wires to pump and compressor

Fridge thermostat (temperature control)

As air warms it expands, switching on cooling system

Evaporator (coldest part of circuit)

Coolant in pipe absorbs heat from air in fridge

Air chamber linked to thermostat

Condenser (warmest part of circuit)

Coolant in pipe gives heat to surrounding air

Fridge thermostat

Electric wires to thermostat

Compressor pressurises coolant

Electric pump

Keeping cool

A refrigerator uses the scientific principles of boiling and condensing under different pressures. A pump circulates a substance called a coolant in the pipes. The compressor outside the fridge compartment squashes the coolant. This makes it condense from a gas into a liquid, and also increase in temperature. Then some pressure is taken off the liquid as it flows through the evaporator pipes inside the fridge. The liquid boils, or changes into a gas, taking heat from the fridge's interior as it does so. This makes the interior cooler. The gas carries this heat out of the fridge and into the condenser pipes. It gives the heat to the surrounding air, becomes compressed into a liquid again, and so on.

Crystals

SOME OF THE WORLD'S MOST VALUABLE ITEMS are a special form of solid matter, called crystals. They include diamonds, rubies, sapphires, emeralds and many other jewels or "precious stones". The atoms or molecules inside these crystals fit together in a certain way because of their shape. They are like bricks in a wall, or clip-together toy building blocks. They can be joined to make larger and larger structures, but always in the same basic shape as the smaller units. A crystal has flat sides called facets, in the form of triangles, squares, rectangles or similar geometric shapes. There are straight, sharp edges between these facets, at specific angles to each other. The natural substances called minerals in the Earth's rocks can often be identified from their crystal shapes. Natural or raw crystals are cut and polished into jewels or gemstones.

Polished crystals
A ruby jewel or gem is a cut and polished version of the raw crystal. Gemstones are valuable because of their beautiful colours, hardness, transparency and shiny, glassy surfaces.

Raw crystals
Natural crystals vary in size, from too small to see except with a microscope, to as big as a house. When they are dug up, they are usually dull and look crushed or distorted.

CRYSTAL SHAPES AND SYSTEMS

Cubic (salt, diamond, garnet)

There are seven basic shapes of crystals, known as crystal systems or groups. These depend on the way that the different atoms fit together inside. The simplest form is a box shape, with all of the facets as equal-sized squares. This is the cubic system. Crystals in this group include common salt (sodium chloride), diamond and garnet. A crystal of common salt which is 1 cubic millimetre in volume – about the size of a pinhead – contains around 70 million atoms. The trigonal shape includes crystals of quartz, otherwise known as sand. Sand grains on the beach are small quartz crystals which have been worn and rounded by rubbing and rolling against each other. Quartz crystals are also used in "quartz" watches (see opposite).

Hexagonal (beryl)

Tetragonal (zircon)

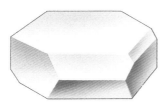

Trigonal (quartz, calcite)

Triclinic (feldspar)

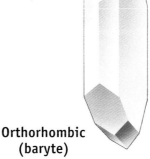

Orthorhombic (baryte)

Monoclinic (gypsum)

See also: Atoms page 14, Metals page 40, Rock cycle page 148

Science discovery

Pierre Curie (1859-1906) helped his wife Marie with research into radioactive substances. He also carried out work on crystals. He discovered that when certain crystals are squashed or distorted, they change the amount of electricity passing through them. Also the reverse happens – passing varying amounts of electricity through a crystal changes its shape. This is the piezoelectric effect. In a quartz watch, a small battery passes electricity through a tiny quartz crystal, which vibrates very fast to mark the time.

Sugar crystals

Sugar, like common salt, is usually in the form of crystals. Under the microscope, these show lines and patterns where they formed. Under suitable conditions, crystals "grow" in size, getting bigger yet keeping their distinctive sharp-edged crystal shape.

Six-sided shape

Every ice crystal in snow has a unique shape

Crystals grow to fill gaps between each other

DOMINUM

Snow crystals

In very cold conditions, high in clouds, water freezes to form tiny ice crystals. These fall as snow. Because of the way they grow, these crystals always have six sides or arms. Yet every one is different.

Crystal scaffolding

The atoms or molecules in a crystal fit together and join like the scaffolding framework of a building. Many smaller, regular, repeated units nest together to form a much bigger structure with angled faces and sharp edges. However, cutting and polishing a crystal can change its shape, like making a curved dome with stepped box-like units of scaffolding.

Water

WATER IS VITAL for life on Earth. All animals and plants need water to survive. Those that live on "dry" land get their water from the soil or from streams, rivers, lakes, puddles, dew or raindrops. Water is also vital for our own lives. We collect and store water for drinking and washing, for our pets and farm animals, and for irrigating our crops. Each person needs to take in at least two litres of water daily, to stay alive and healthy. Like many other substances, water can exist in three different states. Water is the liquid form. Ice is the solid form. Water vapour is the gaseous form. All of these states occur naturally, with ice in cold places and invisible water vapour in the air around us. The natural steam belching from hot springs or geysers is water vapour mixed with tiny floating droplets of hot water.

Floating ice
Most substances enlarge or expand as they heat up, and become smaller or contract as they get colder. But water is unusual. It contracts as it cools down to 4°C. Then, as it gets even colder and freezes into ice, it expands again. This means a lump of ice at 0°C weighs less than the same-sized lump of water at, say, 10°C. So ice – from an ice cube in a drink to a giant iceberg in the ocean – floats on water.

Flowing along a pipe
Liquids such as water flow along channels and through tubes and pipes. But the flow is not smooth and even. The regions of water next to the channel's or pipe's inner surface move more slowly, because they rub against the surface. The region of water in the centre of the channel or pipe flows faster. This variation in speed of movement is called laminar flow. The same happens in a river. Water near the bank flows more slowly than water in the middle. The study of flowing liquids is important in the branch of science and engineering called hydraulics. This deals with how fluids flow and transmit pressures along pipes.

Flow disturbed by bend in pipe

Eddies (whirlpools) at corner

Fast flow in centre

Slow flow near edge

Bend in pipe makes water change direction

Laminar flow restored

Science discovery
Daniel Bernouilli (1700-1782) was an expert in medicine, animals, plants, physics and mathematics. He showed that as water or another liquid flows from a wide pipe into a narrower one, the speed of flow becomes faster – and the liquid also has less pressure. This applies to flowing gases like air, too. This effect is known as Bernouilli's principle. It is used in many kinds of engineering and technology, such as the design of aircraft wings, so they provide a lifting force as they move through the air.

Cirrus clouds (ice crystals)

Cumulonimbus cloud (thunderstorm)

Water for life
An oasis is a small area of water in an otherwise dry place, a desert. The water may be on the surface, as a pool or lake, or underground and reached by plants' roots or our wells. Life can exist in and near the oasis, but not in the desert beyond.

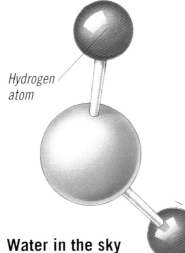

Hydrogen atom

Water in the sky
Clouds are billions of tiny droplets of water or crystals of ice. These are so light that they float.

Water molecules
The smallest particle or molecule of water is made of two atoms of hydrogen (H) and one atom of oxygen (O), combined to form H_2O. The molecule has a particular shape, called a dipole. The two links or bonds between the atoms are at an angle of 105° to each other.

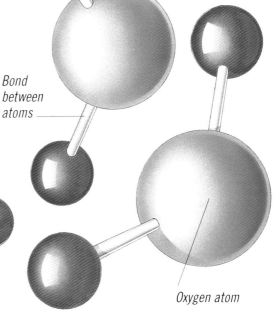

Bond between atoms

Oxygen atom

FLOATING AND SINKING
An object floats because it weighs less than the water it pushes aside, or displaces. A huge ship may be made of heavy metal, but it also contains lots of air. So overall, it is lighter than a lump of water of the same volume. So it floats. A submarine can alter its weight by taking in water to make itself heavier, and dive. To rise again it blows the water out with air from compressed air tanks. This makes it lighter and it floats.

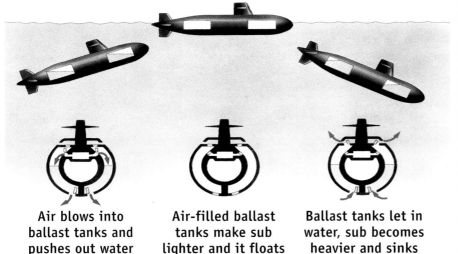

Air blows into ballast tanks and pushes out water

Air-filled ballast tanks make sub lighter and it floats

Ballast tanks let in water, sub becomes heavier and sinks

Water energy
Moving objects and substances have the energy of motion, kinetic energy. So water flowing downhill, pulled by gravity, has kinetic energy. This can be harnessed and turned into electricity in a hydro-electric power station. The energy of a very steep flow of water, the waterfall, wears away the solid rock below.

Dissolving

STIR SUGAR GRAINS into a glass of clear, clean water. They swirl around for a while, then they seem to fade away. Finally they disappear. But if you sip the water, you can still taste the sugar. It has not disappeared – it has dissolved. Its crystals have become smaller, gradually breaking up into their individual molecules or atoms. These are too small to see, but they are present, floating about among the molecules of water.

The substance that dissolves – in this case, sugar – is called the solute. The substance it dissolves in – again, in this case, water – is known as the solvent. The two together, the solute in the solvent, make up a solution. In daily life, water is the most common solvent.

Hotter means more

The warmer a liquid, the more solute can dissolve in it. So you can dissolve more spoonfuls of sugar in a hot drink than in a cold drink. In the cold drink, undissolved sugar settles on the bottom.

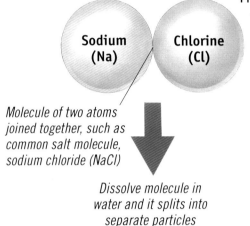

Molecule of two atoms joined together, such as common salt molecule, sodium chloride (NaCl)

Dissolve molecule in water and it splits into separate particles

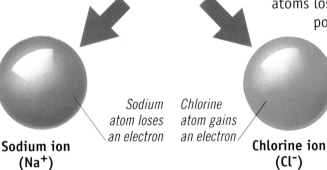

Sodium ion (Na⁺)

Sodium atom loses an electron

Chlorine atom gains an electron

Chlorine ion (Cl⁻)

Atoms to ions

When some substances dissolve, they change slightly. Their atoms are no longer neutral, that is, neither positive or negative. One group of atoms loses their electrons, which are negative, so the atoms become positive. Another group of atoms gains the extra electrons, so they become negative. These particles are no longer known as atoms, but as ions. The positive ions are called cations. The negative ones are termed anions. The formation of ions is very important for all kinds of chemical changes and reactions, and also for producing or using electricity, as shown later in the book.

Dangerous dissolving

There are hundreds of kinds of solvents. Some, like water, are fairly harmless. But the powerful chemical solvents used in industry are not. They dissolve many substances, including our skin and flesh!

Dissolved in the sea

The clean, fresh water from our taps contains very little dissolved substances, apart from those added to kill germs and make it safe. But one sip of sea water shows that it contains dissolved salt. This is the same type of salt as common or table salt, sodium chloride. Sea water also contains many other dissolved substances, including calcium, sulphate and carbonate.

See also: Molecules page 23, Water page 32, Chemical electricity page 84

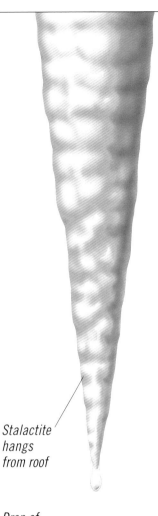

Stalactite hangs from roof

Drop of water full of dissolved minerals

Stalagmite sticks up from floor

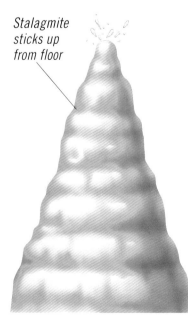

Oil molecules gathered in clumps

Oil molecule

Detergent makes clumps smaller

Dissolving oil

Usually oil does not dissolve in or mix with water. The molecules of oil clump together into drops and float about on the water. But a detergent alters the features of water and makes it a more powerful solvent. It makes the oil drops break up into smaller and smaller clumps, which is called dispersing the oil. We use different types of detergents to wash our clothes, our cooking pots and pans, our eating crockery and cutlery, and also (in the form of soaps, foams and gels) our own bodies. Strong detergents disperse polluting oil slicks.

No more dissolving

Only a certain amount of solute can dissolve in a solvent. A solution which is full of solute is called a saturated solution. Saturation varies with temperature. A hot liquid can hold more dissolved solute than a cold liquid. As a warm saturated solution cools, some of the solute comes out of solution, and reappears as a solid again.

Out of solution

As rain water soaks into the soil and trickles down through tiny cracks in the rocks, it dissolves some of the natural minerals in the soil and rocks. It becomes a mineral solution. Sometimes this solution drips slowly from a cave roof onto the cave floor. As each drip of water falls, it leaves behind its minerals. Over thousands of years the minerals build up into sharp icicle-like shapes of rock – stalactites and stalagmites.

Coloured solute

Some paints are solutions. The solute is the coloured substance, pigment. As the paint dries, the solvent turns into a gas or vapour and floats away. The pigment particles remain as a coloured layer of paint.

Chemical changes

ATOMS ARE NOT FIXED into their molecules for ever. Molecules can come apart, and their atoms then join together again in new, different combinations. This is called chemical change. The atoms in molecules of one or more substances break their links or bonds with each other. They "shuffle their partners" and form links or bonds with other, different atoms. The result is one or more new substances, with different chemical features and properties compared to the original substances. Chemical changes need energy, such as heat, light or electricity, to happen.

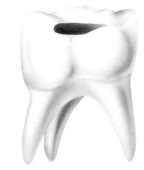

Tooth filling
The silver metal mercury is normally a liquid. But mercury combined with other metals forms an amalgam that sets very hard, for use in dental fillings.

Colour change

In chemistry, an indicator is a substance that changes colour according to the chemical conditions. A common example is litmus, used to find out if a substance is acidic or alkaline (explained on the following pages). The molecules of litmus undergo chemical change when exposed to an acid or alkali. The new molecules have a different colour, so the change is easily visible.

Paper strip containing litmus dye

Neutral (neither acidic nor alkaline) – litmus is unaffected

Acid turns strip red

Acidic – litmus turns red colour

Strip becomes blue

Alkaline – litmus turns blue colour

Fiery change

A familiar chemical change is combustion, or burning. When a substance catches fire, atoms in its molecules break apart from one another. Some link or bond with oxygen in the air. For instance, when wood or coal burn, the carbon atoms in the wood or coal break apart from their molecules and join with oxygen. They form a new substance, carbon dioxide, CO_2. One way of stopping combustion is to prevent oxygen – usually, from air – reaching the fire. A fire blanket or smothering foam does this. The chemical change of joining with oxygen stops, and the fire goes out.

See also: Molecules page 22, Acid and bases page 38, Colours page 124

CHEMICAL BUILDING BRICKS

In a toy building kit, each brick or other shape is a single unit. Likewise, atoms are single units. Bricks fit together or join to each other. In the same way, atoms link or bond to each other. Lots of different bricks fit together to make a certain object, like an aeroplane. Similarly, different atoms fit together too, to form molecules of a certain substance. The bricks can be taken apart and then put together in a different combination or pattern, to make another object, like a house. Atoms in the molecules of one substance can be taken apart from each other, then reassembled to form molecules of a new, different substance, with different chemical features and properties. This is chemical change.

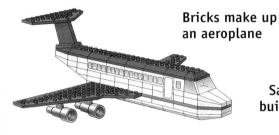

Bricks make up an aeroplane

Same bricks build a house

Science discovery

Henry Cavendish (1731-1810) was exceptionally shy, worked alone, had great wealth, yet rarely spent it. But he made important scientific discoveries. He produced water by exploding oxygen and hydrogen gases together. This caused a chemical change, joining one oxygen atom to two hydrogen atoms. He showed water was a chemical compound, H_2O, not an element as others believed.

Sticky change

An adhesive or glue is used for sticking things together. When it comes out of the tube, it is usually in liquid form. In one type of adhesive, as the liquid "dries", it does not simply turn from liquid to solid. Its molecules undergo chemical change. Their atoms separate from each other, lock into the atoms and molecules of the item being glued, then turn into a solid. In another type of adhesive, resin from one tube is mixed with hardener from another tube. The two seep into the surfaces being joined, and chemically combine or react with each other to bond the surfaces together.

Liquid adhesive turns solid

All change

A high tech object, such as a Grand Prix racing car, is the result of thousands of chemical changes. The metals in the engine parts were once combined with other minerals, in rocks. They have been extracted and purified, and combined with other metals to form alloys with special properties, such as light weight and great strength. The rubber in the tyres was extracted from rubber trees, then heated and chemically combined with other substances, in the process called vulcanizing. This makes it tougher, more elastic and hard-wearing. The plastic parts were made by chemically changing the raw ingredients in natural petroleum, or crude oil.

Acids and bases

TWO SPECIAL KINDS OF CHEMICALS are called acids and bases. An acid is a substance that dissolves (usually in water) and forms ions of hydrogen. This means, as the acid dissolves, each hydrogen atom separates from the rest of its acid molecule and floats freely in solution. It also loses its single electron to become a positive particle called a hydrogen ion, written H^+. These hydrogen ions are available to take part in chemical changes or reactions. Strong acids are corrosive. They dissolve or chemically wear away many other substances. A base is the "opposite" of an acid. It can take up hydrogen ions. Strong bases and alkalis have a slimy feel and, like acids, are chemically corrosive. A base that dissolves in water is known as an alkali.

The chemicals of digestion

Acids and alkalis are not limited to the chemistry laboratory or factory. They are common in daily life, and even in our own bodies. The lining of the stomach makes a digestive juice containing a strong acid, hydrochloric acid (HCl). This chemically attacks swallowed food, breaking it apart and dissolving it, to get nutrients from food. Another digestive part, the pancreas gland, produces strong alkalis. As the acidic food leaves the stomach and goes into the intestine, the alkaline pancreatic juices pour onto it. The acids and alkalis combine and cancel each other. This prevents damage by these powerful natural chemicals.

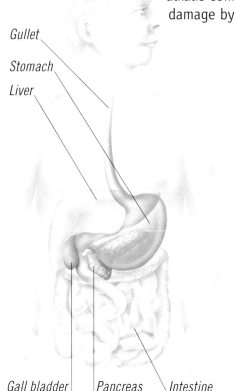

Gullet

Stomach

Liver

Gall bladder   Pancreas   Intestine

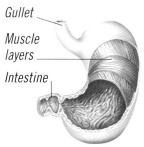

Gullet

Muscle layers

Intestine

Stomach

Stomach lining

Parietal cell

Stomach acid
The stomach's hydrochloric acid is made in microscopic cells, called parietal cells, in its lining. The stomach is protected from attack by its own acid by a thick layer of slimy mucus on its lining.

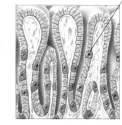

Pancreas duct

Acini

Acinar cell

Gall bladder duct   **Pancreas**

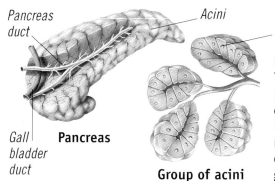

Group of acini

Pancreas alkali
The pancreas makes its powerful bicarbonates and other alkaline digestive juices in thousands of clusters of microscopic cells. Each cluster, shaped like a bunch of grapes, is called an acinus.

See also: Atoms page 14, Dissolving page 34, Chemical electricity page 84

**Lemon contains
citric acid
$C_6H_8O_7$**

**Bicarb contains
sodium bicarbonate
$NaHCO_3$**

NATURAL ACIDS AND BASES

Acids and bases are common in the natural world. The stinging spray that an ant can shoot from its rear end contains formic acid. The ant bites an intruder with its strong pincer-like jaws, then squirts the spray into the wound to cause discomfort and pain. Alkaloids are natural bases found in certain plants, especially in their sap, leaves or seeds. Many have powerful effects on the human body. Some alkaloids are incredibly poisonous, even in tiny amounts. Others can be helpful. The opiate alkaloids extracted from some types of poppies have pain-deadening effects. Their study has helped medical scientists to develop some types of pain-killing drugs. Acetic acid, correctly known as ethanoic acid, has the chemical formula CH_3COOH. Mixed with water, in the proportions of 1 part of acid to 20 parts of water, it is familiar as vinegar. It occurs naturally in the process of fermentation, as fruits go bad or rotten.

An ant's stinging spray contains formic acid

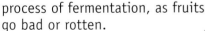

Vinegar contains acetic acid

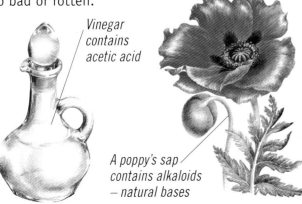

A poppy's sap contains alkaloids – natural bases

Cooking chemicals

Some forms of cooking and flavouring rely on chemical reactions between acids or bases. Lemon juice contains citric acid, which gives it a sharp, sour taste. Lemons, limes, grapefruits and oranges are known as citrus fruits because they contain plentiful amounts of this acid. The "bicarb" used in baking is a base, sodium bicarbonate or bicarbonate of soda. It is mixed with an acid such as vinegar (acetic acid) or cream of tartar (tartaric acid) to form a salt – and also a gas, carbon dioxide. The gas is in the form of tiny bubbles which makes cakes "rise" when baked, for a spongy texture.

Start-up power

Most vehicles, even huge juggernaut trucks, rely on electrical power to start their engines. The electricity is supplied by a type of electrical battery called a lead-acid accumulator, shown below. The acid in this battery is sulphuric acid, with the chemical formula H_2SO_4. It is a very strong acid. A small drip can burn unprotected skin and cause pain and scarring.

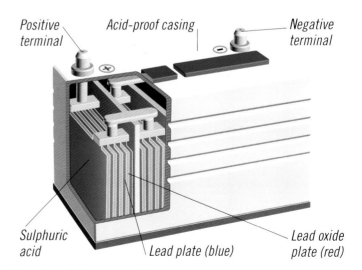

Positive terminal

Acid-proof casing

Negative terminal

Sulphuric acid

Lead plate (blue)

Lead oxide plate (red)

Lead-acid accumulator

This vehicle battery has plates of lead and lead oxide, in a bath of concentrated sulphuric acid. Each pair of plates is called a secondary cell. Chemical reactions between the plates and the acid make electricity flow when the battery is connected into a circuit.

Metals

THERE ARE about 112 known chemical elements. More than three-quarters are metals. A typical metal is hard and shiny, tough and strong, and it conducts or carries electricity and heat well. Metals have thousands of uses in daily life. Often they are mixed or combined with other metals or substances, to form alloys. Almost any machine or device has at least one metal in it. The most widely used metal is iron, but not in its pure form. It is combined with small amounts of the non-metal carbon, to form the group of alloys known as steels. Making alloys is extremely important in industry. Often, alloys of a metal are harder and stronger than the pure metal itself. The science of metals is called metallurgy.

Strong as steel

The world's industries use millions of tonnes of steels each year. Steel plate forms the large panels in washing machines, cars, trains and ships. The stainless steel used for making cutlery and cooking utensils is an alloy with at least one-tenth of the extremely hard, shiny metal known as chromium. Steels with titanium in them form the light but stiff structural sheets in high-speed aircraft. Steel girders make the strong frameworks of skyscrapers, bridges and similar big structures. Other elements mixed with iron to form steels include manganese, phosphorus, silicon and sulphur.

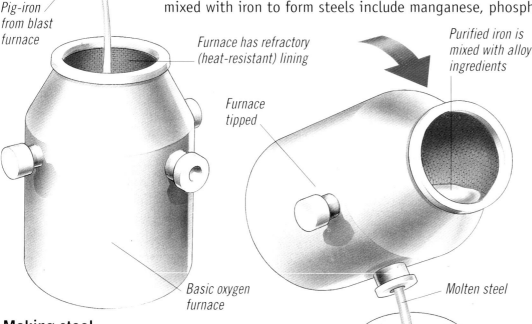

Pig-iron from blast furnace

Furnace has refractory (heat-resistant) lining

Furnace tipped

Basic oxygen furnace

Purified iron is mixed with alloy ingredients

Molten steel

Steel ladle

Molten steel is poured out as brick-shaped ingots to cool

Most valuable metal?
Gold is a famous symbol of wealth. But rarer metals such as platinum and palladium command higher prices for specialised engineering and electronic uses.

Making steel

Iron is extracted from iron-rich rocks, or iron ores, in a blast furnace. The result is pig-iron, which contains various impurities. These are removed by blowing oxygen through the pig-iron, a method known as the basic oxygen process. The steel is so hot that it is in melted or molten form, as a liquid.

See also: Elements page 18, Elements table page 20, Solids page 26

Silvery-white aluminium does not rust

Aluminium

Also called aluminum, this is the most abundant metal on planet Earth (and the third most abundant of all chemical elements). It forms about one-twelfth by weight of the Earth's outer layer, the crust. Pure aluminium is very light but not especially strong. However, combined with other elements, such as copper, magnesium or silicon, it forms extremely strong alloys. Also it does not rust, unlike steel. Aluminium is used for making aircraft, ships, cooking utensils such as saucepans, drinks cans, cooking foil and take-away food cartons.

Recycling metals

Most metals occur combined with minerals and other substances, spread through rocks known as ores. It takes huge amounts of time and energy to dig or mine the ores, and then extract and purify the metals from them. Recycling helps to reduce these problems. For example, recycled aluminium uses only one-twentieth of the energy which is needed to produce aluminium from its ore. Many other metals can also be recycled, including irons and steel, and even the silver and gold used in electrical circuits – and false teeth!

Cans decorated and filled

Cans punched from thin sheet

Cans used, but not thrown away

Cans collected and partly crushed to save space

Can to can

The entire journey around the aluminium recycling circuit, from being a drinks can to another drinks can, may be as short as one month.

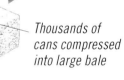

Molten aluminium cooled and pressed into thin sheet

Thousands of cans compressed into large bale

Bales melted to produce molten aluminium

Unsightly mines

Mining metals from surface rocks, known as open-cast mining, can be very unsightly and scar the landscape for hundreds of years.

METALS THROUGH HISTORY

▶ One of the earliest alloys was bronze, a mix of copper and tin. It has been known for thousands of years and was the first widely used substance for tools, after rocks and stones.
▶ Brass is another common alloy, of copper and zinc.
▶ Perhaps the most famous metal is gold. It has been valued and cherished since ancient times because it stays bright and shiny, yet is also easy to work with.
▶ Silver is another long-valued metal. It is the best conductor of electricity of any metal. Silver is also used in jewellery, photographic film and for coins.

Composites

MATERIALS SCIENCE is a fast-growing area of science, especially in engineering. It involves taking various raw or ingredient substances and making them mix, combine or react together in various ways, to produce a new material with specialised properties. Each of the ingredient substances has some useful features, and these all add together to produce the final material. One example is glass-reinforced plastic, GRP. This is made by embedding tiny fibres of glass into a type of plastic. The plastic gives overall bulk and flexibility, while the glass fibres provide extra strength, stiffness and resistance to wear. GRP is used to make boat hulls and light-yet-strong parts for vehicles, aeroplanes, and factory and office equipment.

Composite frame

Nylon-based strings

Composite handle

Bats and racquets
The composite frame of a high tech racquet is extremely light. But it also bends to absorb the energy when the ball hits it. Then it rebounds like elastic to pass this energy back to the ball, so that the ball flies away at maximum speed. The strings are made of another artificial material, such as a specialized form of nylon.

Tests and more tests
Creating a new composite material involves lengthy trials and tests. The carbon fibre composite of a turbine fan, at the front of a jet engine, experiences incredible stresses. It must be tested for hundreds of hours, and then even longer, to destruction. This makes sure it is strong enough to avoid catastrophic failure.

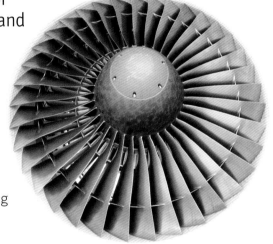

Sails and hulls
A racing yacht's hull is usually constructed from GRP. Varying the direction of the glass fibres gives extra strength and stiffness in a certain direction, with extra flexibility in other directions. The sails are also a composite, able to bend and catch the wind without tearing.

Space tiles
The tiles on the undersides of space shuttles are made of heat-resistant ceramic composites. As the shuttle comes back from space into the Earth's atmosphere, friction with the thickening air generates enormous heat. The tiles keep this heat out of the shuttle's interior. They are checked and renewed as necessary after each mission.

See also: Elements page 14, Crystals page 30, Metals page 40

Ingredient one: fibres

Often called "whiskers", short fibres add the feature of flexibility. They can bend without snapping. Carbon or silicon is often used for such fibres. The huge fan at the front of a modern turbofan jet engine is made of carbon fibre.

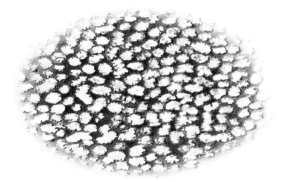

Ingredient two: ceramic

A typical ceramic material is usually made from natural substances such as clay, sand or other minerals obtained from ground-up rocks. It is "fired" in an oven or furnace, to make it hard and able to withstand high temperatures, but liable to cracking.

Ingredient three: metal

Metals are generally hard and tough, able to stand wear and tear. They also conduct heat well, so they disperse or spread out heat from a hot spot. And they deform or change shape slightly under great pressure, rather than cracking. Under the microscope, a metal is formed of tiny grains or crystals.

Making a composite

Most composites are based on a matrix. This is the general surrounding substance in which the various fibres, grains, crystals and other ingredients are embedded. For normal temperatures, a common matrix is some type of plastic. A metal or ceramic matrix can cope with higher temperatures. Making the composite may involve various methods such as mixing, heating, cooling, squeezing at high pressure, passing electricity through the substance, exposure to powerful rays or sounds, and treatment with various chemicals, such as acids, alkalis or solvents.

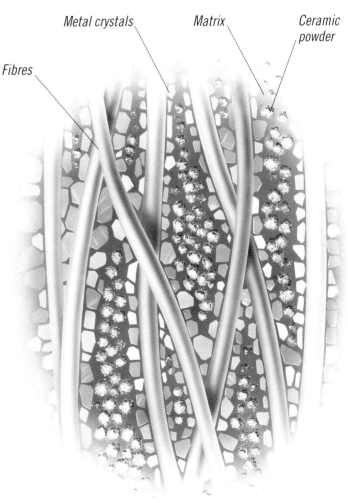

The result: a new composite

The fibres, ceramic powder grains and metal crystals have been mixed or combined into a new composite. If the ingredients are in the correct proportions and laid out in the correct patterns, the composite will have all the desired features. It should be hard and tough, yet flexible, and able to cope with great pressures, stresses and intense heat.

2

Energy, Motion and Machines

Energy is the ability to make things happen and cause changes. It exists in many forms, such as sound, light, electricity and chemicals. Moving objects also possess a type of energy, kinetic energy. Using energy and principles of mechanics and movement, we combine simple machines, such as levers and wheels, into enormously complex ones.

About energy

YOU CAN'T SEE ENERGY. You can't touch it or hold it in your hand. But energy is everywhere. Energy is the ability to do work, to make things happen and to cause changes. There are many different types, or forms, of energy. A hot drink has heat energy. A flash of lightning during a thunderstorm has both electrical and light energy. A lion's roar is sound energy. A racing car speeding around the track has movement energy, which is also called kinetic energy. Even a book lying on a shelf has energy. Because of its position and the pull of gravity, it presses down on the shelf. This type of energy is called potential energy.

Pictures from energy

Machines called scanners make pictures of the insides of the body. They send invisible waves of energy into the body and measure how these waves change as they pass through, or bounce off, the different body parts. A computer then analyses the strengths and directions of the changed waves, and builds up a picture or image. The image on the right of the brain and head was made using the type of scanner called a Magnetic Resonance Imaging, or MRI, scanner.

Radio energy

Radio and television programmes are received by aerials, which pick up invisible waves of energy sent out by transmitters. The waves consist of electrical and magnetic energy, so they are called electromagnetic waves. Some transmitters are fixed to the tops of tall towers, so that the radio waves of energy they send out can travel very long distances.

FORMS OF ENERGY

- ▶ Chemical energy, contained in atoms and molecules.
- ▶ Kinetic energy, in moving objects.
- ▶ Potential energy, from an object's position.
- ▶ Sound energy, when atoms or objects vibrate.
- ▶ Nuclear energy, when atoms join or split apart.
- ▶ Electrical energy, from moving electrons.
- ▶ Magnetic energy, due to magnetic attraction.
- ▶ Electromagnetic energy, in the form of various kinds of rays or waves. These include radio waves, microwaves, heat, light, X-rays and gamma rays.

See also: Magnets page 92, Radio waves page 136, The Sun page 188

Energy from the Sun
The energy we receive from the Sun is called solar energy. It consists mainly of light and heat that travel through space. These forms of energy come from atoms smashing into each other in the centre of the Sun and joining together, or fusing. This process is called nuclear fusion. Energy that comes from the centres or nuclei of atoms is called nuclear energy. The form of nuclear energy in nuclear power stations here on Earth comes from nuclear fission, when atoms split apart.

Soaraway energy
A ski jumper soars into the sky, leaning forwards to cut through the air and fly as far as possible. The jumper gets the energy needed for such a huge leap by sliding down a tall hill faster and faster, changing potential energy into kinetic energy, then leaping from the upturned take-off ramp.

Energy for robots
Vehicle-building robots need energy to move their mechanical arms. This is usually supplied by electricity, which drives electric motors, which tilt and swivel the arms. The movements are controlled with great precision by computer.

Science discovery

Hermann Helmholtz (1821-1894) developed the law of conservation of energy. It says that energy is never created or destroyed. It is simply changed from one form to another. Helmholtz studied various forms of energy, including the newly discovered radio waves. He was also a mathematician and medical researcher.

Movement energy
Anything that moves has kinetic energy. The faster it moves and the more substance or matter (mass) it contains, the more kinetic energy it has. A fast train speeding across the countryside has an enormous amount of kinetic energy.

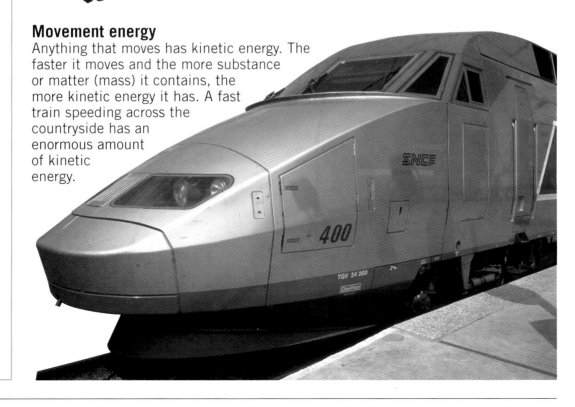

Converting energy

ENERGY CANNOT BE MADE or destroyed. It can only be converted. When anything moves or alters in any way, energy changes its form. A ball at the top of a hill has potential energy because of its position. As it rolls down the hill, some of its potential energy is converted into kinetic or movement energy. When a piece of wood burns, chemical energy stored inside its molecules changes into heat and light energy, and even some sound energy too, as the fire crackles. So energy is constantly changing forms, all around us. One simple event may involve a whole chain of energy conversions.

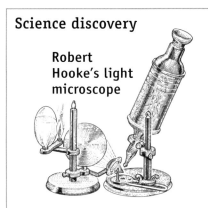

Steam power

A steam train is really solar-powered. Millions of years ago, plants trapped the Sun's light energy, converted it into chemical energy, then died and changed into coal. Burning coal converts this chemical energy into heat, which boils water to make high-pressure steam, which turns the train's wheels.

Generating electricity

A power station produces electricity by changing the energy in its fuel into electrical energy. A gas-fired power station burns gas, converting its chemical energy into heat. The burning gas expands and tries to rush out in all directions – it has kinetic energy. It turns the blades of a turbine, which drives a generator to make electricity. The hot gas also turns water into steam, which drives another turbine and generator. Condensers change the steam back into water so that it can be used again.

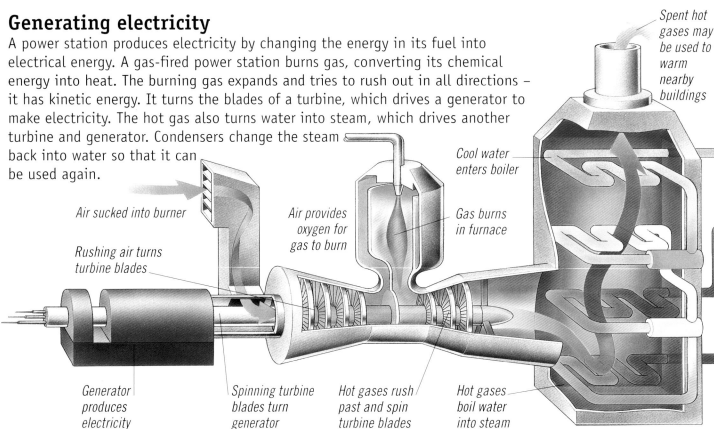

Spent hot gases may be used to warm nearby buildings

Cool water enters boiler

Air sucked into burner

Air provides oxygen for gas to burn

Gas burns in furnace

Rushing air turns turbine blades

Generator produces electricity

Spinning turbine blades turn generator

Hot gases rush past and spin turbine blades

Hot gases boil water into steam

See also: Molecules page 22, Generators page 98, Light page 124

Solar panels

A satellite needs electricity to power its instruments, cameras and radio equipment. Most satellites get electricity from their solar panels. Each panel is covered by thousands of solar cells, which change sunlight directly into electricity. Some of the electrical energy is stored in chemical form, in rechargeable batteries.

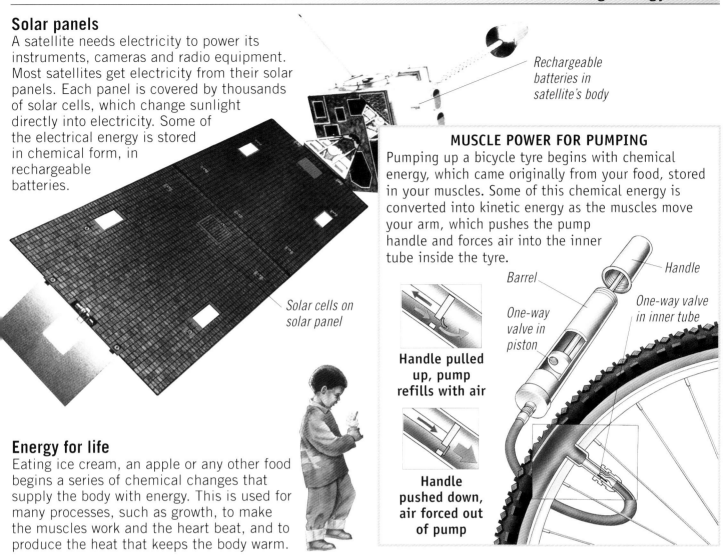

Rechargeable batteries in satellite's body

Solar cells on solar panel

MUSCLE POWER FOR PUMPING

Pumping up a bicycle tyre begins with chemical energy, which came originally from your food, stored in your muscles. Some of this chemical energy is converted into kinetic energy as the muscles move your arm, which pushes the pump handle and forces air into the inner tube inside the tyre.

Barrel

Handle

One-way valve in piston

One-way valve in inner tube

Handle pulled up, pump refills with air

Handle pushed down, air forced out of pump

Energy for life

Eating ice cream, an apple or any other food begins a series of chemical changes that supply the body with energy. This is used for many processes, such as growth, to make the muscles work and the heart beat, and to produce the heat that keeps the body warm.

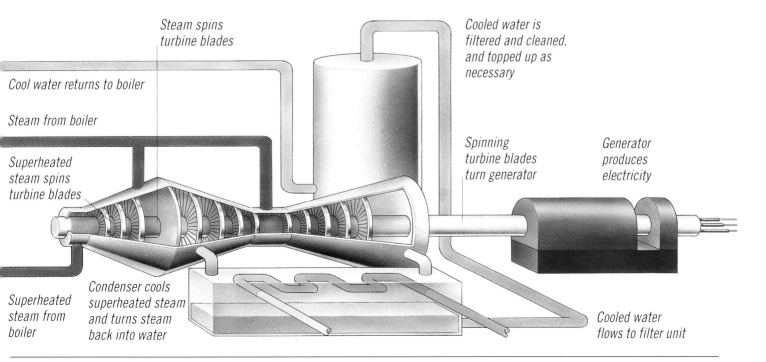

Steam spins turbine blades

Cooled water is filtered and cleaned, and topped up as necessary

Cool water returns to boiler

Steam from boiler

Spinning turbine blades turn generator

Generator produces electricity

Superheated steam spins turbine blades

Superheated steam from boiler

Condenser cools superheated steam and turns steam back into water

Cooled water flows to filter unit

Energy of motion

EVERYTHING THAT MOVES has kinetic energy. But, before a stationary object will move, it has to be given enough energy to start it moving. The bigger and heavier it is, the more energy it needs. This resistance to motion is called inertia. Then, once something has started moving, it tries to keep going. This resistance to stopping is called momentum. Inertia and momentum both show the same principle – whether an object is still or moving, it tries to carry on doing the same. Spinning discs or wheels have momentum which gives them a special feature. As they turn faster, they become more difficult to tilt. This is called the gyroscope effect, and wheels that behave in this way are called gyroscopes.

Frame

Spinning disc

Swivel joints

Science discovery

Until the end of the 19th century, scientists thought that waves of energy were smooth and continuous, like waves on water. Then in 1900, Max Planck (1858-1947) suggested that energy waves, such as light rays and X-rays, might be made from tiny separate packets of energy, called quanta. This means the energy wave is more like an up-and-down chain, made of small but individual links, than an up-and-down continual piece of rope. Planck's quantum theory prepared the way for many more discoveries by other scientists.

Playing with gyroscopes

Stand a toy top upright, and it falls over. But start a toy top spinning, and then stand it upright, and it seems to defy gravity. It stands up all by itself. It stays upright for as long as it continues to spin. This is because a spinning top resists being tilted or pulled over by gravity. It is a form of gyroscope. A real gyroscope has a heavy spinning disc inside a frame and can balance on a pin-point.

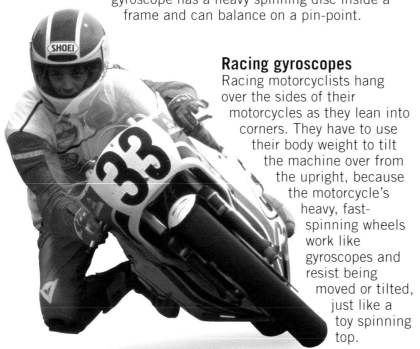

Racing gyroscopes

Racing motorcyclists hang over the sides of their motorcycles as they lean into corners. They have to use their body weight to tilt the machine over from the upright, because the motorcycle's heavy, fast-spinning wheels work like gyroscopes and resist being moved or tilted, just like a toy spinning top.

WHEN MOMENTUM CAN KILL

Mechanical copies of people, called crash test dummies, are used to study the energy conversions involved in car crashes. Injuries in car crashes are caused when the kinetic energy of people's bodies is converted into other forms of energy too quickly, when a car stops suddenly. The momentum of the body keeps it moving until it hits the inside of the car. Safety features like seat belts and air bags work by slowing down these energy conversions. Cars with dummies inside are deliberately smashed into walls or other vehicles. Sensors on and in the dummies measure the forces and pressure involved.

Front impact test crash

See also: Forms of energy page 46, Engines page 66, Electric motors page 96

Transporting nuclear fuel
Fuel for nuclear power stations is dangerous and must not be shaken or spilled. So it is transported inside containers called flasks, designed to withstand almost any accident. They are made from steel and weigh more than 100 tonnes each. Such big, heavy objects can absorb enormous amounts of energy from crashes or fires without bending or cracking. The flasks are usually moved at night, when the rail network is less busy, to reduce the risk of accident.

Keeping your balance
Objects high up have more potential, or positional, energy than those on the ground. So a tightrope walker on a high wire has more potential energy than a person watching from below! If the tightrope walker should slip off the wire, some of this potential energy would change into kinetic energy in the fall.

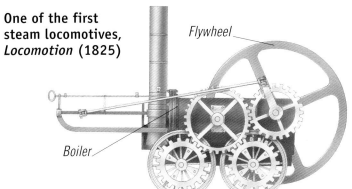

One of the first steam locomotives, *Locomotion* (1825)

Flywheel

Boiler

Steam engines
Steam takes up much more space than water. So when water boils into steam, the steam presses and rushes in all directions. A steam engine feeds the steam into a hollow container or cylinder, where it presses on a piston and pushes this along. The piston then turns a shaft or wheels. The to-and-fro movement of the piston is jerky, so a flywheel is used to even it out, as explained below.

Flywheels
A flywheel is a large, heavy wheel. Once it is turning, it has lots of momentum, and so it spins smoothly for a long time. Flywheels are used to make the small, jerky movements of some engines, like piston-driven steam and petrol engines, smoother and more even. A fast-spinning flywheel also represents a store of energy, in kinetic form. The electro-flywheel works as an electric motor, when electrical energy gets the flywheel spinning at more than 1,000 times each second. It can keep spinning for hours, storing the energy in kinetic form, then work as an electric generator to convert it back into electricity.

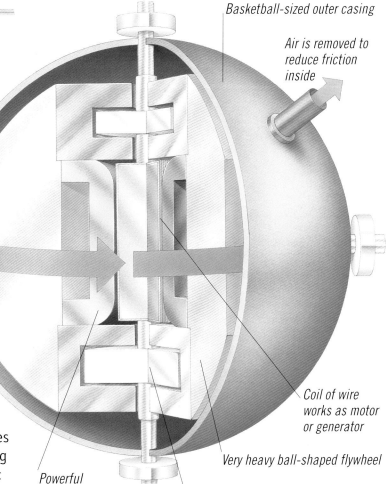

Basketball-sized outer casing

Air is removed to reduce friction inside

Coil of wire works as motor or generator

Very heavy ball-shaped flywheel

Powerful magnets

Low-friction magnetic bearing

Forces and motion

FORCES PUSH, PULL, PRESS and move things. Forces have size or strength – and also direction. A force always acts on an object in a particular direction. If the object is free to move, the force makes it move and speed up, or accelerate, in the direction of the force. When something cannot move, such as a nut in the jaws of a nutcracker, the force can change its shape or even break it apart altogether. When a force pushes against a surface, the result is pressure. The bigger the force, and the smaller the surface area, the higher the pressure.

Fun from forces

A child slides gently to the ground. The force of the child's weight acts straight downwards. But the angle of the slippery slide changes this force into two parts, one acting down and another pushing the child sideways. The steeper the slide, the bigger the downwards part of the force, and faster you go!

Laws of motion

Kick a soccer ball, and you force it to move. Once going, the ball tries to carry on in the same direction at the same speed. But two forces act on it, to change both speed and direction. These are air resistance and gravity. Kicking a ball shows three of the most basic ideas in all of science – the laws of motion.

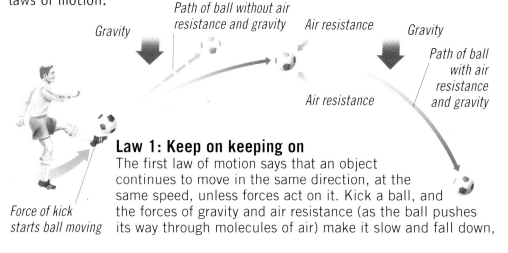

Gravity

Path of ball without air resistance and gravity

Air resistance

Gravity

Path of ball with air resistance and gravity

Air resistance

Force of kick starts ball moving

Law 1: Keep on keeping on

The first law of motion says that an object continues to move in the same direction, at the same speed, unless forces act on it. Kick a ball, and the forces of gravity and air resistance (as the ball pushes its way through molecules of air) make it slow and fall down,

Science discovery

Isaac Newton (1642-1727) was one of the most brilliant of all scientists. One of his greatest achievements was to work out the laws of motion and gravity. These affect everything in the Universe, from atoms and grains of sand, to the Earth, Moon, stars and galaxies in space. Newton also invented a new kind of mathematics, calculus.

Law 2: More means faster

The second law of motion says that the greater the force on an object, the faster the object picks up speed. That is, acceleration of an object is proportional to the force acting on it. So kick harder, and the ball goes faster.

Small force of a soft kick – ball rolls slowly

Large force of a hard kick – ball rolls faster

Roll balls together from opposite directions

Equal but opposite forces mean balls bounce back again

Law 3: Bouncing back

The third law of motion says that when an object hits another, the second object produces an equal force but in the opposite direction. In other words, for every action, there is an equal and opposite reaction. If two soccer balls hit each other, rolling at equal speeds in exactly opposite directions, they bounce apart and roll back the way they came.

See also: Measuring forces page 54, Gravity page 56, Friction page 70

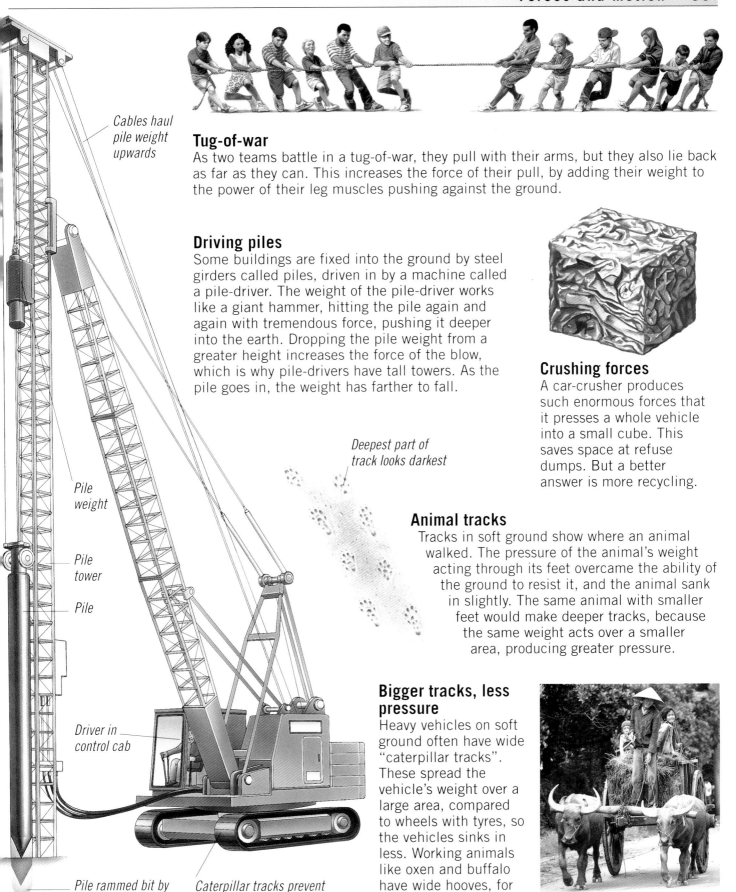

Cables haul pile weight upwards

Tug-of-war
As two teams battle in a tug-of-war, they pull with their arms, but they also lie back as far as they can. This increases the force of their pull, by adding their weight to the power of their leg muscles pushing against the ground.

Driving piles
Some buildings are fixed into the ground by steel girders called piles, driven in by a machine called a pile-driver. The weight of the pile-driver works like a giant hammer, hitting the pile again and again with tremendous force, pushing it deeper into the earth. Dropping the pile weight from a greater height increases the force of the blow, which is why pile-drivers have tall towers. As the pile goes in, the weight has farther to fall.

Deepest part of track looks darkest

Crushing forces
A car-crusher produces such enormous forces that it presses a whole vehicle into a small cube. This saves space at refuse dumps. But a better answer is more recycling.

Animal tracks
Tracks in soft ground show where an animal walked. The pressure of the animal's weight acting through its feet overcame the ability of the ground to resist it, and the animal sank in slightly. The same animal with smaller feet would make deeper tracks, because the same weight acts over a smaller area, producing greater pressure.

Pile weight

Pile tower

Pile

Driver in control cab

Bigger tracks, less pressure
Heavy vehicles on soft ground often have wide "caterpillar tracks". These spread the vehicle's weight over a large area, compared to wheels with tyres, so the vehicles sinks in less. Working animals like oxen and buffalo have wide hooves, for the same reason.

Pile rammed bit by bit into ground

Caterpillar tracks prevent sinking into soft ground

Measuring force and motion

ONE WAY OF MEASURING FORCE is by the way it affects an object. You get an idea of force every time you pick up something, by feeling how much lifting effort you put into overcoming its weight. Bathroom scales show how much your body weight squashes or stretches a coiled spring. To measure movement, we use speed. This is how far an object moves in a certain time. Velocity is speed in a certain direction. A change in velocity is called acceleration when getting faster, and deceleration when becoming slower.

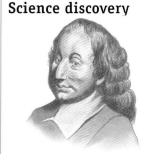
Finding your way underwater

How does a submarine's crew know where they are, underwater? There are no signposts to show the way! They plot their course using gyroscopes and accelerometers. An accelerometer is a heavy weight, with lots of inertia when still or momentum when moving. Each time the submarine turns or tilts, the weight tends to continue in a straight line. Sensitive springs show the forces caused by the difference between the movements of the weight and the submarine around it. A computer uses the information to work out the sub's position, direction and course.

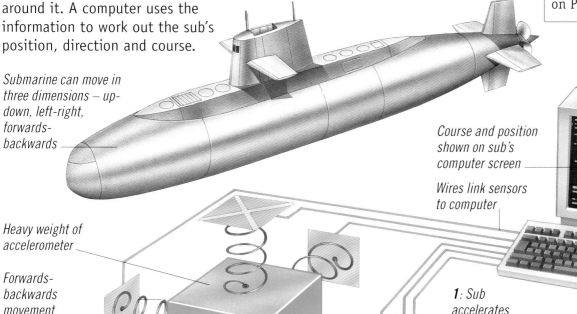

Submarine can move in three dimensions – up-down, left-right, forwards-backwards

Course and position shown on sub's computer screen

Wires link sensors to computer

Heavy weight of accelerometer

Forwards-backwards movement detected here

Sensor springs or special crystals measure changes in force

Side-side movement detected here

Up-down movement detected here

***1**: Sub accelerates forwards*

***3**: Front spring stretches, rear spring squashes*

Heavy weight of accelerometer

***2**: Weight's inertia resists movement*

See also: Forces and motion page 52, Gravity page 56, Sound waves page 112

Sideways forces

As a car speeds around a turn, the driver's body tries to go straight on, according to the first law of motion. So the car presses on the body with a force we call centrifugal force.

G FORCES

▸ Gravity pulls everything at the Earth's surface downwards with a force of one g, or 1g (*g* for gravity).

▸ A pilot in a fast-turning jet plane experiences extra force due to the rapid change in direction. This force may be up to 6g. This means the body feels six times its normal weight.

▸ The body cannot normally cope with such forces. For example, the heart cannot pump blood up to the head and brain against the force. So a person subjected to high g forces may black out after a few seconds.

Club accelerates from rest

Club slows down to rest

Club moves at fastest speed as it strikes ball

Maximum force

A golfer swings a golf club to accelerate the club's lower end, or head. The skill is to make the club's head travel at its fastest speed at the bottom of the swing. This is when the head hits the ball. The faster the club head is going at this time, the greater the force it applies to the ball. So the ball will travel farther. Forces are measured in units called newtons. A normal apple presses down on your hand, due to gravity, with a force of about one newton. A golf club's head hits a golf ball with a force of more than 100 newtons.

Faster than sound

On 15 October, 1997, Thrust SSC (SuperSonic Car) became the first land vehicle to travel faster than the speed of sound. Its two jet engines, borrowed from fighter planes, accelerated it along the smooth, hard sand of Black Rock Desert, USA, to a record-breaking speed of 1,228 kilometres per hour. At the end of the run, a large parachute was released from the rear of the car, to help it decelerate.

Ball receives maximum force

Fin to press car onto ground

Rear road wheel

Jet engine inside streamlined housing

Driver's cab

Side road wheel

Air intake of jet engine

Gravity

WHEN YOU JUMP IN THE AIR, you quickly drop back to the ground. And however hard you throw a ball into the air, it always comes down again. The invisible force that pulls everything downwards on Earth is called gravity. But other objects have gravity, too. In fact, every object has gravity – the force called gravitational attraction.This attracts, or pulls, other objects. So a ball flying through the air pulls the Earth towards it, as well as the Earth pulling the ball. But because the Earth has so much more mass than the ball, and so a much greater inertia (resistance to being moved), it is the ball that moves. Objects like stars are so massive, they have huge gravitational attraction. The Sun's gravity holds all the planets, including Earth, in orbit around it.

Earth and Moon
The Earth and Moon attract each other, but the Earth is much more massive. So the Earth stays almost still compared to the Moon, while the Moon goes around it.

Measuring gravity
Earth's gravity pulls objects down onto its surface. We can measure this force by the amount it stretches the spring in a spring balance. In everyday terms we call it "weight", and we measure it in kilograms or pounds. But in scientific terms, weight is a force and so it should be measured in units called newtons. Bigger objects with more mass (matter or atoms) are pulled more strongly to the Earth. In other words, they weigh more.

Leaning over
The world-famous Leaning Tower of Pisa, in Italy, was slowly being pulled over to one side by gravity. A tall thin object stands upright as long as its top is directly above its base. Then the force of gravity acts straight down through the object. The tower in Pisa was finished in about1350 – but unfortunately, it was built on soft ground. And on one side, the ground was slightly softer than the other. So the tower began to tilt to that side. In recent years, the foundations have been strengthened, and hopefully the Leaning Tower will not lean any further.

Skydiving to the max
Skydivers accelerate towards the ground until the force of gravity pulling them down is balanced by the force of air resistance pushing upwards against them. With these two forces in balance, the skydivers stop accelerating. Their final maximum speed of about 160 kilometres per hour is called their terminal velocity.

See also: Gravity page 56, Planet Earth page 142, Exploring space page 176

Gravity-powered spacecraft

The Cassini-Huygens spacecraft was launched in 1997 to the giant outer planet Saturn. But even the biggest rocket cannot launch a spacecraft straight to Saturn. So the craft uses the slingshot method (below).

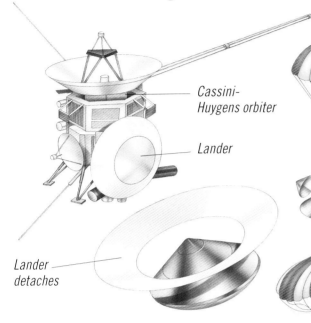

Cassini-Huygens orbiter

Lander

Lander detaches

Small parachute pulls off lander's cap

The slingshot method

The Cassini-Huygens craft was launched not towards Saturn, but at Venus. The gravity of Venus speeds it up until it swings around this planet like a slingshot and heads back to Earth. Earth's gravity gives it another boost, then it slingshots around the Sun, Venus again, and finally Jupiter, before arriving at Saturn.

Large parachute opens

Rings of Saturn

The Cassini-Huygens probe is due to reach Saturn, with its spectacular rings, in the year 2004. The planet's gravity will pull the spacecraft faster and faster towards it. But the angle of the craft's approach should mean that it goes into orbit around Saturn. Then it releases its lander probe. This sends radio signals to the orbiter part of the craft, which relays them to Earth.

Lander drifts down through dense gases of planet Saturn

Lander's heat-shield faces downwards

SWINGING TIMES

Pendulum clocks are driven by gravity. A weight hangs on a cord that is wound around a drum. Gravity pulls the weight down and so the weight tries to turn the drum. Each time the pendulum swings, it lets the drum rotate a small amount, using the escape mechanism. The pendulum also receives a tiny "kickback" from the drum, in return. This tiny kickback on each swing of the pendulum supplies enough energy to keep the pendulum swinging, and the clock ticking, for weeks or even months.

Drum

Cord

Weight

Pendulum

Heat and cold

HEAT IS A FORM OF KINETIC ENERGY. It is the kinetic or movement energy of the atoms in a substance or object. When something is cold, its atoms vibrate, or move about quickly, very little. As the substance or object warms up, its atoms vibrate more and more. Temperature is not the same as heat. Heat is a form of energy. Temperature is a measure of how much heat something contains, or how much hotter or colder it is compared to something else. In normal temperature measurements, the "something else" is when water freezes into ice at 0°C, or boils into steam at 100°C. This is the Celsius (°C) temperature scale.

Hot shots
At high speeds, friction or rubbing with the air causes tremendous heat. So fast planes have outer coverings of metals such as titanium steel, which can withstand very high temperatures.

Measuring temperatures

Very accurate temperature measurements are made by a device called a thermocouple. It consists of two wires made from different metals joined together at their ends. The joined ends are called junctions. If the two junctions are at different temperatures, electricity flows through the wires. The size of the electric current depends on the difference in temperature – the greater it is, the more the current. If one junction is kept at a known temperature, for example, 0°C, the temperature of the other junction can be worked out from the size of the electric current.

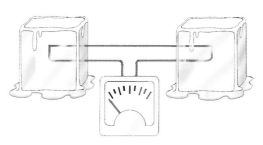

Both junctions at same temperature – no electricity

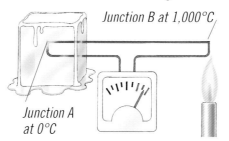

Junction B at 1,000°C

Junction A at 0°C

Junctions at different temperatures – electricity flows

Science discovery

James Joule (1818-1889) was the first person to show that a certain amount of mechanical work, such as turning a handle, produces a certain quantity of heat. In other words, mechanical work and heat are two different forms of the same thing – energy. Joule's investigation of heat led to a new branch of science called thermodynamics, which shows how energy is converted from one form to another.

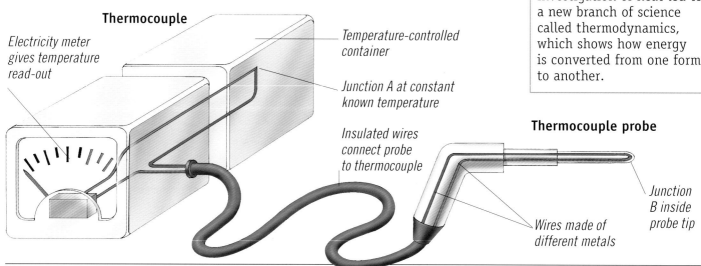

Thermocouple

Electricity meter gives temperature read-out

Temperature-controlled container

Junction A at constant known temperature

Insulated wires connect probe to thermocouple

Thermocouple probe

Wires made of different metals

Junction B inside probe tip

See also: Friction page 70, Electricity page 82, Infra-red rays page 136

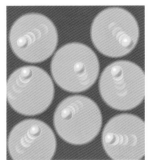

Very hot
In a very hot substance, the atoms or molecules move about a lot. The atoms do not simply swing to and fro, like tiny pendulums. They rush about in all directions, like a small ball (shown in green) bouncing around inside a much larger ball (shown in orange).

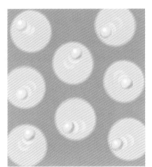

Cooler
When the amount of heat in a substance gets less, this means its atoms and molecules are moving less. We know that the quantity of heat is reduced because the substance feels cooler to the touch, and a thermometer shows that its temperature is lower.

Very cold
A very cold substance has very little heat energy. This means that the atoms and molecules of the substance hardly move around at all. At the lowest possible temperature, which is called absolute zero, they completely cease to move and stay absolutely still.

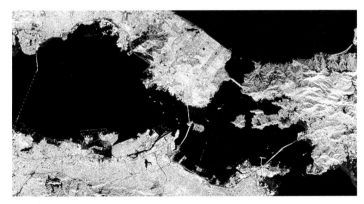

Seeing heat
When we look at things, our eyes detect light rays. These are a form of electromagnetic radiation. As shown later in the book, heat travelling from one place to another is also a form of electromagnetic radiation, known as infra-red rays. Some satellite cameras detect infra-red rays rather than light rays. They take "heat pictures" such as the city shown above. Reds show the warmer parts, blues and black the colder ones.

Keeping out heat
Substances that allow heat energy to pass through them only very slowly, are called thermal insulators. The layers of fibre-glass in the roof of a house are thermal insulation, to keep the warmth inside the house. Firefighting suits are made of a specially flexible thermal insulation material. They also have a smooth surface which reflects some of the heat energy. The surface reflects light rays too, which is why the suits are shiny.

THE RANGE OF TEMPERATURES
In daily life, we experience a very narrow range of temperatures. A cold day might be minus 10°C, while a hot day could be 32°C. The scientific scale for measuring temperature is called the Kelvin scale. Absolute zero is 0 K (minus 273.15°C or minus 459.67°F). Water boils at 373.15 K (100°C or 212°F).

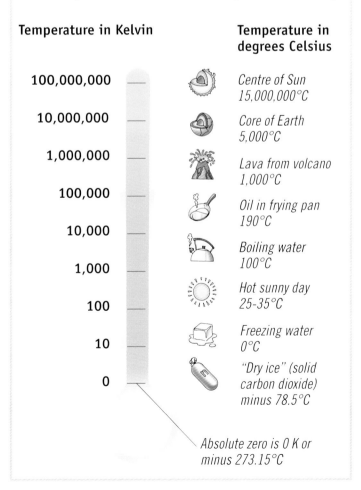

Temperature in Kelvin	Temperature in degrees Celsius
100,000,000	Centre of Sun 15,000,000°C
10,000,000	Core of Earth 5,000°C
1,000,000	Lava from volcano 1,000°C
100,000	Oil in frying pan 190°C
10,000	Boiling water 100°C
1,000	Hot sunny day 25-35°C
100	Freezing water 0°C
10	"Dry ice" (solid carbon dioxide) minus 78.5°C
0	

Absolute zero is 0 K or minus 273.15°C

Helpful machines

IT IS HARD TO IMAGINE A WORLD without machines. It would certainly be a more difficult and less comfortable world, and harder work for people. Machines make tasks easier for us to do, or even do the tasks for us. They lift heavy weights, move heavy loads, fasten things together, pull them apart, wash our clothes, transport people and cargoes, and make or manufacture things – from nails and springs, to cars and planes, to yet more machines. But at a price. Making and using machines depletes the Earth's resources, especially raw materials and fuels.

Progress by machine

One way of measuring "progress" is by the types of machines we use. A region where people have the latest cars, planes, hi-fi systems, computers, power tools and labour-saving household gadgets is said to be modern, developed and progressive. But old-fashioned or outdated machines can have their own charm and attraction.

Simple tool
In olden days, harvest was carried out by human muscle power, using simple tools such as hooks and scythes.

Complex tool

The sequence of events inside a combine harvester is shown by the numbers. One driver can do the same amount of work with this machine, as a hundred people labouring in the field with hand tools. But the combine itself relies on many other people. It needs designers, workshop fitters and welders, sales staff, and service and maintenance engineers.

A combined machine

The combine harvester links together, or combines, all the jobs involved in harvesting crops such as wheat. It is a huge and complex machine. In fact, it is several machines working together. A large diesel engine provides the power to move the combine along the road or field, and to turn all the wheels, cutters, gears, belts and other moving parts. The cutting head snips off the wheat or other crop. The shakers and sorters separate or thresh the valuable grains of wheat from other parts such as the chaff and stalks (straw). On-board bins store the grains as the combine moves to and fro across the field.

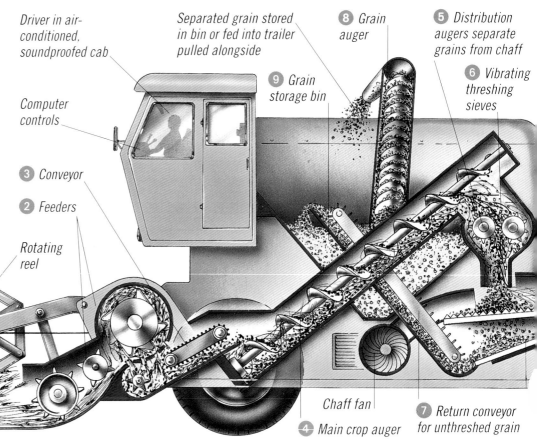

Driver in air-conditioned, soundproofed cab

Separated grain stored in bin or fed into trailer pulled alongside

8 Grain auger

5 Distribution augers separate grains from chaff

Computer controls

9 Grain storage bin

6 Vibrating threshing sieves

3 Conveyor

2 Feeders

Rotating reel

1 Cutter bar

Chaff fan

4 Main crop auger

7 Return conveyor for unthreshed grain

See also: Simple machines page 62, Engines page 66, Earth in trouble page 170

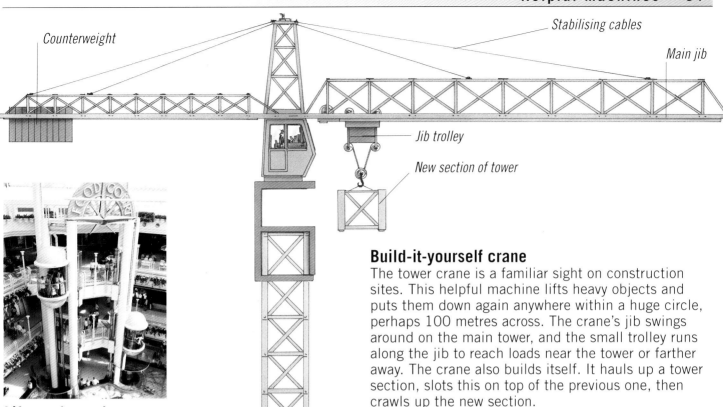

Counterweight

Stabilising cables

Main jib

Jib trolley

New section of tower

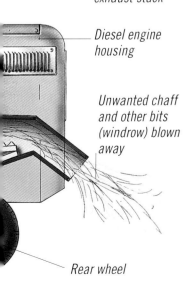

Lifts and escalators

A lift or elevator is a small room hung on cables, that moves up and down. The cables are wound round a drum which is turned by an electric motor. An escalator is a moving stairway, going round and round in an endless loop.

Diesel engine exhaust stack

Diesel engine housing

Unwanted chaff and other bits (windrow) blown away

Rear wheel

Build-it-yourself crane

The tower crane is a familiar sight on construction sites. This helpful machine lifts heavy objects and puts them down again anywhere within a huge circle, perhaps 100 metres across. The crane's jib swings around on the main tower, and the small trolley runs along the jib to reach loads near the tower or farther away. The crane also builds itself. It hauls up a tower section, slots this on top of the previous one, then crawls up the new section.

Science discovery

Some scientific developments, and the inventions resulting from them, are so important that they change people's lives all over the world. In 1903, two brothers from Dayton, Ohio, USA, managed to solve a problem that others had failed to conquer for hundreds of years. They were Wilbur and Orville Wright and the problem was how to build a flying machine. The Wrights made many scientific studies of the shapes of wings, the way propellers work, and how to control an aircraft in flight. They carried out the first true powered airplane flight on 17 December, 1903 at the coastal sand dune area of Kitty Hawk, North Carolina, USA. Their invention of the plane transformed our world.

The Wright's first plane, the *Flyer,* was powered by a small petrol engine that the brothers had designed themselves. They knew that the petrol engines of the time, built for the early motor cars, were too heavy for an aircraft. Over the following years they built improved versions of the *Flyer* and made longer flights.

Soon after the Wright's early flights, many other craft took to the skies. First to fly across the Channel between France and England was Louis Bleriot, in 1909. Soon people began to see the potential for planes as passenger-carriers, beginning the era of fast long-distance travel.

Simple machines

EVERY MECHANICAL DEVICE, even the most complicated giant earth-mover, is made from only four different types of simple machines. These are the lever, the inclined plane or ramp, the wheel and axle, and the pulley. The lever is a stiff beam or bar that pivots at a point called the fulcrum. If the fulcrum is closer to one end than the other, you can use a lever to lift a heavy weight more easily. The inclined plane (ramp or slope) is a machine too. It is usually easier to slide a heavy weight up a slope than to lift it straight up. Place two inclined planes back-to-back and they form a wedge, as in a knife blade, axe or chisel. A wedge wrapped around a rod, in the corkscrew-like shape called a helix, forms a screw. Screws are used to lift things and fasten them together. (Wheels and pulleys are described on the following pages.)

Science discovery
The mathematician and inventor Archimedes (287-212 BC) of Ancient Greece discovered the principle of mechanical advantage that applies to levers and pulleys. These simple machines do not give something for nothing. A lever allows you to move a heavy weight with less effort than by lifting it directly – but the weight does not move very far. In the end, moving the weight the same distance, directly or with a lever, uses the same total amount of energy.

Building the pyramids
The pyramids were built in ancient Egypt about 4,500 years ago, from thousands of blocks of stone – some weighing many tonnes. These may have been levered into place, or dragged up a slope built beside the pyramid, or rolled up on logs. No-one really knows.

Levers at work
The arms of a mechanical digger are made from a series of levers linked together. The arms are moved by oil pumped at very high pressure through pipes, or hoses, into a cylinder. The pressure of the oil pushes a piston along the cylinder and this provides the force, or effort, to move the arm. Cylinders and pistons used in this way are called hydraulic rams.

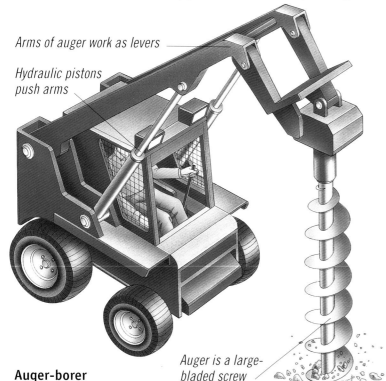

Arms of auger work as levers

Hydraulic pistons push arms

Auger-borer (soil drill)

Auger is a large-bladed screw

Auger bores into ground and pulls earth up and out

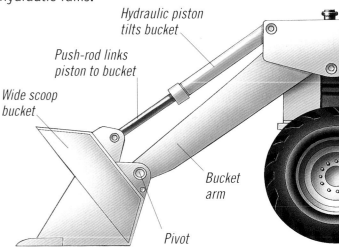

Hydraulic piston tilts bucket

Push-rod links piston to bucket

Wide scoop bucket

Bucket arm

Pivot

See also: Liquids page 26, More simple machines page 64, Engines page 66

DIFFERENT TYPES OF LEVERS

There are three different ways of arranging a lever's effort or moving force, its fulcrum or pivoting point, and its load – the object to be moved or pressed. These different ways are called the three orders of levers. The closer the fulcrum to the load, the easier it is to move the load. But you do not gain any overall advantage, since the load moves less distance.

First order lever

Effort   Fulcrum   Load

In the first order lever, the effort and load are at either end with the fulcrum in the middle, like a see-saw or crowbar. Two such levers sharing the same fulcrum form a pair of scissors or pliers.

Second order lever

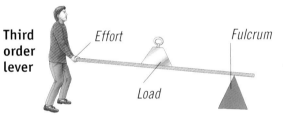

Load   Effort   Fulcrum

In the second order lever, the effort is in the middle, with the fulcrum and load at each end. A mechanical digger's arm uses this arrangement.

Third order lever

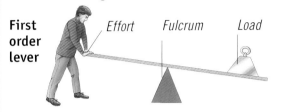

Effort   Fulcrum   Load

In the third order lever, the load is in the middle, between the fulcrum and effort, as in a wheelbarrow or a pair of nutcrackers.

Power of the wedge

A sculptor shapes a piece of stone using a mallet and chisel. The force of the mallet hitting the chisel is passed to the thin, sharp, wedge-shaped chisel blade. The mallet blow's large force acts on a tiny area at the blade tip, producing enormous pressure. The stone gives way and cracks apart.

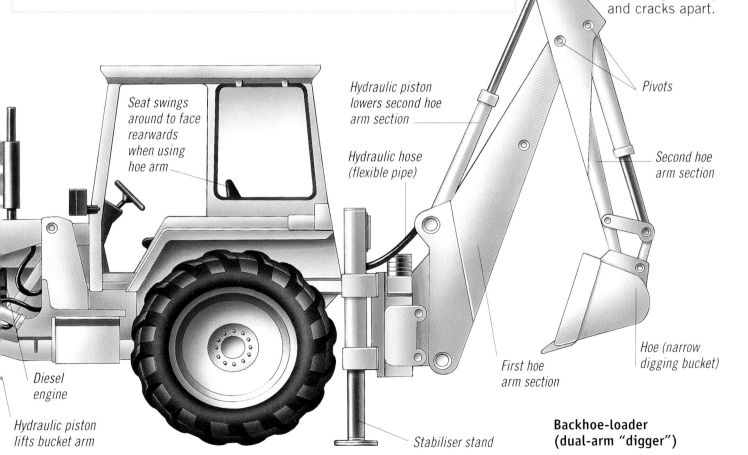

Seat swings around to face rearwards when using hoe arm

Hydraulic piston lowers second hoe arm section

Hydraulic hose (flexible pipe)

Pivots

Second hoe arm section

Diesel engine

Hydraulic piston lifts bucket arm

First hoe arm section

Stabiliser stand

Hoe (narrow digging bucket)

Backhoe-loader (dual-arm "digger")

More simple machines

THE WHEEL IS A SIMPLE MACHINE. It works like a lever. But instead of tilting on a fulcrum or pivot, it turns or revolves around an axle. Wheels enable us to move heavy weights more easily than by dragging or sliding them along. A pulley is a wheel with a groove around its rim, for a cord, rope, cable or chain. By tying a rope around a heavy load, and passing it up over a pulley, the load can be lifted by pulling the rope down. This is easier than pulling up, because you can use your weight as well, for extra force.

The first wheels
The invention of the wheel made it easier to move people and goods on land. The first carts had plank wheels. Spoked-wheeled chariots date from 5,000 years ago.

The ride-on machine

A bicycle is a great example of a collection of simple machines. There are wedges, levers, screws, wheels, pulleys, springs and gears. Each one is slightly different in shape and size, to carry out its job and withstand the stresses and strains placed on it.

Nut and bolt (screw principle) secure saddle

Brakes work by levers to press on wheel rim

Brake handle works as a lever

Spring for suspension

Main road wheel turns on axle

Chain goes around toothed pulleys (cogwheels)

Gears

A bicycle's rear wheel has a set of gearwheels or cogwheels, of different sizes. When you change gear, the chain slips sideways from one gearwheel onto the smaller or larger gearwheel next to it. The smaller the gearwheel, the fewer teeth it has. So the more times it and the rear wheel turn around, for each turn of the front gearwheel, which is attached to the pedals. Low gears, using the larger rear gearwheels, mean pedalling needs less effort. But the bicycle does not move very far for each turn of the pedals.

See also: Helpful machines page 60, Simple machines page 62, Engines page 66

Twisting through air

An aircraft's propeller is a simple machine – a screw. It twists through the air, pushing the air backwards and propelling the plane forwards. This plane, the *Raven*, has a human engine. The propeller is turned by bicycle pedals powered by the pilot.

Tracked vehicles

A bulldozer's wheels act as pulleys. Only two of the wheels are driven by the engine. The rest guide the tracks round and round in an endless loop. To steer left or right, the track on one side moves more slowly than the other track.

Going up – or down?

The drive machinery of a lift or elevator uses two principles of simple machines. One is the pulley – or rather, pulleys. The cable that holds the elevator goes around several pulleys, and is wound by an electric motor. Pulleys are also useful to change the direction of a force, from upwards, to sideways, to down. The second principle is the mechanical advantage of the lever. Again, this involves pulleys. The cable goes around a pulley on top of the lift car, and is then fixed to the top of the lift shaft. This makes it twice as easy for the motor to pull the car up, compared to a cable fixed to the car itself. But for each turn of the motor pulley, the cable moves only half as far, than if the cable was fixed directly to the car.

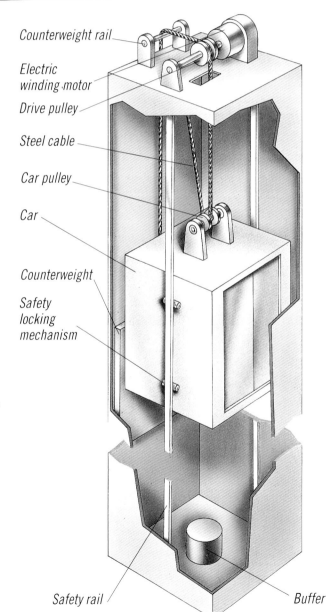

Counterweight rail

Electric winding motor

Drive pulley

Steel cable

Car pulley

Car

Counterweight

Safety locking mechanism

Safety rail

Buffer

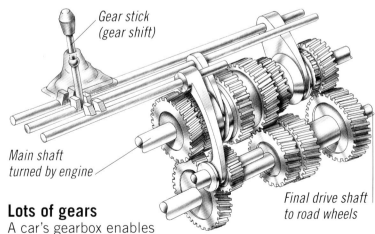

Gear stick (gear shift)

Main shaft turned by engine

Final drive shaft to road wheels

Lots of gears

A car's gearbox enables it to travel at different speeds along the road, even though the engine is turning at the same rate. The gearbox has sets of toothed gearwheels that can be linked together in different combinations. The main shaft is turned by the engine. The final drive turns the road wheels.

Power for machines

SOME MACHINES ARE WORKED by muscle power. But many machines are driven by engines or motors. In order to drive its machine, an engine or motor needs energy, in the form of fuel, which it can convert into the kinetic energy of motion. Electric motors convert electrical energy into the movement energy of a spinning shaft. Other engines and motors use chemical energy stored in fuels such as petrol, diesel, kerosene (jet fuel), gas, coal and wood. The energy is released from the fuel by burning, or combustion. Steam engines burn their fuel in a furnace or firebox outside the engine. Petrol and diesel engines burn their fuel inside, so they are called internal combustion engines.

Under the hood
Most cars have their engines under the bonnet or hood, at the front of the vehicle. The fuel tank is at the rear, and specially designed to resist crushing and prevent spillage.

The petrol engine
Inside a petrol engine, a rod-shaped piston moves down inside a hollow cylinder, sucking or inducing air and a fine spray of fuel into the cylinder through the inlet valve (1). The valve closes and the piston rises, squashing or compressing the mixture of fuel and air inside the cylinder (2). A spark from an electric spark plug makes the mixture combust (burn or ignite). As it burns in a small, short, sharp explosion, it expands and pushes the piston down the cylinder (3). It is this force that turns a car's wheels. Finally, the piston rises again and blows out the burned gases through the open outlet or exhaust valve (4). Several pistons, usually four or six, work in sequence to make the engine run smoothly.

Flywheel

Inlet valve
Exhaust valve
Spark plug
Camshaft
Cam

Cylinder
Piston

Cam belt

Crankshaft

Crank

Connecting rod

Little end bearing
Big end bearing

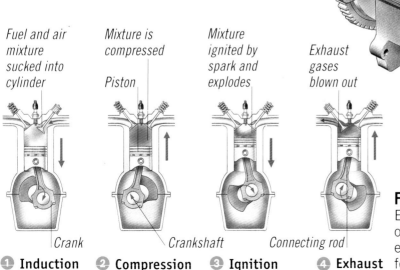

Fuel and air mixture sucked into cylinder

Mixture is compressed

Piston

Mixture ignited by spark and explodes

Exhaust gases blown out

Crank

Crankshaft

Connecting rod

① Induction ② Compression ③ Ignition ④ Exhaust

Four-stroke cycle
Each movement of the piston in the cylinder, up or down, is known as a stroke. In a typical petrol engine, the cycle of events for one piston involves four strokes, so this is a four-stroke engine.

See also: Chemical changes page 36, Electric motors page 96

Science discovery

Engineer Karl Benz (1844-1929) invented a machine that changed the world – the automobile or motor car. There had been steam-powered and petrol-driven vehicles before, but they were unreliable, even dangerous. In 1885 Benz produced the first reliable petrol-engined car. It was a three-wheeled vehicle with a top speed of only 29 kilometres per hour. But it began a new age of travel.

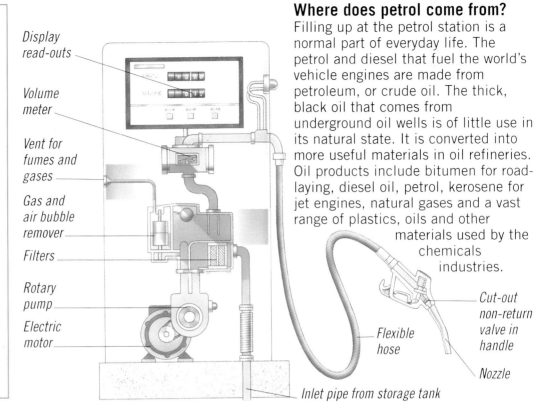

Display read-outs

Volume meter

Vent for fumes and gases

Gas and air bubble remover

Filters

Rotary pump

Electric motor

Flexible hose

Cut-out non-return valve in handle

Nozzle

Inlet pipe from storage tank

Where does petrol come from?

Filling up at the petrol station is a normal part of everyday life. The petrol and diesel that fuel the world's vehicle engines are made from petroleum, or crude oil. The thick, black oil that comes from underground oil wells is of little use in its natural state. It is converted into more useful materials in oil refineries. Oil products include bitumen for road-laying, diesel oil, petrol, kerosene for jet engines, natural gases and a vast range of plastics, oils and other materials used by the chemicals industries.

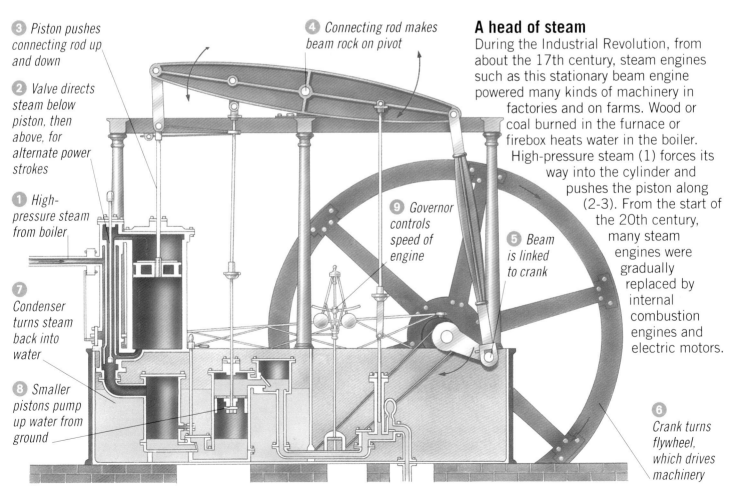

❸ Piston pushes connecting rod up and down

❷ Valve directs steam below piston, then above, for alternate power strokes

❶ High-pressure steam from boiler

❼ Condenser turns steam back into water

❽ Smaller pistons pump up water from ground

❹ Connecting rod makes beam rock on pivot

❾ Governor controls speed of engine

❺ Beam is linked to crank

❻ Crank turns flywheel, which drives machinery

A head of steam

During the Industrial Revolution, from about the 17th century, steam engines such as this stationary beam engine powered many kinds of machinery in factories and on farms. Wood or coal burned in the furnace or firebox heats water in the boiler. High-pressure steam (1) forces its way into the cylinder and pushes the piston along (2-3). From the start of the 20th century, many steam engines were gradually replaced by internal combustion engines and electric motors.

More machine power

JET ENGINES AND ROCKETS have continual explosions going on inside them. A jet engine burns kerosene fuel to produce a jet of hot gases. These blast out of the back of the engine, and thrust the engine – and the plane, car or whatever is attached to it – forwards. A jet engine must take in air from the atmosphere, because this contains the oxygen needed to burn its fuel. So jet engines work only in the air of the Earth's atmosphere. Above the atmosphere, in space, there is no air. Spacecraft engines have to take their own supply of oxygen with them, as a chemical called oxidizer, to burn their fuel. They take off using the most powerful engine of all – the rocket.

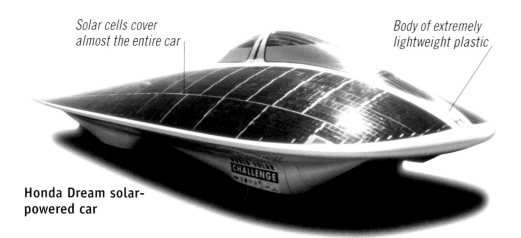

Solar cells cover almost the entire car

Body of extremely lightweight plastic

Honda Dream solar-powered car

Sun power

Vehicles worked by light energy from the Sun – solar power – would be much kinder to the environment than vehicles with petrol or diesel engines. Solar energy produces no air pollution. Solar cells on the car convert sunlight into electricity for the electric motor.

The jet engine

The type of jet engine used in most large passenger planes is the turbofan. The huge fan at the front sucks in air. Some of the air enters the engine and is squeezed by a spinning many-bladed compressor. Fuel sprays into the compressed air and burns. It expands and rushes out of the engine through a turbine, whose spinning drives the compressor and fan. The burning gases provide the main thrust.

Inside the jet

The huge main fan at the front of a turbofan jet engine works like a propeller. It blows some air into the main engine, and some air around the engine. This bypass air helps to add thrust for more forward power. It also works as an "air blanket" to cool and quieten the main engine.

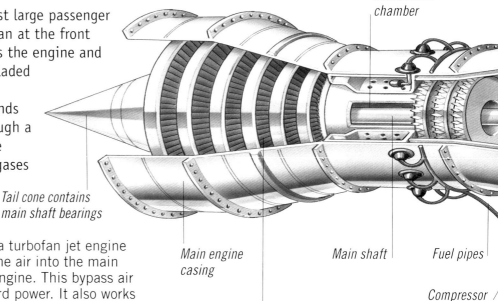

Combustion chamber

Tail cone contains main shaft bearings

Main engine casing

Exhaust turbines

Main shaft

Fuel pipes

Compressor turbines

See also: Friction page 70, Using light page 132, Exploring space page 176

PERPETUAL MOTION MACHINES

Before the science of energy was understood, some people thought it might be possible to build a machine that, once started, would continue working for ever, without fuel. This is a perpetual motion machine. Despite thousands of attempts, no such machine has been made. This is because even the most well-oiled machine loses energy, for example, through friction (rubbing) and heat. So it needs a supply of energy to keep going.

"Falling balls" design runs for days – but not for ever

Rocket science

In a rocket engine, fuel burns with the chemical oxidizer inside the combustion chamber. The hot gases blast out the back, thrusting the rocket forwards, according to the third law of motion – every action has an equal and opposite reaction. A rocket must reach a speed of 28,000 kilometres per hour. This is the speed at which it can enter space and go into orbit around the Earth. A multi-stage rocket has several sets of engines and fuel tanks. These fall away one by one, saving weight as the pull of gravity reduces with height, and less power is needed.

Minimum drag

Fast boats, cars, planes and trains have sleek, streamlined designs. This reduces the problem of resistance or friction with the air, as they push its gas molecules out of the way. The streamlined shape slides past molecules, rather than knocking into them. The slowing effect of air resistance is known as drag. Lower resistance or less drag gives higher speeds and more efficient fuel use.

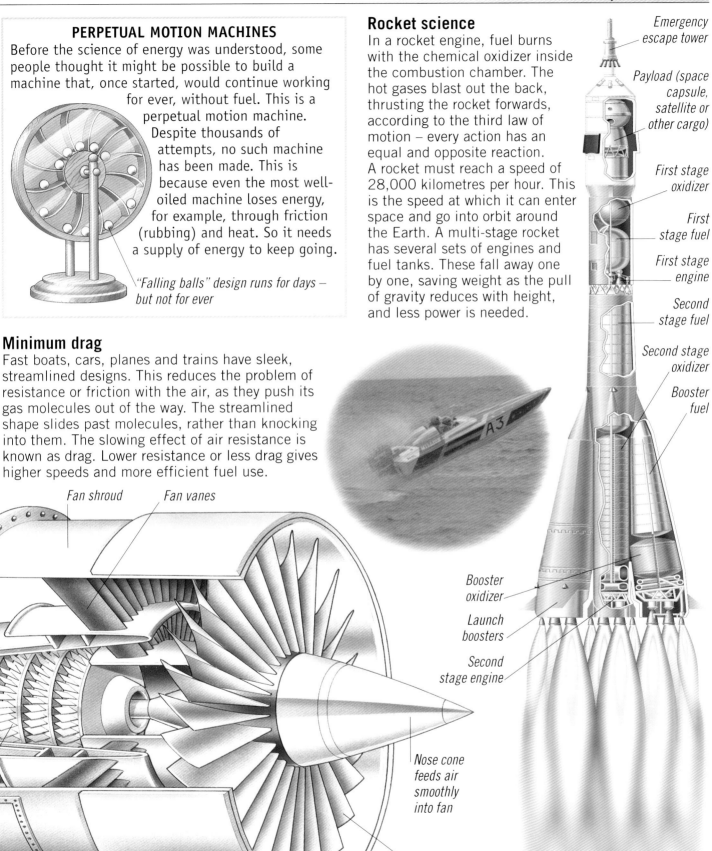

Emergency escape tower

Payload (space capsule, satellite or other cargo)

First stage oxidizer

First stage fuel

First stage engine

Second stage fuel

Second stage oxidizer

Booster fuel

Booster oxidizer

Launch boosters

Second stage engine

Fan shroud

Fan vanes

Nose cone feeds air smoothly into fan

Main fan

Friction

FRICTION IS A FORCE that resists motion. It always acts in the opposite direction to the motion. Friction is caused by the lumps and bumps on two surfaces, rubbing and catching together as they slide across each other. Even the smoothest surface has these tiny lumps. Friction means that objects slow down and lose kinetic energy. This energy does not disappear, but changes into heat. Rub your hands and feel it! In machines, where parts are constantly sliding past each other, a thin film of oil or grease between the parts reduces rubbing, friction and wear. Using oil or grease to reduce friction is called lubrication.

Slow descent
A climber slides or abseils safely down a rope. The rope is wound in and out of steel hoops clipped to the climber's harness. Controlled friction between rope and hoops stops the climber falling too quickly.

BALL-BEARINGS

A bearing is part of a machine specially designed to reduce friction between moving parts. A ball-bearing reduces friction by replacing sliding with rolling. The two grooved collar-shaped parts of the bearing are called races. As the outer race stays still and the inner race rotates, the steel balls between them roll. Wheels often spin on their axles by means of ball-bearings.

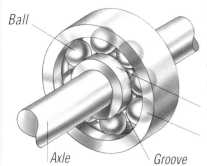

Ball

Inner race

Outer race

Axle

Groove

Riding on air

A hovercraft glides over the water on a cushion of air. When a boat moves through water, the water pushes back against the boat and slows it down. This sort of resistance or friction is called drag (see opposite). In a hovercraft, air blows underneath the boat so fast that its pressure overcomes the boat's weight and lifts it above the surface. The hovercraft's rubber skirt helps to stop the air from escaping too fast and increases the height of the air cushion.

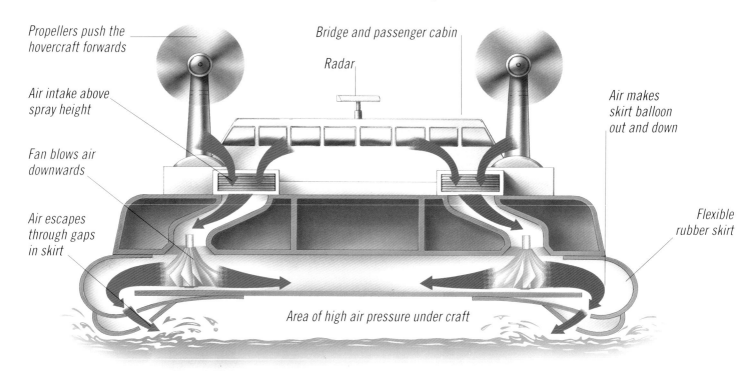

Propellers push the hovercraft forwards

Bridge and passenger cabin

Radar

Air intake above spray height

Air makes skirt balloon out and down

Fan blows air downwards

Air escapes through gaps in skirt

Flexible rubber skirt

Area of high air pressure under craft

See also: Water page 32, Energy of motion page 50, Forces and motion page 52

Vital friction

Friction is often called "the enemy of machines". Yet some machines rely on it, to work effectively. One example is the car brake. Friction between the brake discs and brake pads makes the wheel turn more slowly. Then friction between the wheel's rubber tyre and the road makes the car slow down.

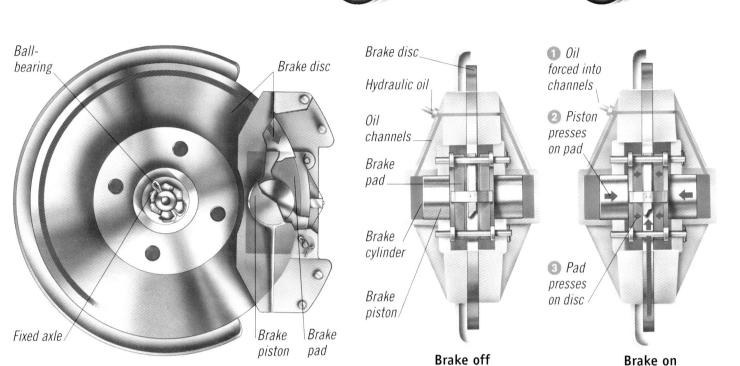

Ball-bearing

Brake disc

Fixed axle

Brake piston

Brake pad

Brake disc

Hydraulic oil

Oil channels

Brake pad

Brake cylinder

Brake piston

Brake off

1 Oil forced into channels

2 Piston presses on pad

3 Pad presses on disc

Brake on

Disc brakes

When a car driver presses the brake pedal, oil is forced through pipes into cylinders on each side of a metal disc, the brake disc, attached to each road wheel. The oil pressure pushes pistons, which press roughed brake pads against the spinning disc. Friction between the disc and the pads slows the disc and wheel.

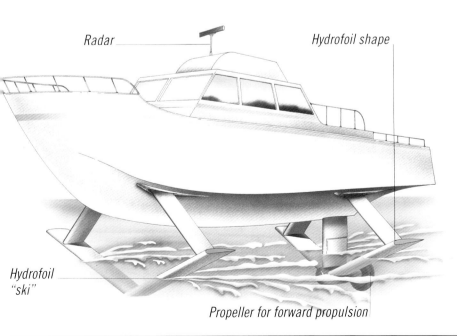

Radar

Hydrofoil shape

Hydrofoil "ski"

Propeller for forward propulsion

Flying through water

A hydrofoil is a boat with "skis". These have the same shape as an aircraft wing, more curved on the upper side than below, and work in the same way. As the boat moves forwards, water must go farther over the upper surface than the lower surface. So it moves faster.This creates lower pressure, and the hydrofoil is lifted upwards. At high speeds the boat rises right out of the water, greatly reducing the drag caused by friction.

Side view of hydrofoil

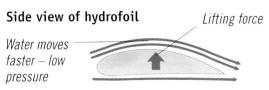

Lifting force

Water moves faster – low pressure

Energy for the world

MOST OF THE ENERGY USED all over the world comes from three sources – oil, coal and natural gas. These are called fossil fuels, because they are made of the rotted, semi-fossilised remains of living things from millions of years ago. Another common energy source is biomass – recently living material or products, such as wood or animal dung. In some parts of the world, biomass in the form of firewood is the only source of energy. Nuclear power is important in some countries, although it brings the problems of nuclear accidents and nuclear waste. Countries with high mountains and plenty of rain can generate electricity from the energy of flowing water. This is hydroelectric power.

Wind energy
Wind, water and muscle power were the main sources of energy for machines, until the steam engine was developed from the 17th century. The traditional windmill works by swivelling its sails into the wind so that they rotate with maximum force. The sails turn an axle that operates machinery inside the mill, such as millstones to grind corn.

Hydro-energy

A hydroelectric power station makes electricity from moving water. The water flows through pipes containing turbines, which spin around and turn generators. As the water pressure pushing against the turbine blades increases, the blades spin more powerfully, and generate more electricity. So, to increase the water pressure, and also to ensure a plentiful year-round supply of water, a dam is built across a river valley. Water piles up behind the dam, filling the valley and forming a lake.

Energy demand
Power stations feed their electricity into a grid or distribution network.

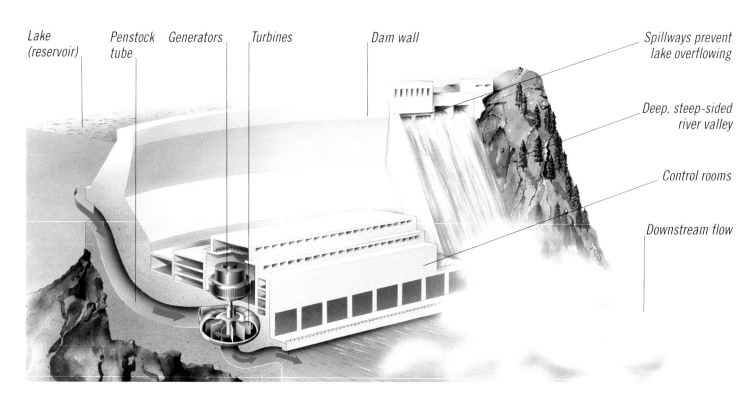

Lake (reservoir)   Penstock tube   Generators   Turbines   Dam wall   Spillways prevent lake overflowing

Deep, steep-sided river valley

Control rooms

Downstream flow

See also: Water page 32, Converting energy page 48, Earth in trouble page 170

Science discovery
Marie Curie (1867-1934) taught herself science by reading books. When she heard about the discovery that uranium produced strange rays, she began to test many substances to see if they also produced such rays. Her word "radioactivity" describes the energies given off by such materials. Marie discovered two new radioactive elements, radium and polonium. Her work helped other scientists to develop nuclear power, as shown on the next page.

Using fossil energy
We are using up fossil fuels millions of times faster than they can be formed. At the present rates of use, known reserves of oil will run out in 100-200 years, and coal in 300-400 years. Also, mining coal which is at or near the surface, open-cast mining, scars on the landscape.

WAVE ENERGY
Waves and tides carry a great deal of energy, which can be converted into electricity. A machine called a duck bobs up and down as waves wash past it. The rocking movement drives a generator, or pumps liquid or gas to spin a turbine that turns the generator. Another wave generator design is the oscillating water column. This is a tall chamber with one end under the water. Waves rise and fall inside the chamber and force the air in it through a turbine at the top. To harness the energy of tides, a dam-like barrier or barrage is built across the mouth of an inlet or bay. The tidal flow spins turbines inside the barrage.

Rocking "duck"

Tilting shafts connected to generator

Each "duck" has its own shaft

Sustainable and renewable energy
Our favourite form of energy is electricity. It can be transported huge distances along wires, and converted into movement, light, heat, sound and other useful forms. But our main sources of energy to make electricity – fossil fuels – will not last for ever. They are not sustainable or renewable, and they cause great pollution. So scientists are developing sustainable or renewable energy sources, which will not run out and which should cause less pollution. They include winds, waves, tides, sunlight, flowing water (hydro-energy) and hot rocks deep underground (geothermal energy). Aerogenerators or wind turbines are modern versions of windmills, making electricity from the energy in moving air.

Many wind turbines form a wind farm or park

Energy and matter

ENERGY CAN CHANGE INTO MATTER (ATOMS), and matter can change into energy. Matter changes into energy in a process called nuclear fission. Some substances, such as certain forms of uranium, have atoms with big, unstable nuclei. When bombarded with atomic particles, such as neutrons, these nuclei split apart. As they do so, they release a burst of energy and more neutrons, so the process can continue. Nuclear fission happens in nuclear power stations. Scientists have also carried out the opposite, and changed energy into matter. In the right conditions, particles of matter can pop into existence, where there was no matter before.

Keeping control
Nuclear reactors have many safety features and bristle with sensors, monitoring circuits and warning devices. But accidents still happen.

Nuclear power

"Nuclear" involves the nucleus, or central part of an atom. In a typical nuclear power station, the nuclei of certain atoms in the fuel split apart. This is nuclear fission. As the nuclei split, they form other substances. But these do not weigh quite so much as the original fuel, which is usually uranium. Tiny amounts of matter or mass have been converted into huge amounts of heat and other energy. Nuclear reactions are so powerful that a lump of uranium the size of your fist can release the same amount of heat as burning a pile of coal bigger than a house.

① Nuclear power station
Nuclear power can produce vast quantities of heat energy, to be converted into electricity. But it also involves dangerously radioactive substances, and produces many kinds of radioactive wastes. Safe disposal of these wastes, which will stay radioactive for many centuries, is a mounting problem.

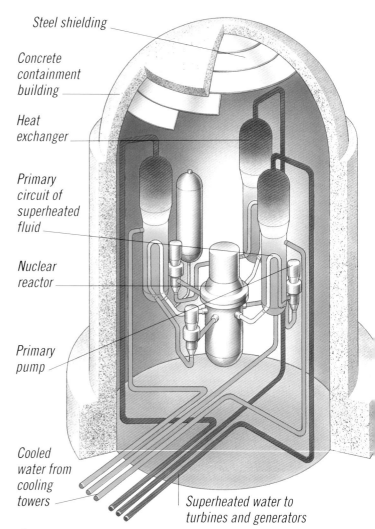

Steel shielding

Concrete containment building

Heat exchanger

Primary circuit of superheated fluid

Nuclear reactor

Primary pump

Cooled water from cooling towers

Superheated water to turbines and generators

② Containment building
Heat from the reactor passes to the primary fluid. This passes it on to superheat water, which flows away to make the steam, that drives the turbines to produce electricity.

See also: Atoms page 14, Inside the atom page 16, The Sun page 188

③ Nuclear reactor

The part of a nuclear power station where the heat is generated is called the reactor. This warms a special primary fluid to extremely high temperatures. The primary fluid is pumped through heat exchangers sited around the reactor, where it superheats water for the turbines.

④ Fuel rod assemblies

The nuclear fuel, such as a form of uranium, is shaped into long rods. In some designs, the fuel is embedded in another substance, the moderator. This slows down atomic particles flying out of the fuel's atoms as the atoms split, so that the particles are more likely to hit other fuel atoms and continue the reaction. Control rods can be lowered into the reactor to slow down the nuclear reactions by absorbing some of the particles.

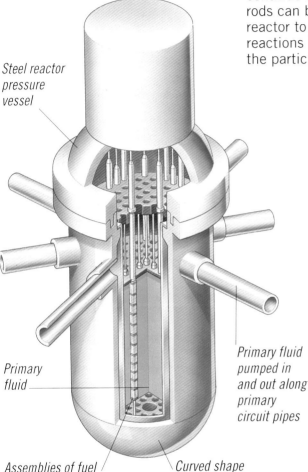

Steel reactor pressure vessel

Primary fluid

Assemblies of fuel and control rods (see above right)

Curved shape withstands enormous pressure

Primary fluid pumped in and out along primary circuit pipes

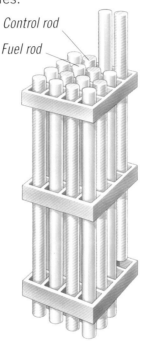

Control rod

Fuel rod

More neutrons given off, in chain reaction

Neutrons hit more fuel nuclei

More neutrons given off

Two nuclei of fission products

Nucleus of fuel atom splits

Neutron

⑤ Nuclear fissions

A nucleus of a fuel atom is hit by a fast-moving particle, a neutron. This makes the nucleus split into two smaller nuclei, which are fission products such as lead. In the process, the nucleus also gives off more neutrons plus large amounts of energy. The neutrons cause more splits, and so on, in a chain reaction. Control rods and moderators keep the chain reaction in check.

Future nuclear power?

Nuclear power stations are huge structures, as shown on the right, and pose various risks, such as radioactive pollution. Far away from Earth, stars also make heat and light by nuclear power. But this involves fusion or joining of nuclei, rather than fission. Scientists are trying to copy this process in experimental nuclear fusion reactors. Nuclear fusion uses hydrogen as fuel, which can be simply made from sea water. And it produces little or no radioactive waste. But practical problems, especially the incredible temperatures, are immense.

3

Electricity and Magnetism

Electricity is a type of energy based on the movement of bits of atoms, called electrons. Magnetism is a mysterious and invisible force that can push or pull. Electricity produces magnetism, and magnetism produces electricity. Together they are the basis of innumerable machines, from motors to computers.

Electrical energy

ELECTRICITY IS AN INVISIBLE form of energy. It is based on the tiny charged particles inside atoms. In an atom's nucleus, particles called protons have a positive charge. Whizzing around the atom's nucleus are electrons, which have a negative charge. Normally, the positive and negative charges balance. If they become unbalanced, an electrical force is produced. This may stay in one place, as static electricity, or move from place to place, as a flowing current. Electricity is so useful to us because it can flow along wires to wherever we need it, and be changed into other forms of energy such as light, heat and movement.

Danger! Electricity!
Electrical energy can be very dangerous. An electric shock from a mains socket, which has a voltage of about 110 or 220 volts, can easily kill a person. The high-voltage (high-tension) electricity carried by cables on pylons is hundreds of thousands of volts. It can "jump" several metres through the air. So stay well clear!

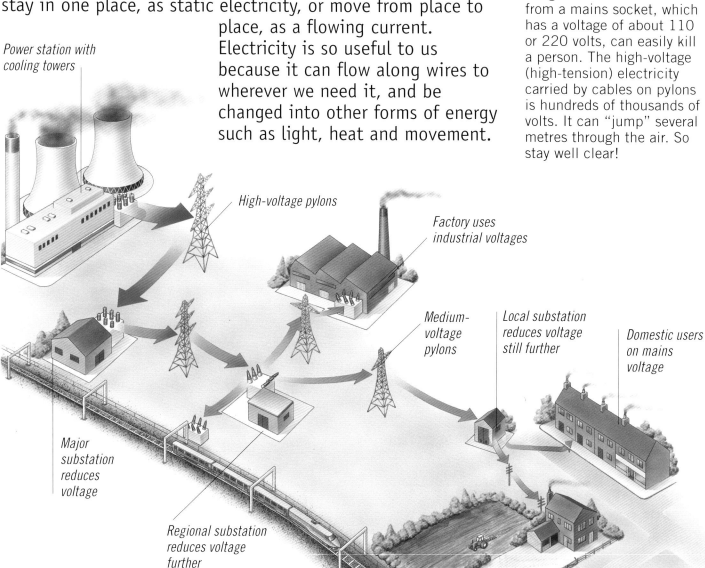

Power station with cooling towers

High-voltage pylons

Factory uses industrial voltages

Medium-voltage pylons

Local substation reduces voltage still further

Domestic users on mains voltage

Major substation reduces voltage

Regional substation reduces voltage further

The electricity network

Power stations turn the energy of movement into electrical energy which is medium strength, or mid voltage. This is changed into more powerful, high-voltage electricity and sent along large cables or wires, high on pylons or buried underground. This network of cables and wires is called the electricity distribution grid. The electricity is changed back into lower-power forms, industrial and mains voltage, for use in factories, farms, offices and homes.

See also: Static electricity page 80, Flowing electricity page 82

Electricity in atoms

Everything is made up of trillions of incredibly tiny particles, called atoms. An atom has a central nucleus containing protons, each with a positive charge, and neutrons, each with no charge, or neutral. Going around the nucleus in empty space are much smaller particles, called electrons, each with a negative charge. When atoms or substances gain or lose electrons, they become electrically charged. Gaining electrons makes them negative. Losing electrons makes them positive.

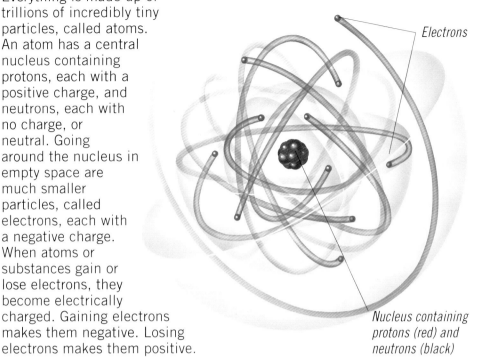

Electrons

Nucleus containing protons (red) and neutrons (black)

Science discovery

Benjamin Franklin (1706-1790) was one of the first people to study electricity in detail. In 1752, he flew a kite fitted with a metal key into a thundercloud. Sparks flew off the key, showing that lightning was a form of electricity. Franklin said that electricity consisted of two states of a mysterious fluid, an idea which is no longer believed.

Electricity at work

If there was a power cut in this city, people would have to manage without most of their lighting and heating, and the machines that make their lives so much easier. Daily routine would grind to a halt and the only sources of energy would be batteries, candles, wood, coal or gas. Yet people managed without electrical devices for thousands of years, and still do in many parts of the world. It is only in the last century or so that electricity has been put to work. One of its great advantages is that it is available at the flick of a switch.

SENSING ELECTRICITY

Sharks have a special sense which allows them to detect weak electrical signals. These are given off naturally by the muscles of their prey and travel well in water. A shark uses tiny sensory pits in the skin of the snout, called ampullae of Lorenzini, to detect the electricity. Other water-living animals can also detect electricity, including elephant-snout fish and squid. Electric eels, electric rays and electric catfish can also make powerful bursts of electricity to stun their prey.

Static electricity

YOU SHUFFLE ACROSS a carpet, touch a metal doorknob – zap! You feel a tiny electric shock as a spark jumps from you to the metal. This sort of electricity is called static electricity. It can make your hair stand on end, attract dust to the television set or stick a balloon to a wall. Static electricity builds up when two different non-metal materials rub together, as shown opposite. It can pull things together or push them apart, because opposite charges attract and like charges repel. Static can be destructive, as in a lightning strike, or useful, as in photocopiers, paint-sprayers and air-ionizers.

Lightning spark
Lightning is a way of releasing the electrical energy that builds up inside thunderclouds. It is a giant spark or discharge of static.

Using static

Photocopies work using static electricity and the attraction of unlike charges. A rotating drum, coated with a material which allows electricity to flow when light shines on it, is positively charged with static electricity. Light from the white areas of the item to be copied shines on the drum and the charge flows away. The black areas keep their positive charge, and attract a negatively charged powder, the toner, which is then transferred to the paper.

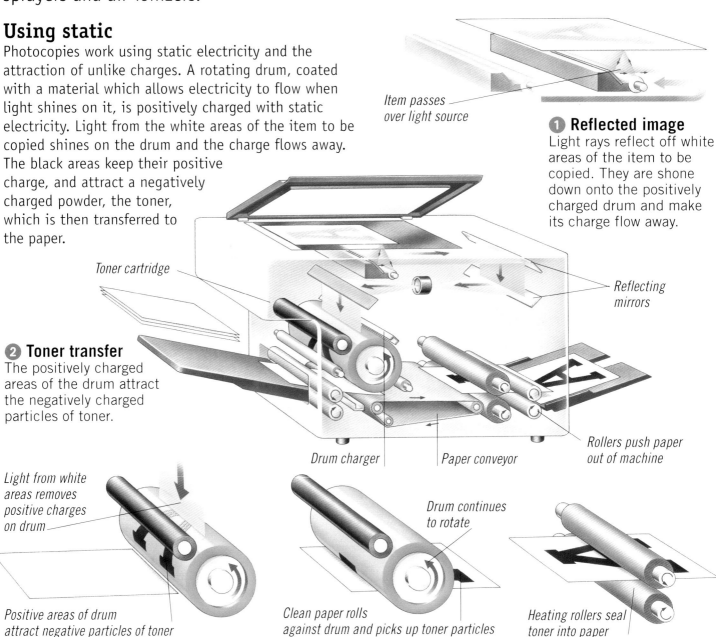

Item passes over light source

1 Reflected image
Light rays reflect off white areas of the item to be copied. They are shone down onto the positively charged drum and make its charge flow away.

Toner cartridge

Reflecting mirrors

2 Toner transfer
The positively charged areas of the drum attract the negatively charged particles of toner.

Drum charger

Paper conveyor

Rollers push paper out of machine

Light from white areas removes positive charges on drum

Drum continues to rotate

Positive areas of drum attract negative particles of toner

Clean paper rolls against drum and picks up toner particles

Heating rollers seal toner into paper

See also: Electrical energy page 78, Mysterious magnets page 92

Gigantic charges

Scientific research equipment such as Van der Graaf generators can produce massive amounts of static charge, measuring billions of volts. These charges are passed through substances and materials to study the effects, or given to atoms and other particles to make them travel at great speed.

Each copy requires the drum to be recharged

❸ Sealing toner

The tiny heat-sensitive particles of toner are "melted" into the paper by heating rollers. Meanwhile the drum is charged again, ready for the next copy.

Science discovery

The first photocopier was made by an American lawyer, Chester Carlson (1906-1968), in 1938. He called his process xerography, from the Greek words *xeros,* "dry" and *graphos,* "writing". At the time, writing was usually with ink and so wet at first. Those first copies took an hour or more to make. But they were valuable documents because they were exact replicas which could be used in law courts. Copying documents by hand might introduce mistakes.

SEPARATING CHARGE

Rubbing or friction makes electrons move. This gives one material a positive charge and the other a negative charge. The charges stay, or remain static, on the surfaces of the materials, until they have a pathway along which they can flow suddenly, or discharge. Static charge can pull things together or push them apart because (similar to magnets) opposite charges attract and like charges repel.

The two materials are brought near to each other. Each has billions of atoms. Each atom has a central nucleus (red) with one or more electrons (blue) going around it. The negative electron is kept near its positive nucleus by electrostatic forces, since unlike charges attract.

The energy of rubbing or friction gives electrons extra energy. This allows some of them to break free from their nuclei and wander off on their own. It is known as "separating charge". Some electrons pass or transfer from one material to the other.

One material has gained extra electrons and so becomes negatively charged. The other has lost electrons and is positively charged. The charges stay on the surfaces of the materials. (In a metal, the charges would be able to spread and disperse into the object.)

Charge-storers

Electronic circuits in hi-fi systems, televisions and computers have fingertip-sized devices called capacitors (shown here as light brown "buttons"). These are used to store static electrical charge. The charge can be released all at once at a certain moment, or in a steady series of steps.

Flowing electricity

WHEN YOU TURN ON A LIGHT, you are using the sort of electricity that flows along wires, like water flowing along pipes. This is called current electricity. It is usually made up of billions of electrons flowing along a wire or through an electrical component. These electrons do not move along a wire by themselves. They have to be pushed along by a difference in electrical state, called potential difference, produced by a battery or a power station. The power of an electric current is used to drive all kinds of machines in our homes, schools and workplaces.

Inside a wire

An electric current consists of billions of electrons, separated from their atoms, flowing along a wire. The electrons "hop" from one atom to the next, travelling in short bursts. Individual electrons move only fractions of a millimetre each second. But, like pushing a row of railway wagons, they have knock-on effects all along the wire. The result is that the effects of electricity travel at the speed of light, 300,000 kilometres per second.

Science discovery

Engineer Nikola Tesla (1856-1943) supported the now-accepted use of alternating current for most practical applications, as shown on later pages. In 1888 he built his first induction motor, which is the type of motor used in many domestic machines and appliances. He also invented a type of transformer, the Tesla coil, which produces enormous voltages and is used in radio technology.

Direct current, DC

In DC, all the electrons move in the same direction, all the time that the electricity flows. This type of current is produced by the batteries in torches, cars and similar devices.

Electrons moving along

Plastic covering or insulation stops electrons escaping from wire

Flow reverses

Flow reverses again

Alternating current, AC

In AC, the direction of electron movement changes many times each second. The electrons move one way, then the other, and so on.

Each atom has a central nucleus (red) and an area where electrons orbit (blue)

See also: Electrical energy page 78, Electricity from chemicals page 84

Electrons have knock-on effects along the whole wire

Keeping electricity in

Electricity passes or flows easily through some materials, mainly the metals that form wires. But it is stopped by other materials, such as plastic. So most wires and cables have plastic coatings, called electrical insulation.

Electrical cables

Electrical power cables are held above ground on pylons or towers, and buried underground in pipes or conduits. They can even be trailed down onto the sea bed by specialised cable-laying ships (above), linking one country with another hundreds of kilometres away. Similar cables are laid to carry telephone messages and electronic communications. But undersea earthquakes or fast-flowing currents of material on the sea bed, called turbidity currents, can snap these cables.

ELECTRICITY IN THE BODY

There are tiny electrical currents and pulses passing naturally through the body all the time. Some are nerve signals, moving around the brain, from the sense organs such as the eyes to the brain, and from the brain out to the muscles. A muscle also makes electrical pulses when it contracts to cause movement. The faint electrical pulses from the brain can be detected on the skin by sensors, strengthened and displayed on a screen or paper chart. The machine that does this is an EEG, electro-encephalograph.

Having an EEG is entirely painless. Sensors stuck on the skin of the head detect faint electrical signals coming naturally and continuously from the brain. The patterns of the signals show if the brain is healthy or if there could be a problem.

Trace of EEG machine showing "brain waves"

Jagged lines indicate electrical nerve signals

ELECTRICAL LETTERS

Electrical engineers and circuit designers use a variety of letters and symbols to describe the different features of electricity, such as its strength or quantity.

A	Amperes (amps), the unit for measuring amount or quantity of electric current.
AC	Alternating current, when the current's direction switches rapidly to and fro.
C	The amount of electrical charge that can be stored, in coulombs.
DC	Direct current, when the current's direction stays the same.
EMF	Electromotive force, the pushing strength of electricity measured in volts.
F	The amount of electrical capacitance, measured in farads.
HZ	The measure of how fast something happens, (such as a.c.) in Hertz.
J	The amount of energy or work, including electricity, measured in joules.
KWH	Kilowatt-hour, how many thousand watts of power are made or used per hour.
P.D.	Potential difference, the pushing strength of electricity measured in volts.
V	Volt, the standard unit for measuring the pushing strength of electricity.
W	Watt, a standard unit of power, including electrical power.
Ω	Ohm, a measure of how much a substance resists electricity passing.

Electricity from chemicals

THE SIMPLEST UNIT for making electricity is called a cell. It makes electricity from chemical reactions and works like a pump to push electrons along wires. A battery has two or more cells and some types, such as car batteries, are rows or "batteries" of single cells, hence our common name "battery" for single and multiple cells. In a primary cell, as electricity is produced, the chemicals are slowly used up. Eventually, the chemicals run out and the battery cannot make electricity any more. In a secondary cell, the chemicals can be replenished or reformed by recharging the cell with electricity.

Electric animal

Muscles produce tiny electrical signals as they work. In the electric eel, these muscles form large blocks along the body. They produce powerful surges of electricity, hundreds of volts, like a "living battery".

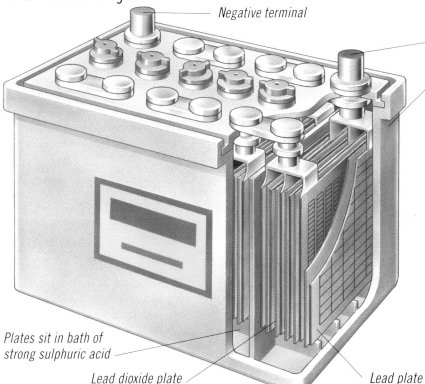

Negative terminal

Positive terminal

Acid-proof casing

Plates sit in bath of strong sulphuric acid

Lead dioxide plate

Lead plate

Car batteries

Also called an accumulator, a vehicle, batteries can be recharged. The chemical reaction which has taken place to make electricity can be reversed by putting electricity back in, so the battery can be used again. In a vehicle the recharging is carried out by an alternator, which is driven by the engine. Most car batteries have six linked cells, each with an output of about two volts. Each cell consists of lead plates, lead dioxide plates and sulphuric acid. Electricity is produced in the reactions between the plates and the sulphuric acid.

Substances such as acids dissolve in water to form charged particles, ions – positive cations (red) and negative anions (blue). In a cell, these form the electrolyte. When other materials, such as metal rods, are put in the electrolyte, they act as electrodes. They attract opposite-charged ions and cause an electric current to flow.

HOW A CELL WORKS

Positive ion   Negative ion

The electrolyte consists of charge particles called ions, positive and negative.

Anode   Cathode

The electrodes are the positive anode and the negative cathode.

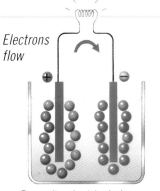

Electrons flow

Opposite electrical charges attract and electrons move, making the current.

See also: Electrical energy page 78, Electrical circuits page 86

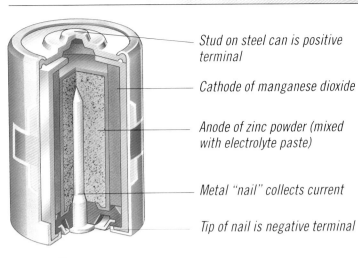

Stud on steel can is positive terminal

Cathode of manganese dioxide

Anode of zinc powder (mixed with electrolyte paste)

Metal "nail" collects current

Tip of nail is negative terminal

Dry cell

"Dry" cells contain an electrolyte paste, rather than the liquid electrolyte in a vehicle battery. The long-life or alkaline dry cell has a combined anode (positive terminal) and electrolyte of powdered zinc in a paste.

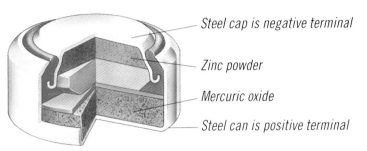

Steel cap is negative terminal

Zinc powder

Mercuric oxide

Steel can is positive terminal

Mercury-zinc "button" cell

This button-sized cell is used in watches, cameras, calculators, hearing aids and similar small devices. The anode is zinc powder and the cathode is mercuric oxide. Most button cells produce about 1.4 volts.

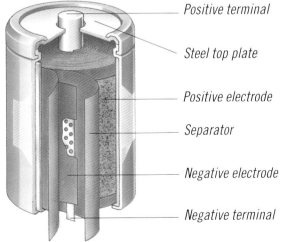

Positive terminal

Steel top plate

Positive electrode

Separator

Negative electrode

Negative terminal

Rechargeable or NiCad dry cell

The secondary or rechargeable dry cell is based on the metals nickel (Ni) and cadmium (Cd), hence the common name of "NiCad".

Science discovery

In 1800, Italian count Allessandro Volta (1745-1827) discovered that two different metals, separated by moist chemicals, could produce a flow of electric charge. This was the first electric cell. Volta piled the cells together on top of each other to make the first true battery, called the Voltaic pile. When he touched a wire from the top of the pile to a wire at the bottom, he got sparks of electricity.

This was the first time that a reliable supply of constantly flowing electrical current had become available. It began a whole new area of science, and sparked off a vast range of new inventions.

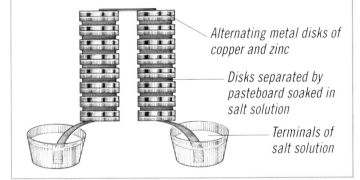

Alternating metal disks of copper and zinc

Disks separated by pasteboard soaked in salt solution

Terminals of salt solution

HEART PACEMAKERS

Sometimes the tiny electrical pulses that make the heart beat naturally do not work properly. An artificial electrical pacemaker stimulates the heart to beat regularly, usually at one beat per second. It is powered by batteries which last at least five years, and sometimes up to 12 years. The artificial pacemaker detects when the heart is not producing its own electrical impulses and fills in the gaps.

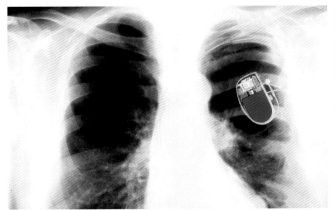

This coloured X-ray shows an artificial cardiac (heart) pacemaker, blue, implanted under the skin at the front of the chest. The heart is just below it, under the ribs.

Electrical circuits

IN SOME MATERIALS, called conductors, the electrons can easily leave their atoms and become free to move. This allows electricity to flow through them with little trouble. In other materials, called insulators, the electrons are held tightly in their atoms. This stops electricity flowing easily. The pathway that an electric current takes as it flows along is called a circuit. The current will only flow if the pathway is unbroken – a complete circuit. If there is a gap in a circuit, with air or another insulator in the way, electricity cannot flow. A switch is a device that makes or removes a gap in a circuit. This allows us to turn the electric current on and off.

Circuits at home
Electricity comes into a house through wires that go into a consumer unit, sometimes called the "fuse box". Then the wires divide into several branches or circuits called ring mains, some for the lighting and some for the power points in the wall sockets. One ring main consists of a cable that runs around the house, to all the power points one by one, and then back to the consumer unit. This allows electricity to reach a wall socket by flowing both ways around the ring, along the cables. This helps to share out the electricity demand around two routes, and avoids the problem of overload.

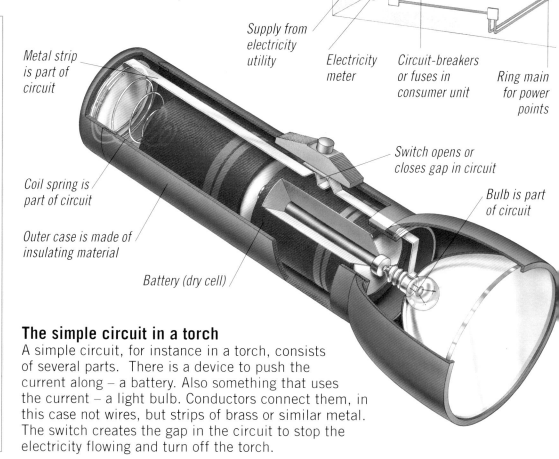

Spur cable to water heater

Supply from electricity utility

Electricity meter

Circuit-breakers or fuses in consumer unit

Ring main for power points

Switch opens or closes gap in circuit

Bulb is part of circuit

Science discovery

Georg Simon Ohm (1789-1854) showed that all conductors, even the best metals, resist the flow of electricity to an extent. The unit of electrical resistance is called the ohm in his honour. Ohm's law says that the current flow through a conductor, in amps, is proportional to the potential difference across it, in volts:
  volts = amps x ohms

Metal strip is part of circuit

Coil spring is part of circuit

Outer case is made of insulating material

Battery (dry cell)

The simple circuit in a torch
A simple circuit, for instance in a torch, consists of several parts. There is a device to push the current along – a battery. Also something that uses the current – a light bulb. Conductors connect them, in this case not wires, but strips of brass or similar metal. The switch creates the gap in the circuit to stop the electricity flowing and turn off the torch.

See also: Electrical energy page 78, Flowing electricity page 82

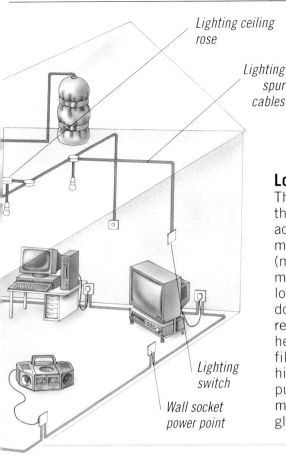

Lighting ceiling rose

Lighting spur cables

Lighting switch

Wall socket power point

Lots of resistance

The large cables that carry electricity across country are made of alloys (mixtures or combinations of metals), to combine strength with low resistance. Electrical energy does not simply disappear due to resistance – it mostly changes into heat. This is why the thin wire filament of a light bulb has a very high resistance. Electricity must push hard to get through it. This makes the filament so hot that it glows with a bright white light.

CIRCUIT SYMBOLS

To save time and avoid confusion, circuit diagrams are drawn with small symbols that represent standard components. This is one of the many examples of the international scientific language of signs and symbols.

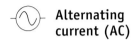 Alternating current (AC)

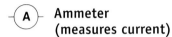 Ammeter (measures current)

 Electrical cell

Fuse

Relay

Switch

 Transformer

Voltmeter (measures p.d.)

——www—— Resistor

Variable resistor (rheostat)

——mmm—— Coil (solenoid)

Capacitor (stores charge)

Preset capacitor

Electrolytic capacitor

Diode

LED (light emitting diode)

Bipolar transistor

Field effect transistor

TYPES OF CIRCUITS

There are many ways of connecting together various components and wires, to make circuits. In a series circuit, the components are joined one after the other. If one component is removed or fails, it breaks the circuit and nothing works. In a parallel circuit, each component has its own "mini-circuit". So if others fail, it still works.

Light bulb

Cell (battery)

Variable resistor

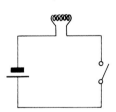

Switch open – no current flows

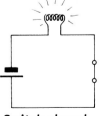

Switch closed – current flows

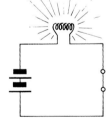

Extra cell in series – twice the current

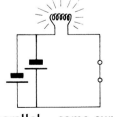

In parallel – same current lasts twice as long

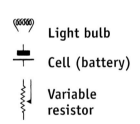

Maximum variable resistance

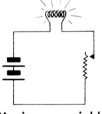

Minimum variable resistance

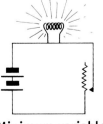

Using electricity

ELECTRICITY IS OUR MOST USEFUL and adaptable source of energy. It can be carried long distances along wires, and changed readily into other forms of energy. At home these include light in electric light bulbs, fluorescent tubes and television sets, movement in motors, pumps and fans, sound in the telephone and music system, heat in the cooker or microwave oven, and even the absence of heat – cold, in a refrigerator or deep-freezer. There are also hundreds of different uses of electricity in industry, from powering machines, tools and robots, to red-hot furnaces and white-hot welding arcs. Hospitals rely on electricity to run X-ray machines, scanners, ventilators, heart-lung machines and other life-saving equipment. Electricity is also vitally important in transport and communications, as shown on later pages.

Science discovery

André Marie Ampère (1775-1836) worked in many areas of science, including physics, chemistry and scientific philosophy. Following the work of Oersted, Ampère made many discoveries about electricity and the electromagnetic effect. He noted that the strength of the magnetic field around a wire was related to the amount of current flowing through the wire and the distance from the wire (Ampère's law). He devised the idea of winding wire into a coil, the solenoid, to increase its magnetic strength. The unit of electric current, the amp (ampère), is named in his honour.

Electricity on the farm

Electrical farming machinery saves time and carries out much heavy work automatically. Milking machines speed up the milking process, and electric conveyor belts move straw and grain. Automatic feeding machines make sure that farm animals receive the right meals at suitable times. Young animals, such as chicks, can be reared in the warmth of electric incubators. Electric heating has extended the growing season for greenhouse crops, and electric clocks control lamps to make "daylight" longer. This encourages flowers to open and fruits to ripen even in winter darkness. Electric sprayers water plants, and the soil itself can be warmed by buried electric wires.

See also: Electrical energy page 78, Electrical circuits page 86

Electric heat

When an electric current flows along a wire, the moving electrons bounce off the metal atoms in the wire and make them move too. This gives the atoms extra energy, which is given off from the wire as heat. The faster the atoms move, the warmer the wire gets, because the heat content of an object depends on the speed of its atoms. Many machines, from electric kettles and toasters to electric fires and furnaces, contain heating elements that work in this way. The heat may move naturally away as rising hot air, which is known as convection. Or fans may blow the heat away as a moving current of hot air, as in a hair-dryer. This is forced convection. Or reflectors help to move heat by bouncing back the infra-red heat rays, as in a radiant electric fire. Electrical heating equipment usually has a thermostat. This cuts off the electric current if the heating element gets too hot, so avoiding the risk of a fire or damage to the machine.

Electrifying factories

During the mid 19th century, some factories began to convert from steam power to electricity. They used a steady supply of current from rows of lead-acid batteries, and the first practical electric motors to work the machinery – like Bonelli's electric-driven silk weaving loom from the 1880s.

A UNIT OF ELECTRICITY

The amount of electricity used by equipment depends on the device or appliance itself, when it is used, and for how long it is used. In general, equipment that turns electricity into warmth, such as kettles, ovens, hobs, immersion water-heaters and electric fires, uses more electrical energy and so costs more. Very bright light-makers, such as halogen spotlights, are also expensive. Equipment that uses microchips and small motors, such as electric toothbrushes and shavers, consumes less electricity. Often, the amount of electrical power (rating or "wattage") used by an appliance is marked on its casing, information plate or label. For example, a typical filament electric light bulb is usually 60 or 100 watts. In many regions, electrical energy is measured in units. One unit of electricity is the amount consumed by a 1,000-watt (1 kW) appliance over a period of one hour, or a 100-watt device over 10 hours. This energy does not disappear. It changes into other forms, such as light, heat, sound and movement. The cost of electricity is usually less at night, when demand is lower.

Filament light bulb 10 hours

Electric drill 2 hours

This chart shows the time in hours that typical appliances would run on one unit of electricity.

Instant shower	.2
Hob with four rings on maximum	.3
Washing machine (cold-fill)	.3
Electric kettle (24 cups)	.5
Clothing tumble-dryer	.5
Large fan-powered space heater	.5
Immersion heater	1
Small convector heater	1.2
Electric mower	1.2
Medium-sized microwave oven (on maximum)	1.2
Hedge-trimmer	1.5
Hand-held hair dryer	1.5
Drill	2
Vacuum cleaner	2
Small television	5
Hi-fi music system	8
Normal (filament) light bulb	10
Deep-freezer	10
Large (1.5-metre) fluorescent tube	15
Small refrigerator	15
Low-energy (compact fluorescent) bulb	25
Shaver	100
Toothbrush	200

Electricity makes magnetism

ELECTRICITY IS CLOSELY RELATED to an invisible natural force called magnetism (which is described in more detail on the following pages). In fact, electricity and magnetism are two aspects of the same force, which modern science views as one of the four fundamental forces in the entire Universe – electromagnetism. When electricity flows through a conductor, such as a length of wire, it produces an invisible magnetic field around the wire. This is known as the electromagnetic effect. Magnets made in this way, by flowing electricity, are called electromagnets.

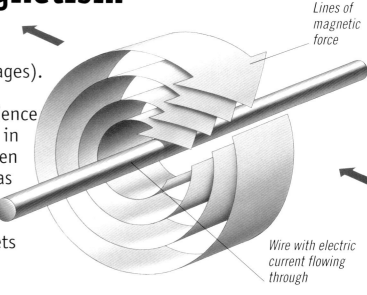

Lines of magnetic force

Wire with electric current flowing through

Invisible force

The magnetic field or force around an electricity-carrying wire goes in a circular direction, curling around the wire.

The electromagnet

A typical electromagnet consists of a coil of plastic-covered wire wrapped around an iron bar, which is known as the core. A coil of wire, or solenoid, produces a stronger magnetic field than a straight length of wire. The wire is connected to a source of electricity such as a battery. As soon as the electric current is switched on, the bar becomes a very powerful magnet. Switch off the electricity, and the magnetism disappears. Most electromagnets use soft iron for the core because this loses its magnetism as soon as the electricity is switched off. A hard steel core would keep its magnetism for a while.

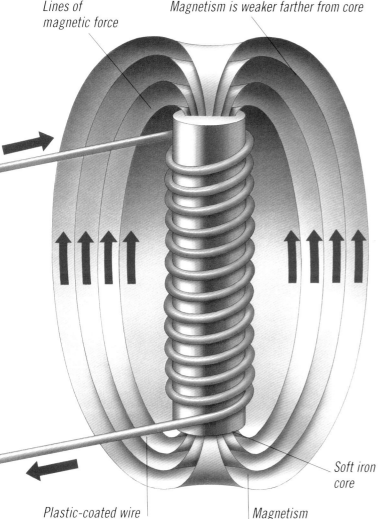

Lines of magnetic force

Magnetism is weaker farther from core

Plastic-coated wire with electric current flowing through

Magnetism concentrated at ends of core

Soft iron core

Science discovery

In 1820, Danish scientist Hans Christian Oersted (1777-1851) noticed that a wire with an electric current passing through it worked like a magnet, making a needle on a nearby magnetic compass move. A compass needle is a tiny magnet and magnets can pull each other together or push apart. Oersted realised that the electric current was producing magnetism, and he was the first to discover the electromagnetic effect. Almost at once, many other scientists began to experiment with this effect.

See also: Flowing electricity page 82, Mysterious magnetism page 92

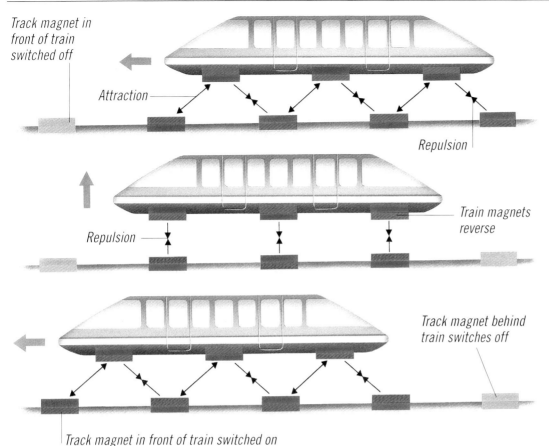

Track magnet in front of train switched off

Attraction

Repulsion

Train magnets reverse

Repulsion

Track magnet behind train switches off

Track magnet in front of train switched on

❶ Along
Electromagnets in the train and track produce pulling (attraction) and pushing (repulsion) forces that propel the train forwards.

❷ Up
The electromagnets in the train reverse their magnetic field for a split second, to produce strong repulsion forces and keep the train up.

❸ Along
The train electromagnets reverse their magnetism again, to propel the train forwards, and so on, many times each second.

Magnetic trains
Electromagnets are used instead of wheels on some trains. The train "floats" a few centimetres above the track, pushed upwards by a magnetic force produced by electromagnets. This type of train is called a maglev, meaning magnetic levitation. There have been many versions of maglev trains. However most of them suffer from practical problems, such as the cost of laying and maintaining the specialised electromagnet-containing track.

Sorting metals
Powerful electromagnets are used in scrapyards to pick out and move certain objects from piles of mixed rubbish. Magnets attract the metal iron, and so steel (which is mostly iron), also nickel and cobalt. This electromagnet is attached to a crane.

Quiet and fast
A maglev train is quiet and fast. There is no noise from the wheels because no part of the train touches the track. Also, the train is not held back by friction with the track. But the maglev system uses large amounts of electricity and relies on complicated switching circuits. However, some maglev projects in progress today may help to make this type of transport more common.

Mysterious magnetism

HOLD A MAGNET near a refrigerator door. You can feel it being pulled towards the door. If you let go, the magnet "sticks" to the door. Yet it does not stick to a plastic beaker, a glass window or a piece of wood. The invisible force of magnetism remains mysterious, even though people have known about it for more than 2,000 years. Magnetism seems to be something to do with groups of atoms, called domains. In non-magnetic materials, the domains point in all directions and cancel each other out. In magnetic materials, all the domains point in one direction and their magnetic forces add up. Magnets attract mainly ferrous materials – those containing iron.

Lines of magnetic force are closest and so magnetism is strongest at the poles

Magnetic fields

Every magnet is surrounded by an invisible magnetic field, which is the space in which the force of its magnetism works. A pattern of imaginary lines provides a picture of this magnetic field. These lines of force show that the magnetic field is strong closest to the magnet but becomes weaker farther away. The power of a magnet is strongest at two points, called the poles, which are usually near the ends of a bar-shaped magnet. There are two poles, called the north and south poles. They are named after the poles of the Earth, to which they are attracted. Unlike poles attract. Like poles repel.

FINDING THE WAY

A compass needle points to the magnetic North Pole and magnetic South Pole of the Earth. This is because the compass needle is a small, thin magnet and the Earth is a giant magnet. So the needle lines up with the Earth's magnetic field. The needle in a compass is balanced on a fine point so that it can turn easily. The magnetic north pole is about 1,600 kilometres away from the true north pole. The magnetic south pole is about 2,400 kilometres away from the true South Pole. The Earth's magnetic poles move a few centimetres each year and the strength of the Earth's magnetism changes slowly over long periods of time.

North or north-seeking end of compass needle

Compass needle points north

Base of compass turned to align north on dial with north-pointing needle

---

See also: Electricity makes magnetism page 90

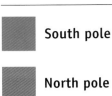

South pole

North pole

Lines of magnetic force become farther apart, or weaker, farther from the magnet

Lines of magnetic force are parallel to the long bar of the magnet

Magnetic animals

Ships and boats use magnetic compasses to help them navigate across the featureless ocean. Certain animals, such as whales, dolphins and sea turtles, and birds like pigeons, swallows, geese and storks, also seem to use the Earth's magnetic field to help them find their direction and route on long journeys. Scientists are not sure how these animals detect the magnetism. It could be connected with tiny particles of iron-containing minerals inside or near the brain, which may form a "living compass".

Science discovery

Charles Coulomb (1736-1806) was an army engineer who turned to the physical sciences in 1791. He studied the attraction and repulsion forces produced by magnets and by objects with electrostatic charge. He invented a torsion balance, based on twisting a piece of stiff wire, that could measure tiny forces accurately. He used this to develop his law, which showed that magnetic forces fade rapidly, by the square of the distance between the magnetic objects.

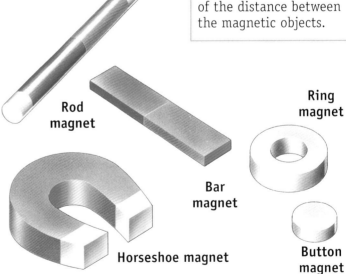

Rod magnet

Ring magnet

Bar magnet

Button magnet

Horseshoe magnet

Lines of magnetic force curve around to pole of magnet

Magnet shapes

Magnets can be made in different shapes. Bar magnets are long and narrow, while horseshoe magnets are curved like the metal shoes on a horse's hooves. Magnets can also be made in rings or thin cylinders, like pencils. A ring magnet can have one pole around the inside of the ring and the other on the outside.

Magnetism to electricity

IN 1831, ENGLISH SCIENTIST MICHAEL FARADAY suggested that if electricity moving in a wire produced magnetism, the opposite might be true – a magnet moving near a wire could produce electricity. He moved a magnet in and out of a coil of wire, and electricity flowed in the wire. This is called electromagnetic induction. The electric current flows only while the magnetic field moves or varies. If the magnet and wire are still, no current flows. Electromagnetic induction is used in hundreds of machines and devices, from audio and video magnetic tape recorders and electric guitar pick-ups, to traffic light systems. It is also used in electric motors and generators, as shown on the following pages.

Lots of induction
A video recorder stores millions of tiny patches of magnetism every second. These are turned back into electrical signals and then spots of light for viewing.

Record-playback head spins at an angle to the tape

Magnetic pattern recorded as series of angled stripes

Tape moves left to right

Record-playback head
In a video recorder, the head spins around one way as the tape moves past it the other way. This increases the passing speed of tape to head, and allows more signals to be stored per second, for better picture quality.

Record-playback head

Tape guide pin

Erase head

Video recorder
A video or audio tape recorder stores electrical signals as tiny patches of magnetism on magnetic tape. The record-playback head is an electromagnet which arranges metal particles on the tape in a pattern that follows the pattern of the incoming electrical signals. When the tape is played, the stored pattern of magnetic patches on the tape move past the tiny wire coils in the record-playback head, and produce electrical signals by electromagnetic induction.

Control panel and display

Tape insert slot

Magnetic tape inside plastic case

See also: Electrical energy page 78. Electricity to magnetism page 90

Science Discovery

American scientist Joseph Henry (1797-1878) observed the effects of electromagnetic induction about one year before Michael Faraday, but he did not publish his experiments and results so quickly. Henry made many advances in the electrical sciences. He devised and constructed an early electric motor, helped Samuel Morse to develop the telegraph, and discovered the laws on which the transformer is based. The scientific electrical unit of inductive resistance, the henry, is named after him.

Batteries, buzzer or bleeper and electronic circuits in handle

Wires in shaft

Buried treasure

A metal-detector can locate certain metal objects, such as coins, medals and goblets, under the ground. The detector contains a coil of wire through which electricity flows from the battery. This creates a magnetic field around the coil, by the electromagnetic effect. Any ferrous or iron-containing object that enters the magnetic field causes it to distort or bend, This has tiny effects on the amount of electricity flowing through the coil, by electromagnetic induction. The variations are detected by a microchip in the handle and turned into a warning buzz or bleep of sound waves.

Coil of wire works as electromagnet

Magnetic field around coil

Magnetic field unaffected by non-ferrous objects such as stones

Metal (ferrous) object in magnetic field causes distortion

Volume and tone knobs

Pick-up selector switch

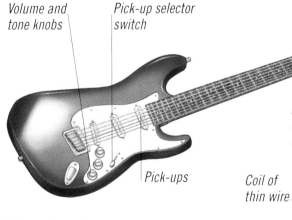

Pick-ups

Pole piece (magnet inside coil)

String

Coil of thin wire

Electric guitar

When a person plays an electric guitar, the strings alone make hardly any sound. We can only hear the guitar loudly because of electromagnetic induction. Plucking the strings makes them vibrate in the magnetic field of the pick-ups beneath the strings. The vibrations change the amounts of electricity in the wire coils of the pick-ups, creating electrical signals that travel along the lead to the amplifier. This boosts the signals, which are then made audible by a loudspeaker.

Wires to volume and tone controls

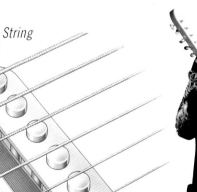

Guitar effects

The electric guitar makes electrical signals which can be manipulated in many ways by electronic devices, to give effects such as echo and distortion.

Electricity to movement

ELECTRICITY AND MAGNETISM work together to produce movement. As a current flows through a wire, it creates a magnetic field around the wire. If there is another magnetic field already present, the two fields interact in the usual way: like poles repel and unlike poles attract. This produces a moving force on the wire. It can be viewed as the force of the magnet pushing or pulling the charged particles which make up the electric current inside the wire. It is called the motor effect and is the idea used in electric motors. An electric motor is a coil of wire turning between the poles of a permanent magnet. When current flows through the coil, a magnetic field is produced that causes a turning movement.

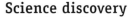
Brush (sliding contact onto commutator)

Coil of wire on shaft

Commutator

North pole of permanent magnet

North pole of electromagnet

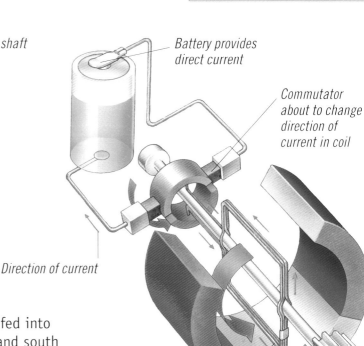

Battery provides direct current

Commutator about to change direction of current in coil

Direction of current

North pole of electromagnet spins, attracted to south pole of permanent magnet

Electric motor
In a simple electric motor, a direct electric current is fed into a coil of wire that sits on a shaft between the north and south poles of a permanent magnet. The current makes the coil into an electromagnet. This turns on its shaft as it tries to bring its north pole close to the south pole of the permanent magnet, and its south pole close to the magnet's north pole, because unlike poles attract. But as the coil turns, a device called a commutator on the shaft reverses the direction of its current. This reverses the poles of the electromagnet, so each pole is pushed away or repelled from the pole it has just passed and attracted to the other pole. After another half-turn the same happens again, and so the coil on its shaft keeps spinning.

Turning force
The permanent magnet is fixed, so the electromagnet tries to move and spins under magnetic attraction and repulsion forces.

See also: Mysterious magnetism page 92, Movement to electricity page 98

Motors big and small

The large electric motors in electric trains are bigger than a person. Each set of wheels has its own motor, so if one fails, the train is largely unaffected. In diesel-electric trains, a diesel engine powers a generator to make electricity that drives the electric motors for the wheels. This means the train can go on tracks which lack an electricity supply in the form of overhead cables or an extra rail. Many motors give continuous rotary or round-and-round motion. But the stepper motors in computer disc drives are specialised to turn the magnetic disc or optical disc (compact disc, CD) by very small, accurate amounts.

ELECTRIC MOTORS

▶ A modern electric motor turns more than 90 per cent of the electrical energy it receives into the energy of movement. This makes it one of the most efficient of all machines.
▶ Many domestic appliances have at least one electric motor. Some have several, for example:
▶ In a washing machine, a large electric motor (using perhaps hundreds of watts of electricity) makes the drum turn round.
▶ Another, smaller motor (using tens of watts) drives the pump that pumps out the dirty water, while an even smaller one turns the programme controller.

The AC motor

Alternating current, as supplied in mains electricity, reverses its direction 50 or 60 times each second – its frequency is 50 or 60 Hz (cycles per second). So an electric motor which runs on AC does not need a commutator, which reverses the current to the coil of a DC motor every half-turn. The AC motor has brushes (sliding contacts) that press onto slip-rings, to carry the electricity to the revolving coil. The motor spins at the same speed as the frequency of the AC changes.

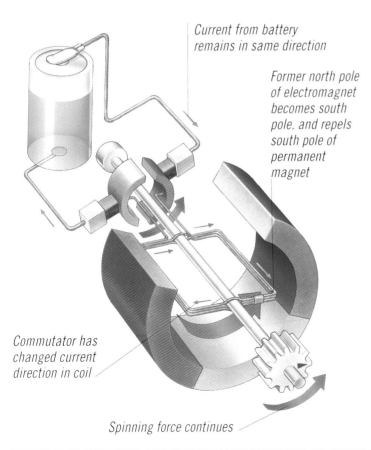

Current from battery remains in same direction

Former north pole of electromagnet becomes south pole, and repels south pole of permanent magnet

Commutator has changed current direction in coil

Spinning force continues

Current goes one way

The current makes the coil into an electromagnet. Its magnetic field interacts with the field of the permanent magnet around it to make the coil turn.

Permanent magnet

Brush

Slip-ring

Current reverses

The current reverses as part of the normal AC system. This swaps the poles of the electromagnetic field around the coil, and so makes the coil continue to spin.

Turning force continues

Movement to electricity

MOST OF THE ELECTRICITY we use today is made in power stations by machines called generators. These use magnets and movement to make electricity. They work in the opposite way to electric motors. Inside a generator, a magnet or electromagnet turns inside a coil of wire, producing electricity in the coil by electromagnetic induction. The energy of movement needed to turn the magnet is provided by energy sources such as steam (made by burning fuel), moving water or the wind.

DC generator

A coil of wire turns, or rotates, between the poles of a permanent magnet. This causes a current to flow in the coil, by electromagnetic induction. The direction of the current in the coil reverses every half turn because each side of the coil alternately passes by the permanent magnet's north pole, then its south pole, and so on. But the commutator changes the connections every half turn, so the current that is generated flows in one direction only, DC.

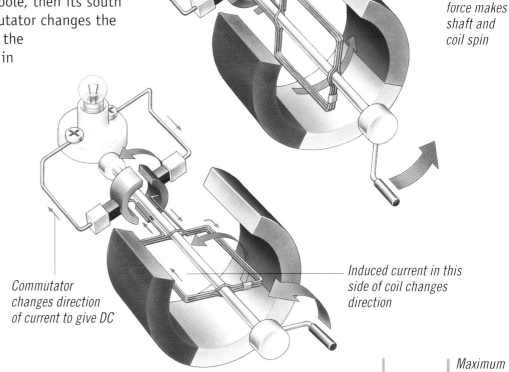

Brush and commutator (as on electric motor)

Current induced in moving coil

Turning force makes shaft and coil spin

Induced current in this side of coil changes direction

Commutator changes direction of current to give DC

Minimum current

Maximum current

Science discovery

In the 1800s, engineer Charles Parsons (1854-1931) designed a steam turbine with angled fan-like blades in which high-pressure steam rotated the same shaft that turned the generator. It was smaller, more efficient and less noisy than earlier piston-engined generators. The steam turbine is now used in power stations and also in ships to drive the propeller (screw).

Not so steady

The DC generator produces DC. But its strength rises and falls as the coil of wire comes near to the pole of the permanent magnet, then moves on. In practice, a DC generator has many coils and also electronic equipment, to smooth out the flow.

See also: Electrical energy page 78, Mysterious magnetism page 92

AC GENERATOR

This device, also called an alternator, works in a reverse way to the AC motor shown on the previous page. Because it does not have a commutator, the induced current it produces becomes reversed every half-turn. This is the basic type of generator used to produce AC in power stations. The spinning speed of the coil controls the frequency, or rate of reversal, of the AC.

The induced current flows one way as the coils pass the permanent magnet's two poles.

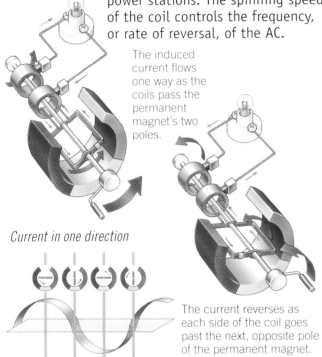

Current in one direction

The current reverses as each side of the coil goes past the next, opposite pole of the permanent magnet.

Current in other direction

Power stations

In a power station, generators the size of juggernaut trucks make electricity. These are often turned using steam or flowing water, which is fed through a pipe and into the turbine, a series of fan-like angled blades. The steam or water pushes on the blades and makes their shaft rotate. At the end of the turbine, the shaft is connected to the generator.

Bicycle dynamo

On some bicycles, the lights are turned on by a simple generator or dynamo. A small wheel touches the bicycle tyre. As the wheel turns, this makes a magnet turn round inside a coil of wire. Electricity is generated in the coil of wire by electromagnetic induction, making the lights glow. But the lights only work if the wheels are turning.

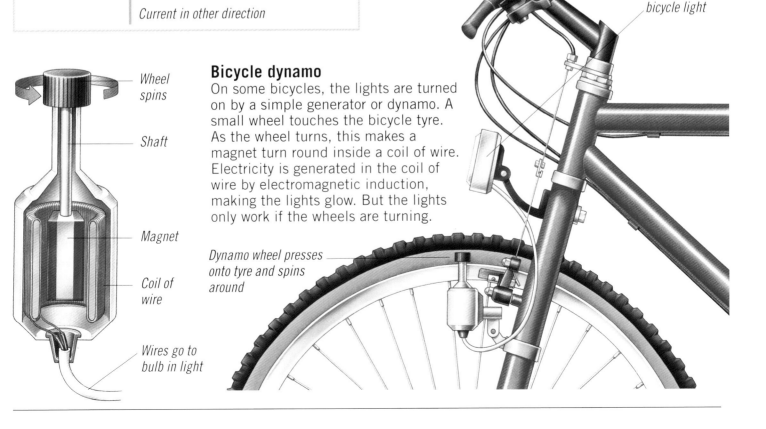

Wheel spins

Shaft

Magnet

Coil of wire

Wires go to bulb in light

Bulb inside bicycle light

Dynamo wheel presses onto tyre and spins around

Electronic information

BY CAREFULLY CHANGING and controlling the flow of electrons in conductors, it is possible to send information around an electrical circuit, a microchip, an electronic device such as a computer – or around the world – in the form of coded pulses, bursts or signals of electricity. These were first used in the electric telegraph, which was developed in the 1830s and 1840s, using the on-off signals of Morse code. Today we also use on-off signals, called binary digital code.

Converting analogue to digital

The wave is "sampled" every fraction of a second. Its height is measured on a decimal digital scale and then converted into binary digits.

BINARY CODE

Binary is a digital code – based on numerals or digits. But it only uses two digits, 0 and 1, unlike our normal decimal number system which has ten digits, from 0 to 9.

Decimal		Binary			
Tens	Units	Eights	Fours	Twos	Units
1	0	1	0	1	0
	9	1	0	0	1
	8	1	0	0	0
	7	0	1	1	1
	6	0	1	1	0
	5	0	1	0	1
	4	0	1	0	0
	3	0	0	1	1
	2	0	0	1	0
	1	0	0	0	1
	0	0	0	0	0

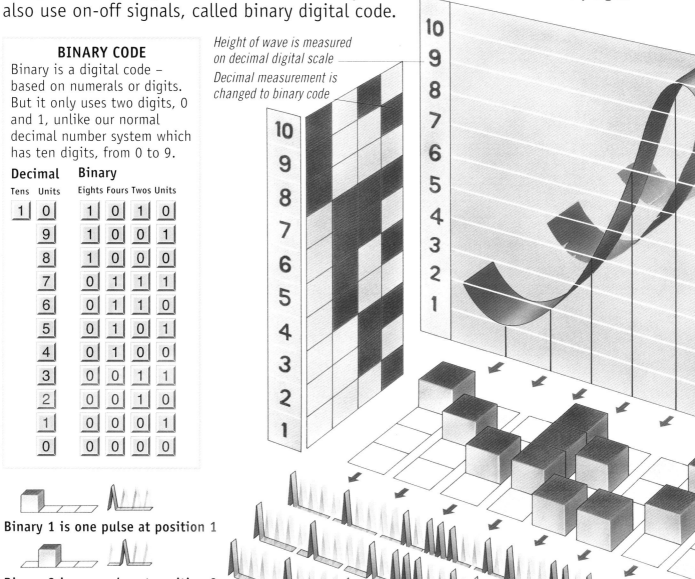

Height of wave is measured on decimal digital scale

Decimal measurement is changed to binary code

Copies of the digital code stay exactly the same. copy after copy

Binary 1 is one pulse at position 1

Binary 2 is one pulse at position 2

Binary 4 is one pulse at position 4

Binary 9 is two pulses at **positions 1 and 8**

See also: Electrical energy page 78, Communications page 102

Analogue

An analogue display or system varies continuously without the step-wise increments or numbers of the digital system. An analogue clock is one with hands. With an analogue stopwatch, it is difficult to tell the exact time elapsed, since the hand may be between divisions.

Digital

A digital display or system has step-wise increments or numerals, such as 1, 2, 3 and so on. These numbers are fixed quantities and do not vary, and there are no "in-betweens". A digital stopwatch shows the exact time, to the nearest minute, second, one-tenth of a second and so on.

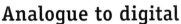

Analogue to digital

A wave is an analogue system. It goes up and down continuously, always varying if only by a very slight amount. Pulses of electronic signals make up a digital system. They are in a code which is all-or-nothing. Making copies of an analogue system, such as the recording on an ordinary audio cassette, can introduce errors. Copies of a digital system remain exactly the same. Changing analogue to digital is called digitization. A computer or CD player works using digital information.

Copies of the analogue wave become faded, changed and distorted

Analogue wave

Height of wave is measured by sampling many thousands of times each second

Decimal-to-binary conversion changes digital system based on tens (decimal) to digital system based on twos (binary)

Ones

Twos

Fours

Eights

Binary code is represented as tiny pulses of electricity

Science discovery

After beginning his career as a portrait painter, Samuel Morse (1791-1872) thought of the idea for the electric telegraph after hearing a conversation about the newly discovered electromagnet. This was in 1832, while he was returning by ship to North America, after studying art in Europe.

He devised a code of short and long electrical signals, dots and dashes, for different letters and numbers. Morse probably made his first working model of the telegraph by 1835 and opened the first permanent telegraph line in 1844, between Baltimore and Washington in the USA. The first message he sent was: "What God hath wrought!"

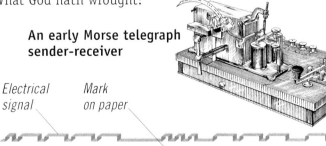

An early Morse telegraph sender-receiver

Electrical signal

Mark on paper

Number 1   Letter S   Letter O   Letter N

Snippet of Morse code

Communications

MODERN COMMUNICATIONS DEVICES give almost instant access to almost any information, almost anywhere in the world. Most work using electricity and magnetism, and some use light too. Telephones and televisions rely on converting sounds or pictures into electrical signals, which are sent long distances through wires at high speed – the speed of light, 300,000 kilometres per second. Information can also be converted from electrical signals into pulses of electromagnetic waves – laser light – and sent along fibre-optic cables. Or it is changed into radio waves and sent to local networks, or up to satellites in space and then back down to Earth again. The light or radio signals have to be converted into electrical signals before they can be turned back into sounds or pictures again.

The electronic age
In the last 170 years, electrical information has revolutionised the way we communicate. Long-distance or telecommunications networks can pass messages around the world in seconds. These amazing achievements all started with the electric telegraph, which developed into the modern telex system. The telephone network has now developed to carry pictures, computer data, electronic mail and many other forms of information.

Fibre-optics

An optical fibre is a rod of glass or similar transparent material, which is thinner than a hair and can flex or bend. It is contained in a protective sheath that also separates it from other optical fibres around it. The fibre carries information as coded flashes of laser light. Because these hit the inside of the surface of the rod at a very shallow angle, they bounce off or reflect back into the rod, by total internal reflection. This means the laser pulse zig-zags along the inside of the fibre, even if it is bent. The flashes carry information in digital form. As with electrical information, a flash or pulse is 1 in binary, and no flash or pulse (a gap) is 0. The digital information can represent numbers, letters, words, sounds and pictures. Thousands of optical fibres are bundled together in one casing as a fibre-optic cable.

Strong waterproof outer covering

Steel core gives entire cable strength against stretching or kinking

Fibre made of special glass

Laser light pulses inside fibre

Different colours or wavelengths of light carry different messages

Outer sheaths protect cable from knocks and kinks

Each fibre has a colour-coded protective casing

See also: Electronic information page 100, Computers page 106

Science discovery

In the 1920s, Vladimir Zworykin (1889-1982) devised the iconoscope or television transmission tube, and the kinescope, or television receiver. These two inventions formed the first all-electronic television system and provided the trigger for the development of modern television. The modern television picture tube is basically Zworykin's kinescope. The first regular television broadcasts began in 1936 in London, England. Zworykin also helped to develop a colour television system and the electron microscope.

Telecom network

A mobile phone sends and receives messages by radio waves. The radio waves travel to and from a transceiver (transmitter/receiver) station which connects the calls into the standard telephone network. Countries are divided up into different areas, called cells, and each cell has its own transceiver station. In an area where a lot of people live, there are many small cells because there are likely to be many people using mobile phones. In sparsely populated areas, the cells are larger.

Network of cells

Satellite in geostationary orbit

Ground station uplink to satellite

Cell transmitter-receiver

Satellite downlink to ground station

Inside a mobile phone

A "mobile" is a low-power radio transmitter-receiver. It has a mouthpiece to change sound waves into electrical signals (like a microphone), and an earpiece to change electrical signals into sound waves (like a loudspeaker).The transmitter-receiver only needs to send and pick up waves from the nearest cell tower, which is usually just a few kilometres away. However hills or tall buildings may block the radio signals. Also, in areas where the cell towers are farther apart, the signals may be too weak to travel to and from the phone.

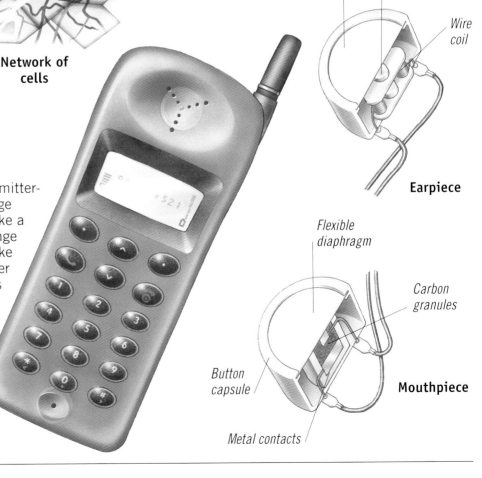

Flexible diaphragm *Magnet* *Wire coil*

Earpiece

Flexible diaphragm

Carbon granules

Button capsule

Metal contacts

Mouthpiece

Electronic machines

IMAGINE WHAT LIFE WOULD BE LIKE without all the electronic devices that people in developed countries tend to take for granted. You would not be able to phone your friends, watch television, play computer games or listen to music from a compact disk. In an office, people would not be able to communicate with each other by phone, fax, computer disk or e-mail (electronic mail). In a factory, there would be no computer-controlled robots, safety sensors or automatic ordering and payment systems. All of these devices have a common "language" – tiny pulses of electricity, as electronic signals. These are manipulated by electronic components such as microchips and used to represent, process and transmit information.

Sending a fax
Fax is short for "facsimile", a copy or reproduction. Fax machines use the phone network to send and receive written or printed material, including words, photographs, maps and drawings. A scanner changes the marks on paper into a code of electrical signals and sends these along the telephone line – as shown below.

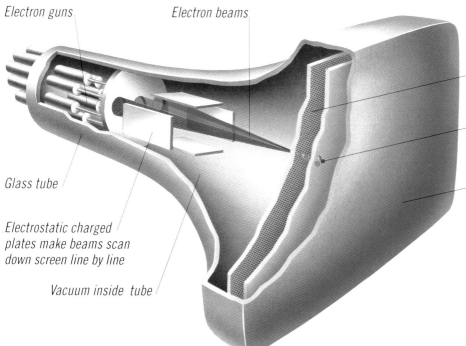

Electron guns

Electron beams

Glass tube

Electrostatic charged plates make beams scan down screen line by line

Vacuum inside tube

Wires and cables of telecom network

Shadow mask

Phosphor dots on screen

Screen cover

Television
The main part inside a television is a glass vacuum tube (containing no air) with the screen at the front. Electron guns fire beams of the atomic particles called electrons at the screen. In a colour television, there are three electron guns, one for each primary colour of light - red, green and blue. The screen is covered with tiny phosphor dots, which glow red, blue or green when struck by the electrons. From a distance, our eyes merge the coloured dots into a complete picture.

Shadow mask
Electrons themselves have no colour. Between the electron guns and the screen is a plate, the shadow mask, with thousands of tiny holes. As the electrons pass through each hole, they can strike only the phosphor dots of the correct colour.

Electron beams

Shadow mask

Phosphor dots

See also: Electronic information page 100, Communications page 102

Science discovery

Rene Descartes (1596-1650) was a scientific thinker, mathematician and physicist. He combined the branches of mathematics called geometry and algebra into cartesian geometry which is the basis of the charts and graphs we know today, and is also used in the design of electronic components and circuits. Descartes also thought long and deeply about what we know or think we know, and how and why we know it. His famous saying was *Cogito, ergo sum* – "I think, therefore I am."

TOWARDS THE COMPUTER

▶ **1930s** Mathematician Alan Turing put forward the idea of an electronic computer which could manipulate data according to instructions in a program.

▶ **1949** John von Neumann's computer EDVAC was the first to use binary arithmetic and store its operating instructions internally. This design forms the basis of today's computers.

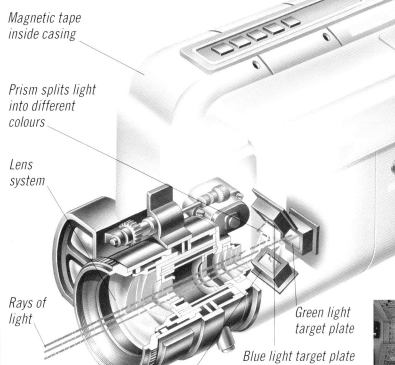

Magnetic tape inside casing

Prism splits light into different colours

Lens system

Rays of light

Green light target plate

Blue light target plate

Red light target plate

Eyepiece for viewing

Camcorder

In an ordinary camera, light causes a chemical change in photographic film. In a camcorder (camera-recorder), the light is focused onto target plates called CCDs, charge-coupled devices. These are covered in a material that conducts different amounts of electricity according to the amount and colour of light falling onto it. The image on the target plate is changed into a code of electronic signals which are recorded on magnetic tape.

Receiving a fax

The receiving machine changes the electrical signals back into a pattern of marks on a piece of paper. All this takes only a few seconds.

Information displays

In the past, information displays and control consoles had rows of lights and dials. Today, screens are more common. They can show more adaptable graphic displays of information such as charts and diagrams, and change these if information which is more important suddenly becomes available.

Computers

A COMPUTER IS AN ELECTRONIC MACHINE that manipulates, changes and processes information, or data, of all kinds – not only numbers but also words, patterns, pictures, animations, sounds and so on. The data is processed according to a sequence of instructions called a program, which tells the computer what to do. Inside a computer, the program and data are in digital form, as patterns of tiny electrical signals that pass around the many circuits and microchips. Computers can deal with vast amounts of information in a very short time. For example, a supercomputer can work out all the consequences of more than 200 million chess moves every second.

Science discovery

In the 1830s English mathematician Charles Babbage (1792-1871) designed several kinds of programmable mechanical calculators. His machines used gearwheels to do the calculating and had more than 2,000 moving parts. Due to engineering and money problems, Babbage's machines were never finished at the time. But modern computers still use his basic ideas.

Supercomputers

A supercomputer must work so fast that its main processing and memory circuits are supercooled to many degrees below freezing. Supercooling reduces the resistance of the conductors in the electronic circuits.

Parts of a PC

The Personal Computer, PC, has several major parts. These are the computer itself, a monitor screen (which works in much the same way as a television) as the main output device, and input devices such as a keyboard. Extra devices which can be plugged into the computer, like scanners or graphics tablets, are known as peripherals.

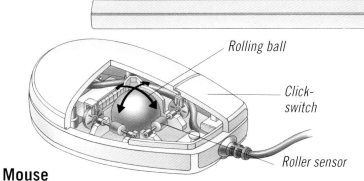

Switch contact under key

Special function keys

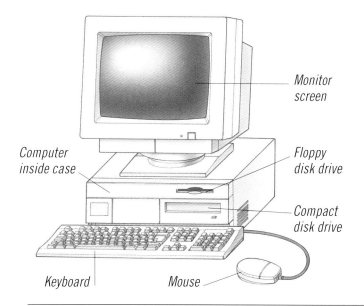

Monitor screen

Computer inside case

Floppy disk drive

Compact disk drive

Keyboard

Mouse

Rolling ball

Click-switch

Roller sensor

Mouse

The mouse is a small case for a rolling ball. As this moves on the desktop, rollers track the ball's motion and use it to control a pointer or cursor on the screen. One or more click-switches on the mouse select items or boxes on the screen. The wire to the main computer is the mouse's "tail".

See also: Electronic information page 100, Communications page 102

Networks

Computers can be linked together in networks, providing they have the necessary connections to carry electronic signals between them. Networks can use existing means of communication, such as telephone lines and satellites, or their own private wires and cables (LAN, local area network). Networking allows people to share information or programs. In a token ring network, all the devices or nodes, such as computers, printers and fax machines, are connected to a central loop.

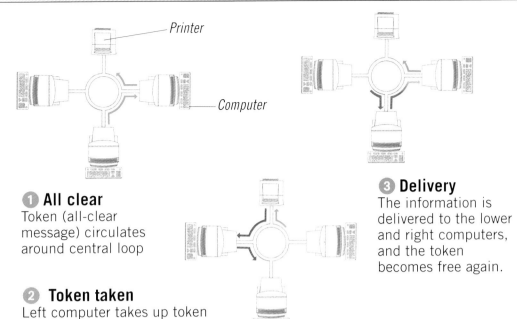

Printer

Computer

① All clear
Token (all-clear message) circulates around central loop

② Token taken
Left computer takes up token since it has information to send.

③ Delivery
The information is delivered to the lower and right computers, and the token becomes free again.

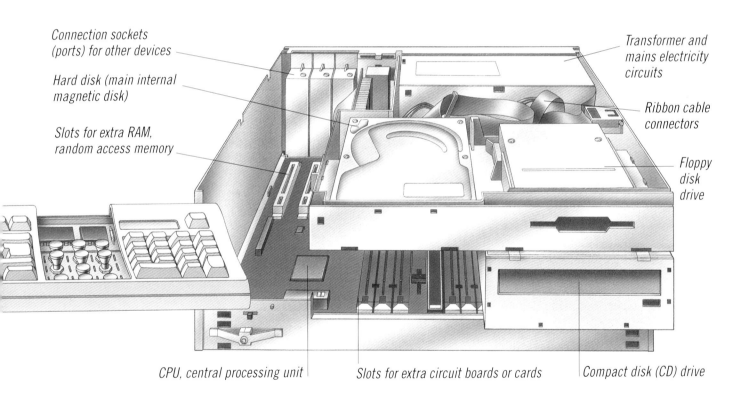

Connection sockets (ports) for other devices

Hard disk (main internal magnetic disk)

Slots for extra RAM, random access memory

Transformer and mains electricity circuits

Ribbon cable connectors

Floppy disk drive

CPU, central processing unit

Slots for extra circuit boards or cards

Compact disk (CD) drive

Inputs to the PC

The modern PC is several machines working together as a system. The actual computer consists of sets of circuit boards and other electronic components. Information goes into the computer via input devices such as a keyboard, mouse, scanner or microphone. These are linked to the BIOS, basic input/output system, which feeds information to and from the central processing unit, CPU, the main microchip which does the manipulations. The CPU is linked to the main working memory, random access memory or RAM, which also stores the program, a special list of instructions.

Outputs from the PC

The results of a computer's calculations or processing are fed to output devices, such as a monitor screen, printer or loudspeaker. Magnetic disks of various kinds work as memories to store information fed out from the computer and put it back in later.

4

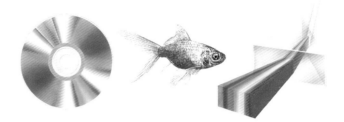

Sound and Light

Some types of energy are in the form of up-and-down waves. They include sound and light – but the nature of their waves is very different. Sound is moving atoms and molecules. Light is combined electricity and magnetism. Both are sensed by the body, and are used to convey information.

About waves

SOUND AND LIGHT are both forms of energy. They are very different forms of energy – sound is made by something moving, while light is a mixture of electrical and magnetic energy. But sound and light are similar in that they both travel in regular up-and-down curved patterns, called waves. These are similar to ripples on a pond or the waves you make if you shake a rope up and down. In science, a wave is a travelling change, disturbance or fluctuation that passes energy from one place to another. Sound can travel only by moving particles of matter, such as the atoms or molecules that make up a substance. So sound cannot exist in, or travel through, the nothingness of a vacuum, such as space. Light, on the other hand, does not need matter or substance. It exists as tiny packets or parcels of energy called photons. These can travel through a substance such as air or water, and also through a vacuum.

Peak or crest (highest point) of first wave

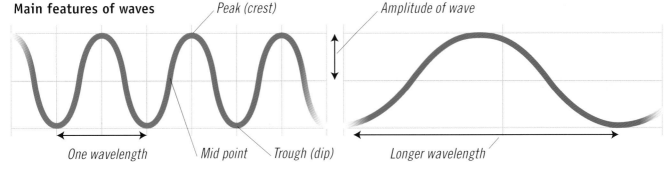

Main features of waves   *Peak (crest)*   *Amplitude of wave*

One wavelength   *Mid point*   *Trough (dip)*   *Longer wavelength*

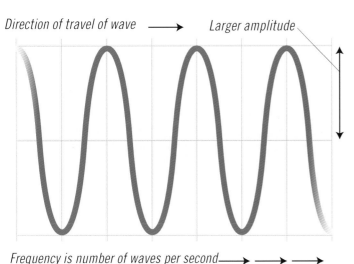

Direction of travel of wave ⟶   *Larger amplitude*

Frequency is number of waves per second ⟶ ⟶ ⟶

Features of waves

All waves have certain features. The highest part is the peak (crest). The lowest part is the trough (dip). The height of a wave, from its mid point up to its peak, or from the mid point down to its trough, is the amplitude. For sound, bigger amplitudes (taller waves) make louder sounds. For light, they make brighter lights. The number of waves passing a place or point in one second is called the frequency of the wave. The distance along one complete wave – for example, from one peak to the next – is the wavelength. For waves travelling at the same speed, the shorter the wavelength, the more waves pass a place during a given time. So shorter waves have higher frequencies.

See also: Sound waves page 112, Using sounds page 122, Light page 124

Similar, but different

The watery ripples on a pond, after a stone is thrown in, help us to imagine the shape of sound and light waves. However, the sizes of these waves are very different. Light waves rise and fall several hundred million million times every second, and there are millions of peaks and troughs in one centimetre. Sound waves are much bigger. Each of the sound waves in a low hum is a metre or more long. Also, light waves travel a million times faster than sound waves.

Waves spread out, or emanate, from their central source

INVISIBLE AND INAUDIBLE

Our experience of sights and sounds is affected by the limits of our own sense organs – our eyes and ears. There are forms of light, such as infra-red and ultra-violet, which our eyes cannot detect. But the eyes of many animals can see them. Some animals can see well at light levels which are so low, we think it is completely dark. A cat may peer into the night, obviously watching intently. Yet we see only blackness. Also, there are sounds which are too quiet, or too low-pitched, or too high-pitched, for our ears to register. But dolphins, bats and many other animals can hear (and make) them. A dog or a horse may prick up its ears at a sound which is so faint, we hear nothing.

UV on flowers
Bees see lines called honey guides on flower petals. The lines show up only in ultra-violet (UV) light. They guide the bee to the honey in the centre of the flower.

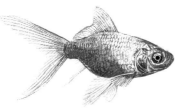

IR in water
Goldfish see infra-red (IR) light, which is less filtered out by water, compared to normal light.

Common dolphin emits fast, high-pitched clicks and squeals

US at night
Bats such as the horseshoe bat send out very high-pitched (ultrasonic, US) squeaks through the nose and mouth. They detect the reflections or echoes with their large ears.

Sound waves

A SOUND WAVE starts with something moving. The something can be any state of matter – solid, liquid or gas. Usually, it is a solid. The object moves to and fro, or vibrates. It pushes and then pulls against the particles of the substance around it, which can also be any state of matter, but is usually air. The moving object squashes the molecules of air closer together, and then stretches them farther apart. These molecules push and then pull the ones next to them, and these do the same, and so on, passing on the wave of energy. So a sound wave is a series of invisible squashes and stretches that ripple through the air.

Sound source
(loudspeaker)

Sound wave

Atoms and
molecules of air

Region where atoms
and molecules are
squashed close together
– high air pressure

Region where atoms and
molecules are pulled farther
apart – low air pressure

Musical sounds
All sound waves are made in the same way, by vibrating objects. Whether they are harsh and unpleasant, like the roar of traffic, or musical and pleasant, depends on how different sound waves are combined.

Sound on the move
Sound travels through substances when the particles they are made of – atoms, or atoms joined together into molecules – move back and forth. Each atom or molecule hits another and then returns to its original position. The energy is passed on from one to the next, as though moving along links in a chain. But the atoms or molecules themselves only move short distances from their central positions. We picture sound as a wave, but really it is areas of particles closer together and farther apart, rippling outwards from the source. In air, these ripples are regions of high and low air pressure. As the particles collide, tiny amounts of energy are lost from the wave each time. So the wave gradually fades with distance.

See also: Light page 124, Deep space page 196

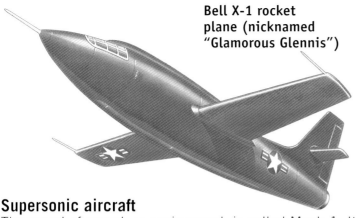

Bell X-1 rocket plane (nicknamed "Glamorous Glennis")

Supersonic aircraft

The speed of sound, or sonic speed, is called Mach 1. It varies with the pressure and temperature of the air, but is about 1,200 kilometres per hour. Something that travels faster than sound is known as supersonic. Twice the speed of sound is Mach 2, and so on. Some planes can reach Mach 3 or more. The first person to fly faster than the speed of sound was Captain Charles "Chuck" Yeager in a rocket plane, the Bell X-1. It blasted through the sound barrier in 1947. Supersonic aircraft overtake their own sound, which spreads out behind them in a shock wave that we hear on the ground as a sonic boom.

Ocean sounds

Sound travels through water at about 1,430 metres per second – five times faster than it travels through air. Many water-living animals use sounds for communication. The deep or low-frequency calls of the great whales travel for hundreds of kilometres through the seas. Male humpback whales sing to attract females. Each individual has its own song and repeats it with small variations for hours on end. Mother great whales and their babies, or calves, also make clicks and squeals.

Atoms and molecules farther from sound source vibrate with less energy

Region of high air pressure corresponds with peak of wave

Region of normal air pressure corresponds with mid point of wave

Region of low air pressure corresponds with trough of wave

THE DOPPLER EFFECT

Have you noticed how the noise of a speeding vehicle, like a motorcycle, car, train or plane, seems to be constant as it approaches you – then as it goes past, the noise drops or falls in pitch, to a lower note? As the vehicle moves towards you, it travels a small distance closer between sending out each sound wave. So for you, the sound waves are squashed closer together and make a high sound. As the vehicle passes, it now travels a small distance away between sending out each sound wave. So the sound waves are more stretched out, and make a lower sound, as shown on the next page.

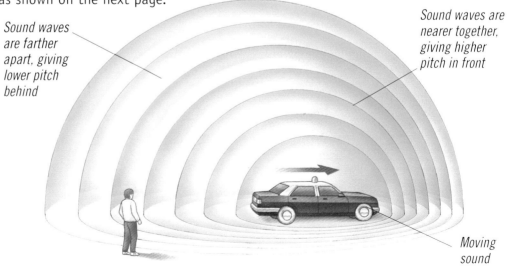

Sound waves are farther apart, giving lower pitch behind

Sound waves are nearer together, giving higher pitch in front

Moving sound source

The Doppler effect is named after the Austrian scientist Christian Doppler, who first discovered it in 1842. It is especially noticeable with high-pitched sounds such as sirens. It happens with any form of waves, including light waves, when it is called "red shift".

High and low sounds

THE PITCH OF A SOUND means how low or high it is. In a music band, the bass drum's deep boom is low-pitched, while the triangle's shrill tinkle is high-pitched. Pitch depends on how many times the sound source moves to and fro, or vibrates, each second. This is the same as the frequency – how many sound waves are produced each second. The frequency of a wave is measured in units called Hertz, Hz. For example, the note of middle C, in the middle of a piano keyboard, has a frequency of 261 Hz. Frequency is related to wavelength, since higher frequencies have shorter waves. The length of a middle C sound wave is 126 centimetres.

What sounds can we hear?

We hear many sound frequencies, from the shrill notes of bird song to the deep growl of traffic. But, because of the way our ears work, we do not hear all of the sounds around us. Our ears pick up frequencies from about 20 to 20,000 Hz (Hertz, vibrations per second). We hear sounds below 80 Hz as low, deep booms, thuds or rumbles. Frequencies below about 30 Hz may not be heard clearly, but if they are powerful enough, we can feel them as vibrations in the air and ground. Our ears are most sensitive in the range from 400 to 4,000 Hz. (Human speech tends to be around 300-1,000 Hz.) Sounds above about 5,000 Hz are extremely high-pitched squeaks, hisses and screeches. As people get older, their ears become less sensitive to high notes. So a young person can hear a bat's very high-pitched squeaks, while an older person cannot.

Science discovery

The unit of frequency for waves, Hertz, is named after physicist Heinrich Hertz (1857-1894). The unit is used for sound waves, and also for other waves, such as radio and light waves. In fact, Hertz worked mainly with radio waves, rather than sound. He was the first to make radio waves in a laboratory experiment. But he died before he could expand his work and make radio into a practical form of communication.

Animal ears

Compared to many animals, humans can hear a wide range of frequencies. However some animals hear frequencies which are too high-pitched for our ears. These are called ultrasonic sounds.

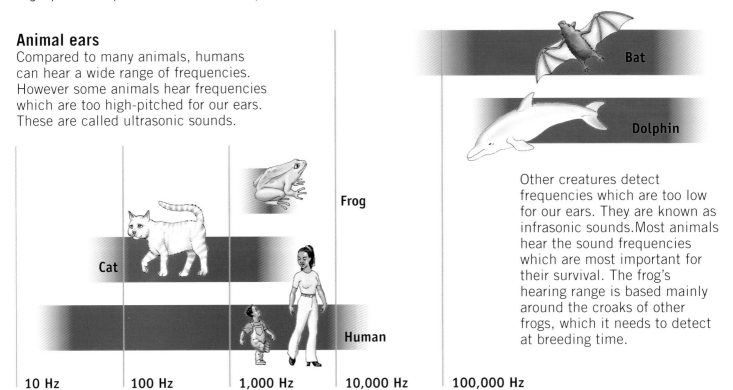

Bat

Dolphin

Frog

Cat

Human

10 Hz   100 Hz   1,000 Hz   10,000 Hz   100,000 Hz

Other creatures detect frequencies which are too low for our ears. They are known as infrasonic sounds. Most animals hear the sound frequencies which are most important for their survival. The frog's hearing range is based mainly around the croaks of other frogs, which it needs to detect at breeding time.

See also: Solids, liquids and gases page 26, Sound waves page 112

Musical notation

We can hear sound waves, but not see them. Also sounds soon fade away in time. So we write or print a visual version of sounds and musical notes, known as musical notation. This helps people to remember the music and also preserves the music over time. The notation has symbols for the pitch (frequency), length (duration) and loudness of the sounds.

Crash cymbal

Ride cymbal

Hi-hat cymbals

Snare drum

Floor tom-tom

Bass drum

Mounted tom-tom

Hi-hat foot pedal

Musical instruments

Anything that can produce sounds of different timing or pitch is a musical instrument. The three main types of musical instruments produce their sounds in different ways. Stringed instruments, like the guitar and violin, are plucked or rubbed. Percussion instruments, such as drums, are tapped or hit. You blow a wind instrument, like a recorder or trombone.

Elephant sounds

About two-thirds of the noises that elephants make are too low for the human ear to detect. They are infrasonic sounds. They include more than 20 different types of rumbling calls, powerful enough to communicate with elephants more than 5 kilometres away.

Unwanted noise

Noises are generally unpleasant, unwanted jumbles of sound waves. They may be from loud music, machinery such as saws and drills, and vehicles, trains and planes. Noisy surroundings make it hard for people to think, relax or sleep. This can lead to stress or illness. Very loud or prolonged noise can damage hearing, as shown on the next page.

Sounds in solids, liquids and gases

In general, sounds travel farther and faster through solids than through liquids, and farther and faster through liquids than through gases such as air. This applies especially to low-pitched or low-frequency sounds. In a gas, the molecules are far apart. So much of the sound energy is lost in pushing the gas molecules about until they bump into other gas molecules. In a liquid or solid, the molecules are much closer together, so they bump into each other more easily as they vibrate with sound energy. This means the sound moves more quickly. So we sometimes feel the vibrations of a big sound source like a truck through the ground, before we hear it.

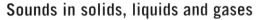

Loud and soft sounds

LOUD SOUNDS ARE LOUD because the atoms or molecules carrying them vibrate by large amounts, representing lots of energy. Soft or quiet sounds have much smaller vibrations. The loudness or volume of a sound is the strength of that sound as it reaches the ear. This is slightly different from the intensity of a sound, which is the amount of energy flowing along in the sound waves. Intensity depends on both pitch (frequency) and height (amplitude) of the sound wave. The loudness of a sound might be perceived as different from one person to another, but the intensity of the sound energy is the same for everyone.

Ear protection

People who work in noisy places, like textile factories or airports, or who use noisy machinery, protect their ears with ear-defenders. Continual higher-pitched sounds such as whines are most damaging to the ears.

Atomic explosion 200 dB

Blue whale grunting 170 dB

The decibel scale

The measurement scale which compares the intensities of sounds – which are similar to their loudness or volume – is called the decibel scale. Its units are decibels (dB), named after Alexander Graham Bell, who invented the telephone. A measure of 10 dB is the faintest sound that the human ear can detect, such as the rustling of dry leaves. Normal conversation measures about 60 decibels. Sounds become physically painful above about 130 dB. Even in the loudest sounds carried through air, the atoms and molecules of air do not move very much, only fractions of a millimetre.

Jet plane nearby 140 dB

Warning!

Warning signs show that loud noises might cause damage to the ear and loss of hearing, which could even be permanent.

Dangerously loud music 120 dB

Legal limit

In some regions, local regulations restrict sound levels in public places to 100, 90 or even 80 dB.

| 200 Decibels | 175 Decibels | 150 Decibels | 125 Decibels |

See also: Sound waves page 112, Making and detecting sounds page 118

HOW MANY DECIBELS?

Some examples of decibel levels are shown in the chart below. Here are some more:

▶ 180 dB   Rocket launch about 50 metres away
▶ 160 dB   Rocket launch about 200 metres away
▶ 140 dB   Huge machinery such as steelworks
▶ 110 dB   Road drill (pneumatic jackhammer)
▶ 100 dB   Nearby clap of thunder
▶ 80 dB   Speeding train
▶ 20 dB   Just audible whisper
▶ 10 dB   Faint rustle of wind in long grass

ANIMAL EARS

Some animals, like rabbits and horses, have large ear flaps that they can tilt and swivel. They do this to locate the source of a sound. Humans cannot swivel their ears this well! But if you hear a sound, you can turn your head until the sound waves reach both of your ears at the same time and with the same volume. Then you are facing the source of the sound.

Insects such as butterflies have sensitive hairs on their bodies, which can pick up certain sound wave frequencies in the air

Rabbits turn their ears to where the sound is loudest

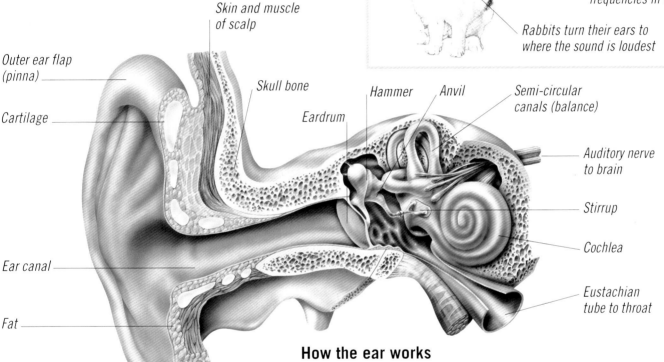

Skin and muscle of scalp

Outer ear flap (pinna)

Cartilage

Skull bone

Eardrum

Hammer   *Anvil*

Semi-circular canals (balance)

Auditory nerve to brain

Stirrup

Cochlea

Ear canal

Eustachian tube to throat

Fat

Ear lobe

How the ear works

The human ear has three main parts – the outer, middle and inner ear. The outer ear is like a funnel collecting sounds from the air. It leads to a tube, the ear canal, which ends in a flexible, circular eardrum. Sounds make the eardrum vibrate and this, in turn, makes three small bones in the middle ear vibrate too. The bones pass the sound vibrations to the cochlea in the inner ear, where they are changed into nerve signals that go to the brain.

Chainsaw 100 dB

Loud conversation 70 dB

Soft conversation 50 dB

Bird song 30 dB

Ticking watch 10 dB

| 100 Decibels | 75 Decibels | 50 Decibels | 25 Decibels |

Making and detecting sounds

THE NATURAL WORLD IS FULL of sounds, such as the wind, leaves rustling, waves lapping, and animal sounds like birds singing and insects buzzing. Some natural sounds even come from our own bodies – chewing, swallowing, coughing, sneezing, breathing, the heart beating and bubbles of gas gurgling through the intestines. A doctor can listen to these sounds using a stethoscope, to check the body's health and detect any signs of illness. Besides these natural sounds, our world is full of man-made sounds too. They come from machines, cars, trains and planes. Some of these man-made sounds are given off as part of the workings of moving and vibrating objects, such as hammers, drills, motors and engines. Other sounds, like those from radios, televisions and music systems, are produced by a device which is purpose-made to recreate sounds – the loudspeaker.

Tiny speakers
Headphones have a tiny version of a loudspeaker for each ear. The padded ear covering cuts out most of the noise from the surroundings. This lets the listener concentrate on the sounds from the headphones.

The microphone

A microphone is the man-made version of our own ears. It does the same job – changes the energy of a pattern of sound waves into the energy of a similar pattern of electrical signals. There are several kinds of microphones and they work in different ways. The carbon button version is found in a telephone mouthpiece, and is shown later in the book. A piezoelectric microphone is based on a small crystal and uses the piezoelectric effect, explained earlier in the book. The moving-coil microphone shown here relies on electromagnetism. Sound waves are changed to physical vibrations of a wire in a magnetic field. This produces electrical signals in the wire by the process of electromagnetic induction.

Wind cover

Grille allows sound waves through

Diaphragm (vibrating cone-shaped piece of card or plastic)

Iron core joined to diaphragm

Ring-shaped magnet

Iron core inside coil

Coil of wire

Connecting wires to amplifier

Moving-coil microphone

THE POWER OF SOUND

- ▸ The power of an amplifier in a music or hi-fi system is measured in watts.
- ▸ A small music system for a typical bedroom might have a power output of 10-20 watts.
- ▸ A larger domestic system for a bigger room would have a power output of 50-100 watts.
- ▸ A sound system for a small hall with 100-200 people needs an output of around 1,000 watts, or 1 kW (kilowatt).
- ▸ A sound system for a huge outdoor event with thousands of people might put out 50-100 kW.

Inside a microphone

The microphone is an "electric ear". A small rod or core of iron has a coil of wire wound around it. The core is fixed to a thin cone-shaped diaphragm, which is very flexible. When sound waves hit the diaphragm, it vibrates – just like the eardrum in the ear. The coil of wire also vibrates, and because it is inside a ring-shaped magnet, electrical signals are generated in the wire.

See also: Sound waves page 112, Electronic machines page 104

Controlling sound

A large hall such as a gymnasium usually has flat, hard walls, floor and ceiling. These surfaces reflect sounds very well, giving any sound a confusion of loud echoes. This is very unhelpful when trying to listen to music. So concert halls have sound-absorbing surfaces such as thick carpets and drapes on the walls and ceiling. Specially designed acoustic baffles and reflectors around and above the stage direct only the desired sounds out to the audience.

Science discovery

Alexander Graham Bell began his working life as a teacher of children with hearing and speaking problems. He studied the human voice, speech and sound waves in great detail. At the time, messages were sent long distances by telegraph. This produced on-off electrical pulses, in Morse code, which were then sent along wires. Bell realized that a pattern of sound waves could be converted into a corresponding pattern of varying electrical signals. These would travel along a wire, as in the telegraph, and change back into sound waves again. In 1876 Bell made a device that did this – the telephone. The first words spoken over the telephone were Bell asking for help from his assistant Mr Watson in the next room, after spilling acid on his clothes.

Alexander Graham Bell (1847-1922)

One of Bell's early telephones, around 1878

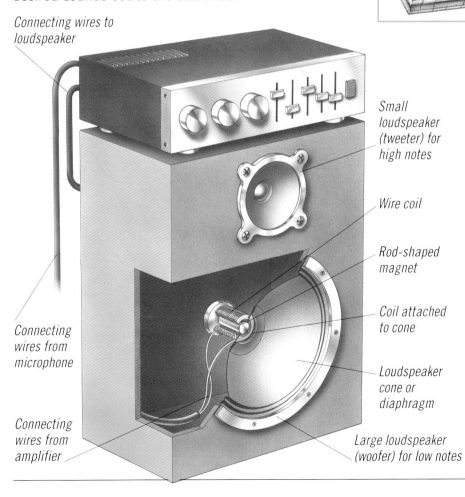

Connecting wires to loudspeaker

Small loudspeaker (tweeter) for high notes

Wire coil

Rod-shaped magnet

Coil attached to cone

Loudspeaker cone or diaphragm

Connecting wires from microphone

Connecting wires from amplifier

Large loudspeaker (woofer) for low notes

The amplifier

The electrical signals from a microphone, or from a cassette tape, vinyl disc or CD player, are very small. So are the signals from an electric instrument such as an electric guitar. They are not powerful enough to drive a loudspeaker. An amplifier is an electronic device that amplifies the signals – makes them much stronger. The tone or equalisation controls make different pitches, or frequencies, of sounds louder or softer.

Inside a loudspeaker

The loudspeaker works in the reverse way to the microphone. Electrical signals from the amplifier pass through the coil of wire and make it into an electromagnet, creating a varying magnetic field around it. This interacts with the steady magnetic field from the permanent magnet. As a result the coil moves or vibrates. It is attached to the loudspeaker cone or diaphragm, so this vibrates too, producing sound waves in the air.

Storing sounds

FOR CENTURIES, PEOPLE could only record sounds by writing words or musical notes. Today's technologies enable us to store the actual sounds we hear. Sound waves can be converted into patterns of magnetic patches on tape, wavy grooves on a vinyl record, or micro-pits on compact discs (CDs). Storing and reproducing sound rely on converting sound waves into electrical signals, which are then converted again into the form of storage.

Sounds on tape

The sounds are converted into electrical signals by a microphone, or fed in as electrical signals from another source, to an electromagnet in the record-playback head (shown below). The signals produce a varying magnetic field which turns the metal particles on the tape into tiny, invisible magnets. The pattern of the micro-magnetic patches matches the pattern of sound waves.

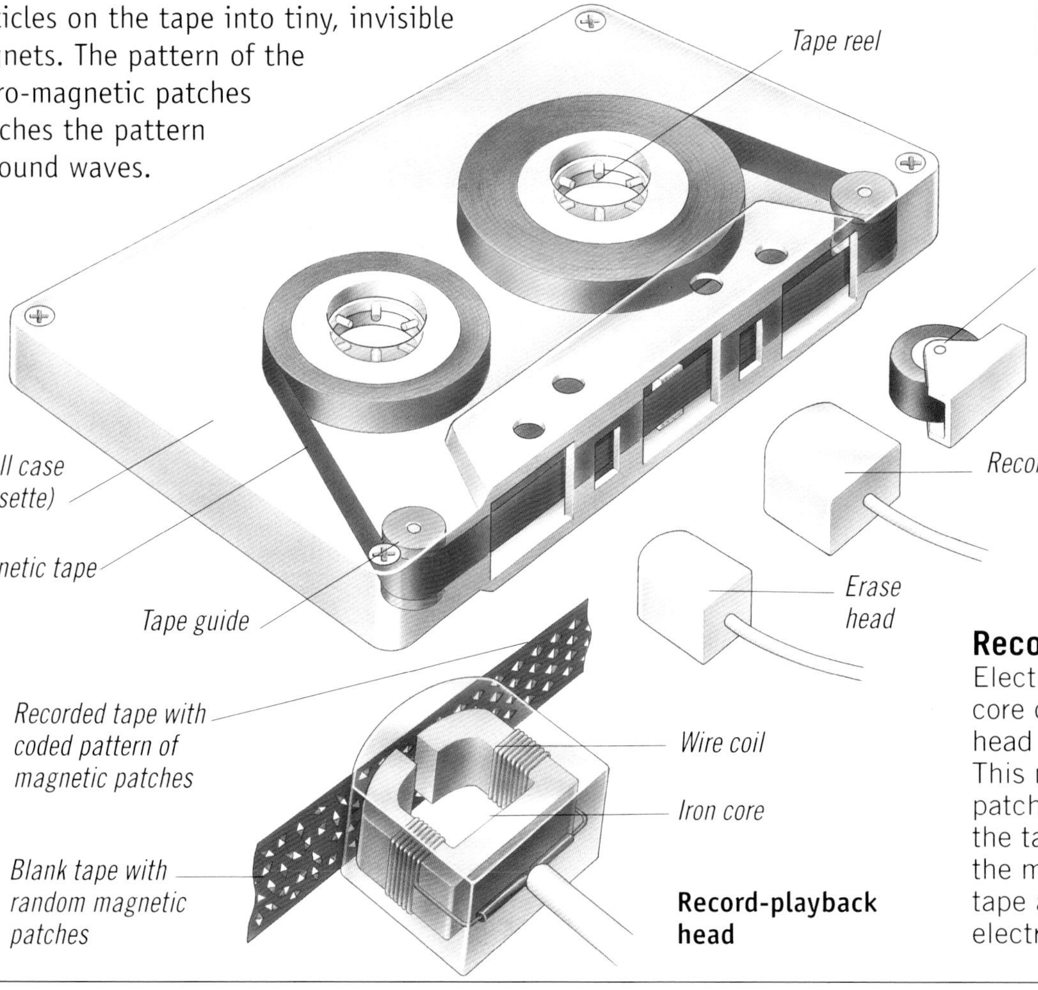

Microscopic pits give rainbow effect on compact disc

Tape reel

Tape drive roller

Record-playback head

Small case (cassette)

Magnetic tape

Tape guide

Erase head

Recorded tape with coded pattern of magnetic patches

Wire coil

Iron core

Blank tape with random magnetic patches

Record-playback head

Record, play

Electrical signals turn the iron core of the record-playback head into an electromagnet. This makes tiny magnetic patches on the tape. To play the tape, the head picks up the magnetic pattern on the tape and turns it back into electrical signals.

See also: Making and detecting sounds page 118

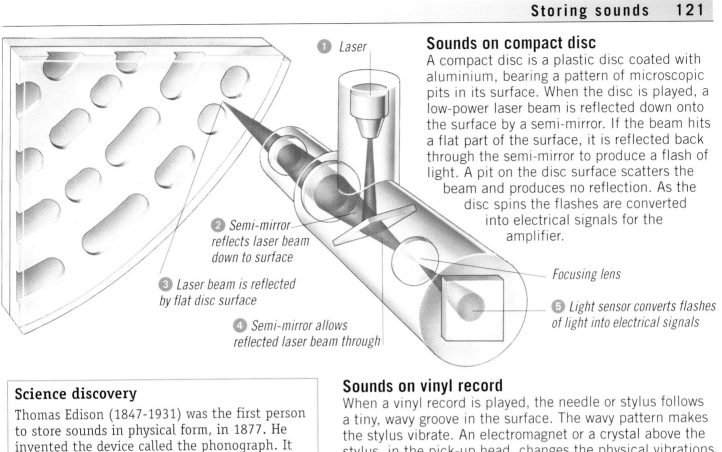

❶ *Laser*

❷ *Semi-mirror reflects laser beam down to surface*

❸ *Laser beam is reflected by flat disc surface*

❹ *Semi-mirror allows reflected laser beam through*

Focusing lens

❺ *Light sensor converts flashes of light into electrical signals*

Sounds on compact disc

A compact disc is a plastic disc coated with aluminium, bearing a pattern of microscopic pits in its surface. When the disc is played, a low-power laser beam is reflected down onto the surface by a semi-mirror. If the beam hits a flat part of the surface, it is reflected back through the semi-mirror to produce a flash of light. A pit on the disc surface scatters the beam and produces no reflection. As the disc spins the flashes are converted into electrical signals for the amplifier.

Science discovery

Thomas Edison (1847-1931) was the first person to store sounds in physical form, in 1877. He invented the device called the phonograph. It scratched grooves on a wax cylinder to record sounds, and played them back by running a needle along the grooves. The first recording was Edison himself saying the nursery rhyme *Mary had a Little Lamb*.

Sounds on vinyl record

When a vinyl record is played, the needle or stylus follows a tiny, wavy groove in the surface. The wavy pattern makes the stylus vibrate. An electromagnet or a crystal above the stylus, in the pick-up head, changes the physical vibrations into electrical signals for the amplifier and loudspeaker. Deeper grooves make louder sounds, and more frequent or shorter waves in the grooves make higher frequency sounds.

Each side of the record has one long groove in a tight spiral

Stylus ("needle")

Wavy groove in vinyl record's surface

Using sounds

SOUNDS ARE VITAL. We use them to communicate, learn and convey ideas, thoughts and plans, either face-to-face or with telephones. Musical and natural sounds such as bird song affect our emotions, making us happy or sad, worried or relaxed. Loud sirens or bells warn us of danger. The sound-only radio provides entertainment, information and amusement, while the television becomes much less interesting without its sound! We cannot hear ultrasound with our ears, but it can be detected by microphones and shown as patterns on a screen. This allows us to "see" inside the body, under the sea or into machinery. Ultrasound can also weld metals and plastics, make electronic circuits and clean tiny, delicate components.

Ship's radar works in air

The power of speech
The effects of spoken words are enormous, especially when delivered with passion and emotion. Famous speeches, such as Martin Luther King's 1963 plea for civil rights, "I have a dream ...", change the course of history.

Testing materials
Ultrasound can detect tiny flaws in metals, plastics and other materials used to make parts and components – from bridge bolts to aircraft wings. Pulses of ultrasound are reflected by micro-cracks, which could grow when the part is under stress. The ultrasound patterns are shown on a screen.

Outgoing sonar pulses or "pings"

Sound waves travel at 1,430 metres per second in water

Sound waves spread out from source

Animal communication
Roaring lions, howling wolves, barking dogs, chattering monkeys – these are a few examples of animals using sounds to communicate with each other. Sometimes we can gather the meaning of the sound, even if the animal is unfamiliar. A growl or hiss is usually threatening.

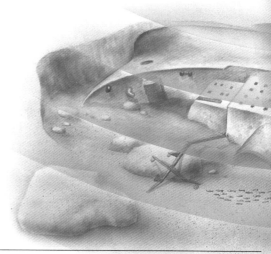

See also: About waves page 110, Sound waves page 112

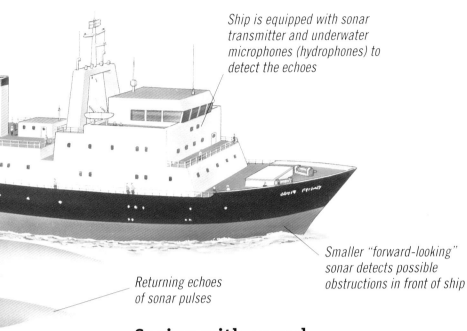

Ship is equipped with sonar transmitter and underwater microphones (hydrophones) to detect the echoes

Returning echoes of sonar pulses

Smaller "forward-looking" sonar detects possible obstructions in front of ship

Science discovery
Ernst Mach (1838-1916) was a science philosopher. He was interested in the aims of science, the nature of theories and facts, and what experiments prove. He also studied sight, hearing and the features of waves. The Mach number referring to the speed of sound is named after him. It is a useful idea because the actual speed of sound varies with changes in density, temperature, pressure and other conditions.

Seeing with sound
Ships use sonar to search for objects such as wrecks, submarines, rocks, icebergs, whales and shoals of fish under the sea. Sonar is also used to measure the depth of water and map the sea bed. Sonar stands for SOund Navigation and Ranging. It involves sending pulses of ultrasound (very high-pitched sound) down through the water. The sound waves bounce, or reflect, off objects and come back as echoes. We know how fast sound travels in water, so timing the echoes gives the distance to the object. Analysing the details of the echoes shows the nature of the object – whether it is large or small, and hard or soft. Radar works in a similar way to sonar, but it uses radio waves that travel through air. (Radio waves do not travel far in water.)

Ultrasound waves reflect off objects such as seabed wrecks

Sounds on screen
Sonar uses ultrasound, which is too high-pitched for our ears. Microphones convert the ultrasounds into electrical signals. Electronic equipment turns these signals into sounds of lower pitch, that we can hear as eerie "pings", and also into patterns of lines and colours on monitor screens.

Light

WE SEE LIGHT, and only light. We use light every day, in endless ways. But describing light is more difficult. It's a type of energy caused by a combination of electrical and magnetic fields. In some ways, light travels as waves, so it has typical wave features. For example, the colour of light depends on how long its waves are. However, in other ways, light seems to be a stream of tiny particles or packets of energy, called photons. Scientists have come to accept these two ways of understanding light. They call it the "wave-particle duality" of light. Nothing travels faster than light – it flashes along at almost 300,000 kilometres each second.

Invisible light

Light with waves which are shorter than the waves of violet light, is called ultra-violet light, UV. Our eyes do not detect UV, so we cannot see it. But too much UV can cause sunburn and also damage our eyes.

Rainbow colours

A rainbow is caused by light from the Sun shining through raindrops. The raindrops separate out the colours in white light, so we can see them. The major colours in a rainbow are red, orange, yellow, green, blue, indigo and violet. They are always in the same order. These colours are called the spectrum. Each is light of a different wavelength. Red light has the longest waves, orange is slightly shorter, and so on. Violet has the shortest waves.

Colours of spectrum merge into each other

Clear and fuzzy

Some substances let most of the light pass straight through them. These clear materials, such as air, window glass or water, are called transparent. Other substances let some light through, but the waves are scattered and bounced around. So the view is fuzzy or blurred. These translucent substances include frosted glass, mist, net curtains and tracing paper. A substance that lets no light through is known as opaque.

Science discovery

One of the first scientists to study light in a scientific way was Alhazen (965-1038). At the time, most people believed that light came out of the eyes and shone onto objects, so that we could see them. Alhazen worked out the correct explanation – that light from a light source, such as the Sun or a candle, reflected off objects and went into the eye. He also studied coloured lights, mirrors and lenses. His work helped later scientists to develop the microscope, telescope and other optical, or light-based, devices. Sadly, for a person who helped to explain so much about light, lenses and how eyes work, there is no known portrait of Alhazen. So we do not know what he looked like.

An early compound microscope (one with more than one lens)

See also: Television page 104, About waves page 110

COLOURS AND FILTERS

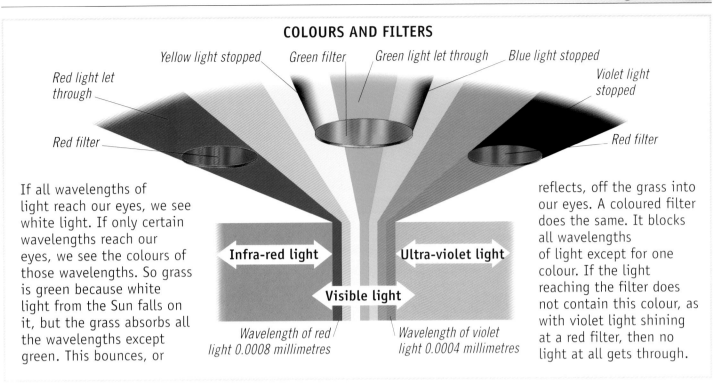

Yellow light stopped · Green filter · Green light let through · Blue light stopped

Red light let through

Violet light stopped

Red filter

Green filter

Red filter

Infra-red light

Ultra-violet light

Visible light

Wavelength of red light 0.0008 millimetres

Wavelength of violet light 0.0004 millimetres

If all wavelengths of light reach our eyes, we see white light. If only certain wavelengths reach our eyes, we see the colours of those wavelengths. So grass is green because white light from the Sun falls on it, but the grass absorbs all the wavelengths except green. This bounces, or reflects, off the grass into our eyes. A coloured filter does the same. It blocks all wavelengths of light except for one colour. If the light reaching the filter does not contain this colour, as with violet light shining at a red filter, then no light at all gets through.

Mixing colours

Most colours of light can be made by mixing together just three colours – red, blue and green. These are called the primary colours of light. Added together in different proportions, they create other colours. Red and green light together make yellow. Red and blue light together make magenta (pink). Green and blue make cyan (light blue). Yellow, magenta and cyan are called the complimentary, or secondary, colours of light. Red, blue and green all added together make white light.

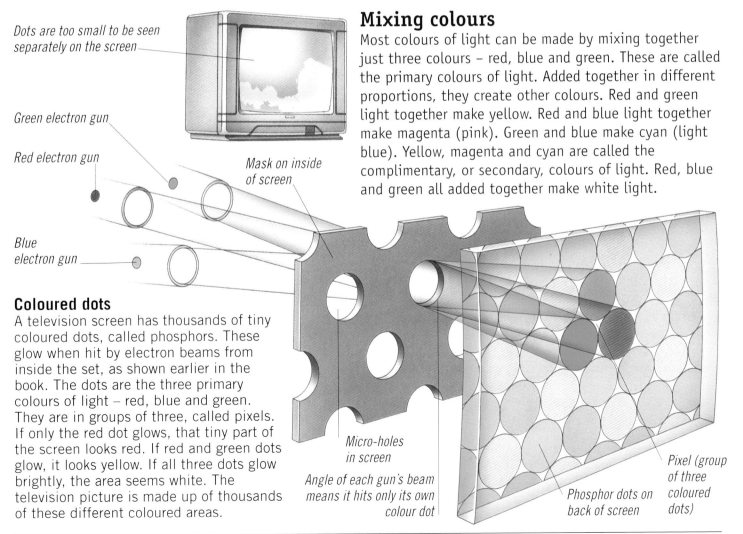

Dots are too small to be seen separately on the screen

Green electron gun

Red electron gun

Mask on inside of screen

Blue electron gun

Micro-holes in screen

Angle of each gun's beam means it hits only its own colour dot

Phosphor dots on back of screen

Pixel (group of three coloured dots)

Coloured dots

A television screen has thousands of tiny coloured dots, called phosphors. These glow when hit by electron beams from inside the set, as shown earlier in the book. The dots are the three primary colours of light – red, blue and green. They are in groups of three, called pixels. If only the red dot glows, that tiny part of the screen looks red. If red and green dots glow, it looks yellow. If all three dots glow brightly, the area seems white. The television picture is made up of thousands of these different coloured areas.

Reflected light

WHEN LIGHT HITS certain kinds of surfaces, it bounces back from the surface, like a ball bouncing off a wall. This is called reflection. Most objects do not give out their own light. We see them because they reflect light from something else, into our eyes. For example, the Moon does not produce its own light. It shines because it reflects the Sun's light. A very smooth and shiny surface, like a mirror, reflects most of the light falling onto it, without scattering. So it produces a bright, clear reflection. On a rough surface, light is scattered or reflected in all directions, producing poor reflections. The colours of objects also depend on reflections. A white object reflects all the colours of white light shining on it. A completely black object reflects no light at all.

Funny reflections
A curved fairground mirror has a wavy surface. It produces distorted, amusing images. The surface of this mirror curves inwards in some places and outwards in others.

CURVED REFLECTIONS

A curved mirror changes the shape of its reflection. A convex (bulging or outward-curved) mirror makes things look smaller. A concave (bowl-like or inward-curved) surface makes things look bigger. Concave mirrors can also turn things upside down. Curved mirrors have many uses. The driving mirrors of a car are convex, to give a wider view. Shaving mirrors are concave to give a magnified image. You can see how curved surfaces change reflections by looking in both the convex and concave sides of a shiny new spoon.

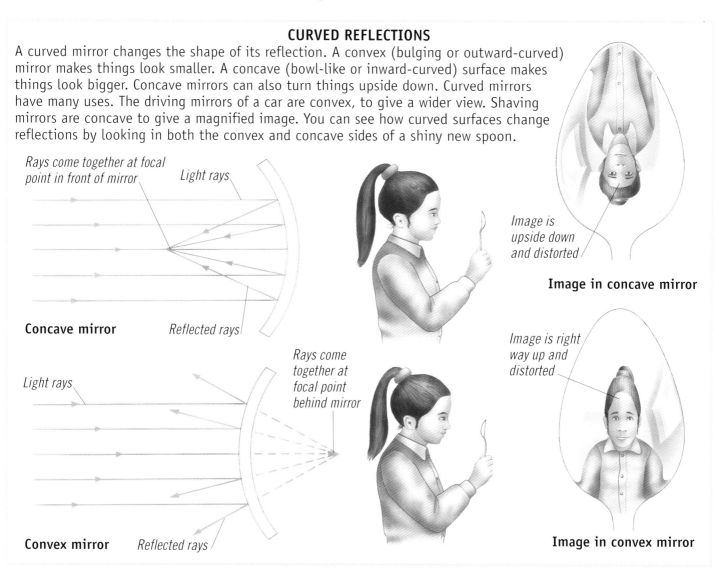

Rays come together at focal point in front of mirror

Light rays

Concave mirror   Reflected rays

Light rays

Rays come together at focal point behind mirror

Convex mirror   Reflected rays

Image is upside down and distorted

Image in concave mirror

Image is right way up and distorted

Image in convex mirror

See also: Light page 124, Refracted light page 128

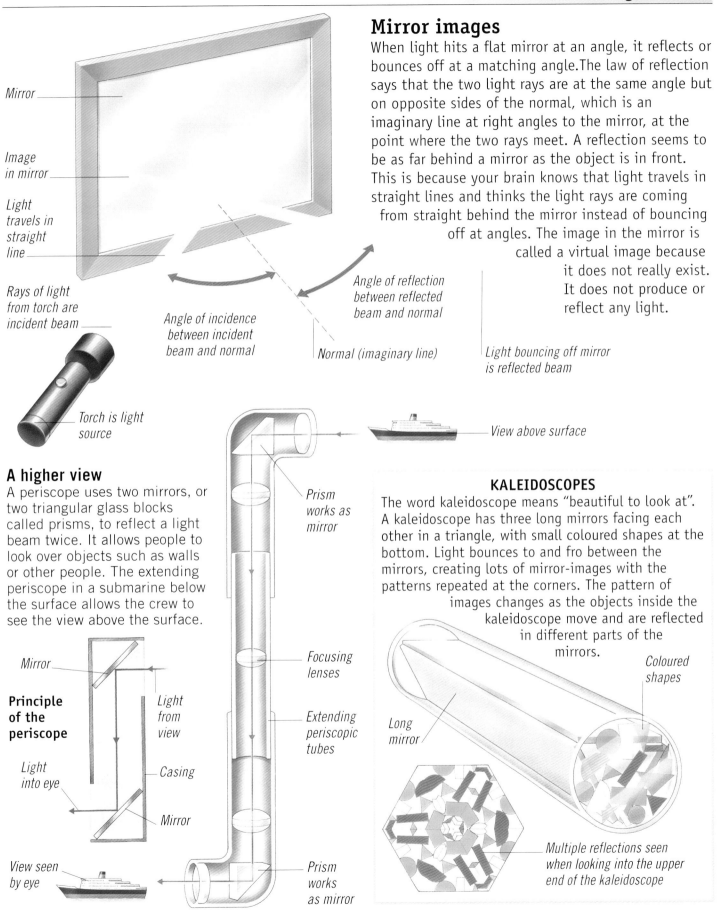

Mirror

Image in mirror

Light travels in straight line

Rays of light from torch are incident beam

Torch is light source

Angle of incidence between incident beam and normal

Normal (imaginary line)

Angle of reflection between reflected beam and normal

Light bouncing off mirror is reflected beam

Mirror images

When light hits a flat mirror at an angle, it reflects or bounces off at a matching angle.The law of reflection says that the two light rays are at the same angle but on opposite sides of the normal, which is an imaginary line at right angles to the mirror, at the point where the two rays meet. A reflection seems to be as far behind a mirror as the object is in front. This is because your brain knows that light travels in straight lines and thinks the light rays are coming from straight behind the mirror instead of bouncing off at angles. The image in the mirror is called a virtual image because it does not really exist. It does not produce or reflect any light.

A higher view

A periscope uses two mirrors, or two triangular glass blocks called prisms, to reflect a light beam twice. It allows people to look over objects such as walls or other people. The extending periscope in a submarine below the surface allows the crew to see the view above the surface.

Mirror

Principle of the periscope

Light into eye

Light from view

Casing

Mirror

View seen by eye

View above surface

Prism works as mirror

Focusing lenses

Extending periscopic tubes

Prism works as mirror

KALEIDOSCOPES

The word kaleidoscope means "beautiful to look at". A kaleidoscope has three long mirrors facing each other in a triangle, with small coloured shapes at the bottom. Light bounces to and fro between the mirrors, creating lots of mirror-images with the patterns repeated at the corners. The pattern of images changes as the objects inside the kaleidoscope move and are reflected in different parts of the mirrors.

Coloured shapes

Long mirror

Multiple reflections seen when looking into the upper end of the kaleidoscope

Refracted light

WHEN LIGHT PASSES from one transparent substance, such as air, to another, such as glass, it appears to bend where the two substances meet. This bending is called refraction. It happens because light has a different speed in each substance, or medium. Light travels fastest – the "speed of light" – through space or a vacuum. It goes slightly slower through air. In water, it travels much slower, only about three-quarters of its speed in a vacuum. In glass, it travels even slower. Refraction is used in hundreds of devices, from eye contact and spectacle lenses to giant telescopes.

White light (mixture of all colours)

Prism refracts light

Splitting white light

A triangular, flat-sided block of clear glass or plastic is called a prism. As a beam of white light enters a prism, it slows down, because light travels more slowly through the glass or plastic. But not all of the colours in the white light slow down by the same amount. Those with shorter waves slow down more than the colours with longer waves. This makes the colours separate into a spectrum. Red light, with the longest waves, slows down the least and so bends or refracts the least.

Clear glass prism

Light refracts as it enters the prism

Light refracts again when leaving the prism

Violet light is slowed the most and so refracts the most

Red light is slowed the least and so is refracted the least

Raindrop "prism"

White light from the Sun

Refracted light makes rainbow

Raindrop prisms

In a rainstorm, millions of raindrops act as tiny prisms to break up sunlight into its spectrum of colours. This forms a rainbow in the sky. You can only see a rainbow when the Sun is shining from behind you – and when it is raining!

Science discovery

Willebrord Snell (1580-1626) was the first person to investigate refraction in a scientific way. He found that each substance has a characteristic light-bending power, called its refractive index. This is a comparison of the angle of the light ray entering the substance, with the angle of the light ray once it is inside. The more a substance bends light, the higher its refractive index.

See also: Reflected light page 126, Using light page 132

LENSES

Any piece of transparent material with smoothly curved sides is called a lens. A convex lens is thicker in the middle than at the edges. A concave lens is thinner in the middle than at the edges. Convex lenses bend the light rays inwards so that all the light is concentrated at one point, called the focus. Convex lenses make things look bigger, as in a magnifying glass, but you see a smaller area of view. Concave lenses do the opposite, bend light rays outwards and make things look smaller.

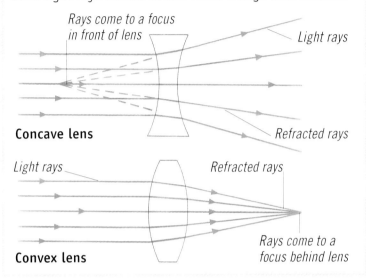

Rays come to a focus in front of lens

Light rays

Concave lens

Refracted rays

Light rays

Refracted rays

Convex lens

Rays come to a focus behind lens

Odd refractions

Refractions of light in water can have some strange effects. They make a straw in a watery drink appear cut in half. If the drink is in a glass, the glass's own refractions add to the effect. Refraction also makes the bottom of a swimming pool or pond look nearer than it really is.

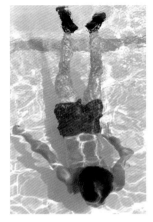

Ripple effect

Water's smooth surface works like a mirror to reflect light from above. It also refracts light from below, coming from objects in the water out into the air. The ripples on water's surface have two effects. They cause reflections from the surface to be distorted. They also distort the refractions.

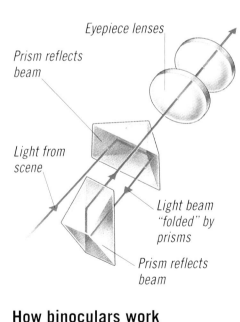

Eyepiece lenses

Prism reflects beam

Light from scene

Light beam "folded" by prisms

Prism reflects beam

Prisms inside protective casing

Focusing control knob

Small eyepiece lenses at rear

Large objective lenses at front

Two sets of prisms and lenses produce views for both eyes, allowing judgement of distance

How binoculars work

Binoculars make small faraway things look larger. The prisms turn the image so that it is the right way round and also the right way up for the eyes. The prisms also lengthen the light path between the lenses by sending the light to and fro. Making a longer light path between the lenses increases the magnifying that the lenses can do, and the prisms fit this longer path into a shorter distance. A telescope does a similar job to binoculars, but lacks prisms and so is longer.

Detecting light

WE SEE BY TWO MAIN KINDS of light. One is daylight, from the Sun. This star is 150 million kilometres away, but its light takes only eight minutes to reach us, because light travels so fast. The other main kind of light source is the electric lamp. There are various types, such as filament bulbs and fluorescent tubes. Other light sources include fires, candles, gas lamps and oil lamps. We see when light from a light source bounces or reflects off other objects, and enters our eyes. The eye is an amazingly complex, delicate body part that senses light rays and provides us with a view of our surroundings, in great detail and full colour.

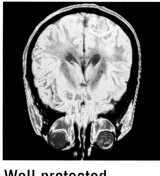

Well protected
The rear three-quarters of the eye is well protected inside a deep bowl of bone, the eye socket or orbit, in the skull. The front quarter is protected and cleaned by the eyelids.

How the eye works

The eye is about the size of a golf ball. It has a lens inside which is as small as a pea. Light enters the eye through a hole called the pupil. From the outside this looks like a black dot in the middle of the eye. The light rays pass through the lens, which focuses them onto a thin layer, the retina, at the back of the eye. The retina contains light-sensitive chemicals which change the energy of light into the energy of tiny electrical nerve signals. These go along the optic nerve to the brain. About two-thirds of the information in the brain, about what we know and learn, comes in through our eyes as words and pictures.

Down side up
Because of the way the eye's lens works, it focuses an upside-down image on the retina. But from the moment we are born and first look at our surroundings, the brain never knows any different. So we learn to see without problems.

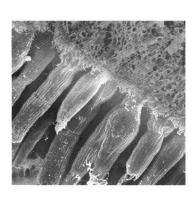

Light micro-sensors
Two types of microscopic cells in the retina convert light into nerve signals. Seven million cones (greenish-blue in the micro-photo above) work only in bright light, but see fine details and colours. About 120 million rods (taller and bluer) see only greys, but function well in dim light.

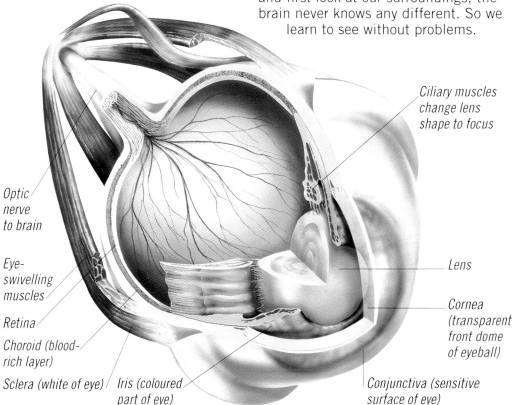

Optic nerve to brain

Eye-swivelling muscles

Retina

Choroid (blood-rich layer)

Sclera (white of eye)

Iris (coloured part of eye)

Ciliary muscles change lens shape to focus

Lens

Cornea (transparent front dome of eyeball)

Conjunctiva (sensitive surface of eye)

See also: Refracted light page 128, Using light page 132

Science discovery
Antoine Henri Becquerel (1852-1908) discovered radioactivity when he placed a uranium-containing substance near a plate of glass coated with light-sensitive photographic chemicals. The plate became cloudy and dark, even though it was wrapped up and there was no visible light. The cloudiness was due to radioactivity given off by the uranium. Becquerel also studied fluorescence. He built an early fluorescent light, although practical tube-shaped lamps were not made until the 1930s.

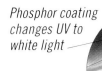

Phosphor coating changes UV to white light

UV light hits phosphor coating

Mercury vapour inside tube

Electricity gives mercury atom energy

Mercury atom gives out energy as UV light

High-voltage electricity flows through gas

Pins connect to electricity supply

Glass tube

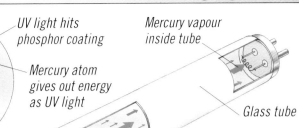

Fluorescence
Under certain conditions, atoms take in an invisible form of energy, and give it out as visible light. This is fluorescence. A fluorescent light is a glass tube filled with mercury vapour. When electricity flows through the gas, the mercury atoms take up the electrical energy and give it out as invisible ultra-violet rays. These rays hit a phosphor coating inside the tube. The phosphor atoms convert it to white light.

Light from burning
Some chemicals give off very bright light when they burn. Many are used in fireworks. Magnesium metal was used in old-fashioned camera flash guns. It burns with a sudden brilliant white light.

Inside a camera
The single-lens reflex (SLR) camera uses the same lenses both for checking the view and taking the photograph. Light comes into the camera through the lens, reflects off a mirror, and reflects around the inside of a prism into the eye. When you press the shutter, the mirror swings quickly upwards, so the light can shine onto the light-sensitive photographic film.

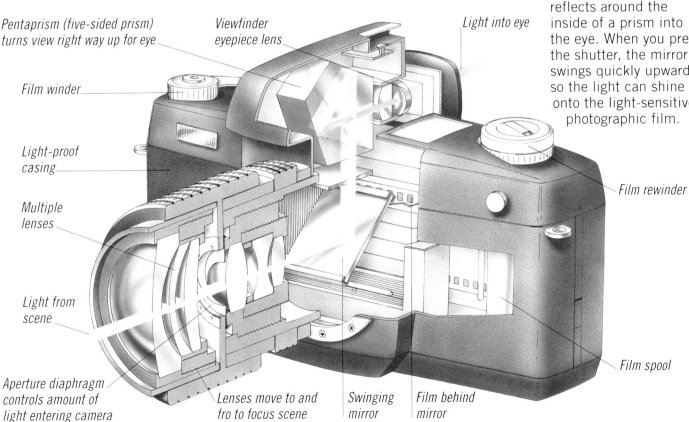

Pentaprism (five-sided prism) turns view right way up for eye

Viewfinder eyepiece lens

Light into eye

Film winder

Light-proof casing

Multiple lenses

Light from scene

Aperture diaphragm controls amount of light entering camera

Lenses move to and fro to focus scene

Swinging mirror

Film behind mirror

Film rewinder

Film spool

Using light

ELECTRIC LIGHTS, MICROSCOPES, telescopes, televisions, cameras, solar panels – we use light in hundreds of ways every day (and night). Artificial lights are especially important at night in our homes, on vehicles, for advertising and to help the emergency services. Optical instruments use lenses and mirrors to change the sizes of images and make them clearer. Flashes of light can also be used to send messages. These vary from the simple on-off pattern of a torch beam, to the millions of flashes per second of laser light in optical fibres, carrying information for television programmes, telephone calls and computer communications.

The microscope

A light microscope uses two sets of lenses to make very small objects look hundreds of times bigger than they really are. A compound microscope magnifies in two stages. Light from a mirror reflects up and through the object (which must be very thin and partly transparent) into the powerful objective lens. This gives the first magnification. The eyepiece lens then enlarges this further, like a magnifying glass.

Eyepiece lenses

Barrel

Focusing knob

Fine-focus knob

Objective lenses

Tilt adjustment

Heavy base

Rotating turret

Other objective lenses for different magnifications

Object on piece of glass (glass slide)

Mirror reflects light up through object

Science discovery

Antonie van Leeuwenhoek (1632-1723), a cloth trader from Holland, was one of the first microscopists. He made hundreds of simple (one-lens) microscopes, grinding and polishing the tiny glass lenses himself. Some of the lenses were hardly larger than rice grains. The magnifying power of his microscopes varied from about 70 to more than 250 times. Van Leeuwenhoek saw and drew pictures of microbes such as bacteria, and the living cells in blood and body fluids.

Dust-sized grains of plant pollen seen under the light microscope

View through a microscope

A light microscope can magnify objects to 1,000 or perhaps 2,000 times. More than this, and the image is too faint and blurred to be useful. An electron microscope, which uses beams of electrons instead of light rays, can produce much greater magnifications.

See also: Optical fibres page 102, Using the EMS page 138

TELESCOPES

Telescopes give close-up views of distant objects, from a satellite or space station orbiting the Earth, to stars and galaxies billions of kilometres away in deep space. Because very large glass lenses tend to have tiny flaws, most modern astronomical telescopes use mirrors. They are called reflector telescopes. The largest mirrors are more than 5 metres across.

In a refracting telescope, two lenses or sets of lenses refract or bend the light rays. A large lens at the front collects and focuses the faint light. A smaller eyepiece lens makes the image larger so it can be seen more clearly.

Reflecting telescopes use mirrors to reflect the light. A large concave (dished) mirror collects and concentrates the light rays. A second mirror reflects the light onto a small eyepiece lens, at the side of the telescope, which makes the image look larger.

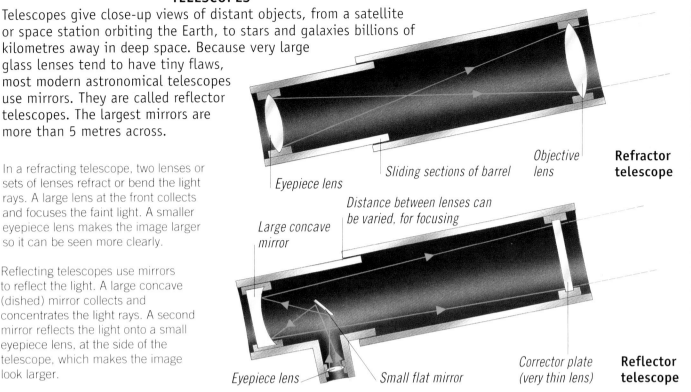

Eyepiece lens | *Sliding sections of barrel* | *Objective lens* | **Refractor telescope**

Large concave mirror | *Distance between lenses can be varied, for focusing*

Eyepiece lens | *Small flat mirror* | *Corrector plate (very thin lens)* | **Reflector telescope**

Light at night
Without light, the night-time scene would look very different. People would not be able to travel around, go for meals, carry out work, visit friends and family or pursue leisure interests. Advertising signs would not brighten the scene. More seriously, the emergency services would have difficulty attending an accident or disaster, and hospitals would not be able to treat injured people.

Seeing into space
The kinds of telescopes that detect light rays are called optical telescopes (shown below right). They are usually built on mountains, high above the dusty, hazy air near the ground. They are also sited far away from the bright lights of towns and cities, which would out-shine and blot out the very faint light from stars. Other types of telescopes detect not light waves, but radio waves coming naturally from space. They have large dishes (shown below left) and are called radio telescopes.

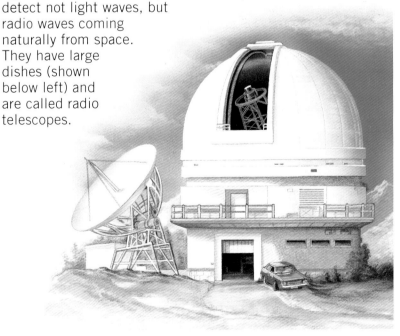

Laser light

ORDINARY LIGHT, FROM the Sun or an electric lamp, is a mix of many different wavelengths, or colours. Also the waves are jumbled and rise and fall out of step with each other. Laser light is different. Its waves are just one wavelength, or colour, and these waves are all in step with each other, rising and falling together. The result is an intense beam of a single colour, that does not spread out or fade like ordinary light. Laser light is even brighter than sunlight. It has so much energy that it can "burn" through metal. Lasers are used in hundreds of ways, in industry, medicine and surgery, to make holograms, read bar codes and compact discs, and send messages along fibre-optic cables.

Industrial lasers
Long-wavelength lasers focused onto a surface produce intense heat. This heat can easily cut through fabrics for clothing, and even solid metals such as steel. It can also melt or weld together pieces of metal.

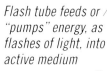

Flash tube feeds or "pumps" energy, as flashes of light, into active medium

Fully-silvered mirror

Active medium (in this laser, ruby crystal)

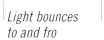

How a laser works

"Laser" stands for Light Amplification by the Stimulated Emission of Radiation. Laser light is made by feeding energy, such as ordinary light or electricity, into a substance called the active medium. As the active medium takes in the energy, its atoms start to release light of a particular wavelength. When light from one atom strikes its neighbours, they also release identical bursts of light. The light energy builds up as it is reflected to and fro by special mirrors at each end of the laser. Eventually, the light becomes so intense that some of it escapes through one of the mirrors and forms the laser beam.

Light bounces to and fro

Part-silvered mirror

Laser beam

Science discovery

Engineer and physicist Theodore Maiman (1927-) built the first working laser in 1960. It generated laser light by energizing or "pumping" a ruby crystal with light from a camera-type flash tube. The whole device was only a few centimetres long, but worked very well. Maiman had developed earlier research into lasers and also masers, which use microwaves rather than light, by Nikolay Basov and Charles H Townes.

Big and small
High-powered industrial lasers fill whole rooms. Lower-powered lasers are used in medicine to cut through body parts, especially in delicate surgery such as inside the eye. The heat of the beam seals blood vessels to reduce bleeding from the cut. Semiconductor lasers that read computer and music CDs are about the size of large rice grains.

See also: Light page 124, Fibre-optics page 102

Fun with lasers

The most spectacular light shows are produced by beams of laser light. The colour of the light depends on the chemical elements in the active medium. The medium can be a solid, such as a crystal, a liquid, or a gas such as argon or carbon dioxide. Laser light can travel huge distances without spreading or fading – even to the Moon and back. Like ordinary light, laser light goes in perfectly straight lines. So laser beams are used as "rulers" for surveying and to line up large structures like skyscrapers, tunnels and bridges.

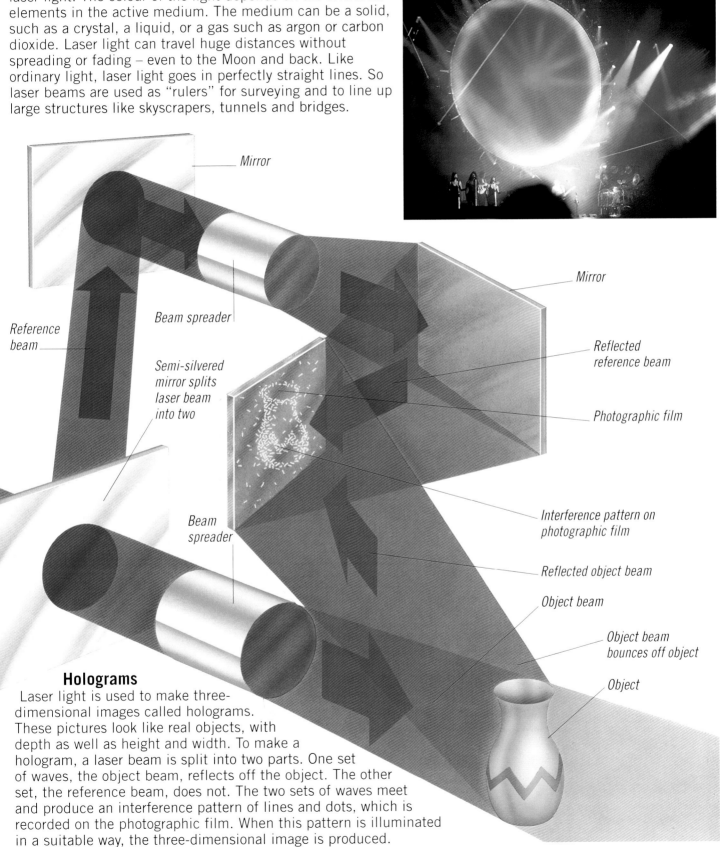

Mirror

Beam spreader

Reference beam

Semi-silvered mirror splits laser beam into two

Beam spreader

Mirror

Reflected reference beam

Photographic film

Interference pattern on photographic film

Reflected object beam

Object beam

Object beam bounces off object

Object

Holograms

Laser light is used to make three-dimensional images called holograms. These pictures look like real objects, with depth as well as height and width. To make a hologram, a laser beam is split into two parts. One set of waves, the object beam, reflects off the object. The other set, the reference beam, does not. The two sets of waves meet and produce an interference pattern of lines and dots, which is recorded on the photographic film. When this pattern is illuminated in a suitable way, the three-dimensional image is produced.

Beyond light

LIGHT IS IN THE FORM of combined electrical and magnetic rays, known as electromagnetic or EM waves. But it is only one form of EM wave. There is a whole range of EM waves, called the electromagnetic spectrum, EMS. The waves are all ripples of electromagnetic energy. They all travel at the same speed. They can all pass through space. They differ mainly in their wavelengths, and so in their frequencies (number of waves per second). We can see the visible light part of the EM spectrum, but the other waves are invisible to our eyes. However we can detect them in various ways. For example, we can feel the warmth of infra-red waves.

Seeing EM waves

Our eyes see only the light part of the EM spectrum. So we use electronic devices to detect other waves and convert them into light. This air traffic control screen shows radar "blips" as spots of light. The blips represent reflections or echoes of radio waves, bouncing off nearby aircraft.

How high, exactly?

Modern EM equipment is amazingly complex and accurate. A satellite's microwave-based radar can beam the waves down to the ground, receive and time their reflections, and work out the satellite's height – to the accuracy of the nearest 10 centimetres.

The electromagnetic spectrum

This diagram shows the whole range of electromagnetic waves, spread out in their spectrum. Radio waves have the longest wavelength and lowest frequency. Gamma rays have the shortest waves. Most of these waves exist naturally, on the Earth or coming from the Sun and space. We have also been able to work out ways of making and using most of the waves in some way, as shown on the following pages.

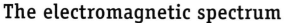

Radio broadcast | Television programme | Radar dish | Microwave oven

Long radio waves

The longest radio waves measure many kilometres from one wave peak to the next. They carry mainly radio programmes.

Shorter radio waves

These are used for FM radio and television broadcasts (VHF and UHF, Very and Ultra High Frequency). Their waves are a metre or less.

Shortest radio waves

Some television and radar systems (see above) use shorter radio waves, where each wave is only tens of centimetres long.

Microwaves

Microwaves are used in microwave ovens, to generate heat, and also in radar and satellites. They are a few centimetres long.

See also: About waves page 110, Light page 124, Reflected light page 126

Heat pictures

Infra-red (IR) photographs show the heat given off by objects. Their colours are not real. They represent the types and proportions of infra-red waves given off or reflected from each object. These values are then changed into colours we can distinguish. IR images from planes or satellites, as shown on the left, can be used in many ways. Clean, clear water appears black, but polluted water is more blue. In forests, younger trees can be picked out from older ones. In farmland, healthy crops normally appear bright red. A duller colour warns of drought, disease or attack by pests.

WAVES OF SURPRISE

- Radio waves of short wavelength are reflected by the billions of water droplets in a cloud. This is how a weather satellite's radar system produces images of cloud cover over the regions below.
- Natural X-rays from space cannot penetrate far into the Earth's atmosphere. So X-ray telescopes must be carried above the atmosphere, on a rocket or satellite, or even under a high-altitude balloon.
- Gamma rays are very dangerous to living things. They are used to kill germs, and to sterilise medical instruments and equipment.

Science discovery

In about 1894, Guglielmo Marconi (1874-1937) became interested in the "electric waves" which scientist Heinrich Hertz had studied. Marconi decided to build his own equipment for making and detecting the waves, and for sending messages by them. In 1896 he sent radio signals across his garden, in 1899 across the Channel between France and England, and in 1901 across the Atlantic between England and Newfoundland. Regular public radio broadcasts began in the 1920s.

Atoms by X-rays

X-rays help to work out atomic structures, in the technique of X-ray diffraction. The rays are beamed through the object, when they are scattered or diffracted (bent). They form a pattern of lines and curves on an X-ray-sensitive film or screen. The details of the pattern show the sizes and shapes of the atoms and molecules in the substance, and also how they are arranged. This helps to work out the structures of metal alloys, medical drugs, plastics and even virus germs.

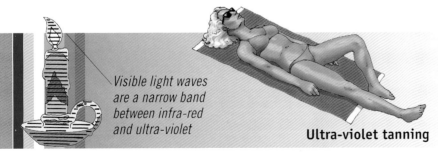

Visible light waves are a narrow band between infra-red and ultra-violet

Ultra-violet tanning

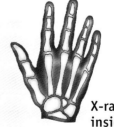

X-ray image of inside the body

Infra-red
At a millimetre or less in length, these carry heat. They are given off by anything hot, such as a fire, the Sun or your own body.

Ultra-violet
Even shorter than light waves, ultra-violet rays can be harmful. They cause the skin to go red (sunburn) and then darken (suntan).

X-rays
Each wave is less than one millionth of one millimetre long. X-rays pass through or penetrate soft substances such as human flesh.

Gamma rays
These are the shortest EM waves and so they have the highest frequency, with a million million million going past each second.

Using the EMS

WE USE THE DIFFERENT KINDS of electromagnetic waves for many different purposes. Our radio transmitters generate artificial radio waves that carry radio and television programmes in coded form, by varying the height or frequency of the waves. Microwaves cook food and also carry satellite communications, beaming information up and down from ground stations here on Earth. X-rays can be used to look inside the bodies of people and animals. They also see inside suitcases and luggage, at security checks. We are also learning about our world, space and the Universe, by detecting and studying the natural EM waves which are all around us.

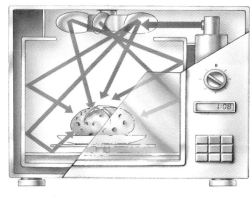

The microwave oven

In a microwave oven, a device called a magnetron produces microwaves about 12 centimetres long, which strike a spinning fan. The fan reflects the waves onto the food from all directions. The waves pass into the food, hit molecules of water and make them vibrate. This causes the heat.

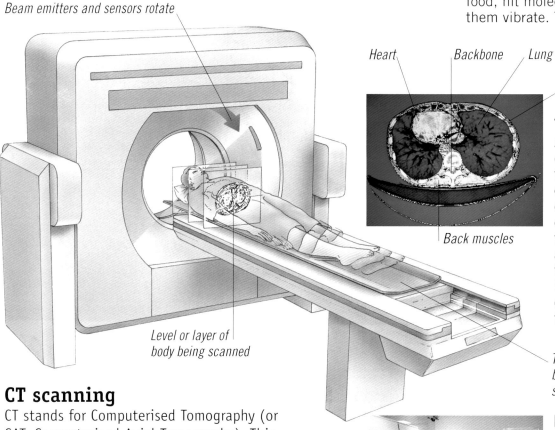

Beam emitters and sensors rotate

Level or layer of body being scanned

Heart   Backbone   Lung

Rib

Back muscles

Table slides body through scanning beams

The CT scan

A CT scan shows different body parts and tissues in different colours or shades, depending on their density. A hard, heavy tissue like bone is almost white. Fluid-filled areas such as blood vessels are much darker. This is a scan at the level of the chest.

CT scanning

CT stands for Computerised Tomography (or CAT, Computerised Axial Tomography). This form of medical scanner uses very weak X-ray beams that rotate around the person. Sensors detect the strengths of the beams as they pass through the body, showing how much of the beam energy has been absorbed by different parts, such as muscles and bones. A computer analyses the results and builds up a series of pictures showing "slices" through the body.

Having a scan

CT scanning is painless and harmless. The person lies still on the table as the X-ray emitters and sensors rotate around the body. The table moves along slowly so the beams pass through each level.

See also: Beyond light page 136, The atmosphere page 152

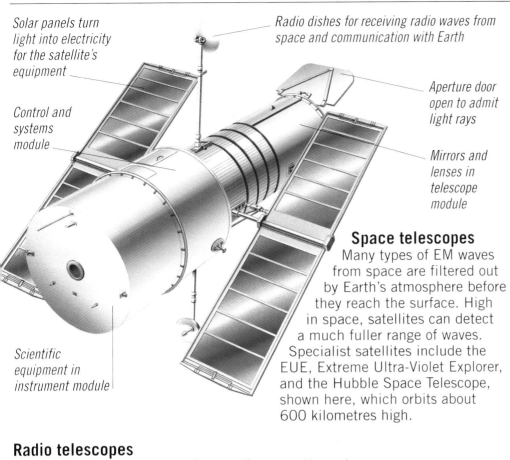

Solar panels turn light into electricity for the satellite's equipment

Radio dishes for receiving radio waves from space and communication with Earth

Control and systems module

Aperture door open to admit light rays

Mirrors and lenses in telescope module

Scientific equipment in instrument module

Space telescopes

Many types of EM waves from space are filtered out by Earth's atmosphere before they reach the surface. High in space, satellites can detect a much fuller range of waves. Specialist satellites include the EUE, Extreme Ultra-Violet Explorer, and the Hubble Space Telescope, shown here, which orbits about 600 kilometres high.

Radio telescopes

The Sun and other stars send out radio waves through space. To detect them on Earth, astronomers use radio telescopes. The huge dishes face the sky to collect and focus the waves. Radio telescopes have to be large, because radio waves are many kilometres long. The largest single-dish radio telescope is at Arecibo, Puerto Rico. The dish is built into a natural hollow in the jungle and is 305 metres across. As the Earth moves, the dish turns to point at a different part of the sky. An alternative is to use an array of many smaller dishes linked by computers. The dishes are spaced out to receive parts of the same waves in different places.

Science discovery

Christiaan Huygens (1629-1695) discovered the rings of planet Saturn and also devised the first pendulum clock to keep accurate time. In 1678 he proposed the theory that light travelled in waves. He said these waves were vibrations of microscopic particles which made up a mysterious substance, "ether". Many people of the time believed that the ether existed everywhere, even in space. The notion of ether was eventually disproved. But Huygens' basic idea of light as waves helped later scientists to discover its true nature.

5

Earth and Life

Our home is a giant ball of rock, 12,800 kilometres across, spinning through space. Its surface is constantly changing. Daily, weather patterns move over sea and land. Yearly, volcanoes erupt and earthquakes split the landscape. Over millions of years, rocks buckle into mountains and great continents drift around the globe.

Planet Earth

To an astronaut high in space, the Earth looks like a small, mainly blue ball with white areas of cloud and green or brown land. Here on the ground, our world is huge and daunting. The Earth is a slightly flattened sphere measuring about 12,800 kilometres across (diameter) and 40,000 kilometres around (circumference). Almost three-quarters of its surface is not earth at all, but covered with water.

Radio antenna (dish)

Satellite maps
Every part of the land has been photographed and measured by survey satellites, such as Landsat and Spot. They detect differences of less than 10 centimetres.

Mapping Earth
Every hill, valley, stream, cliff and pool has now been mapped on the Earth's land surface. So have the mountains and trenches below the waves, on the sea bed (as shown later) using sound waves in echo-sounding or sonar. Maps such as this one distort the sizes of the land masses, as explained below, making those near the poles seem larger. The only way truly to represent an Earth map is to put it onto the same shape as the Earth itself – a ball or globe.

MISSHAPEN MAPS
A true map of the Earth depicts a curved or spherical surface. As soon as this is flattened out to put it onto a page, distortions occur. The way this flattening and transfer is done is called the map's projection. Different projections make the continents look different shapes – compare Antarctica (in white) on these two examples. The various projections each have their own uses, such as showing round-the-world voyages or the relative areas of land and sea in a particular region.

Lambert's equal area projection

Wagner's VII projection

Old maps
About 4,000 years ago the Ancient Egyptians developed the science and art of map-making, or cartography. They needed maps to plot the route and floods of the River Nile, and to plan their journeys across the Mediterranean Sea. As the Greeks and Romans extended their empires, maps became more important. In medieval times the Earth's whole surface was still unknown. The edges were shown with the heavens, fanciful waterfalls or beasts such as dragons. Most people still believed the planet was flat.

See also: Inside the Earth page 144, Earth in space page 174

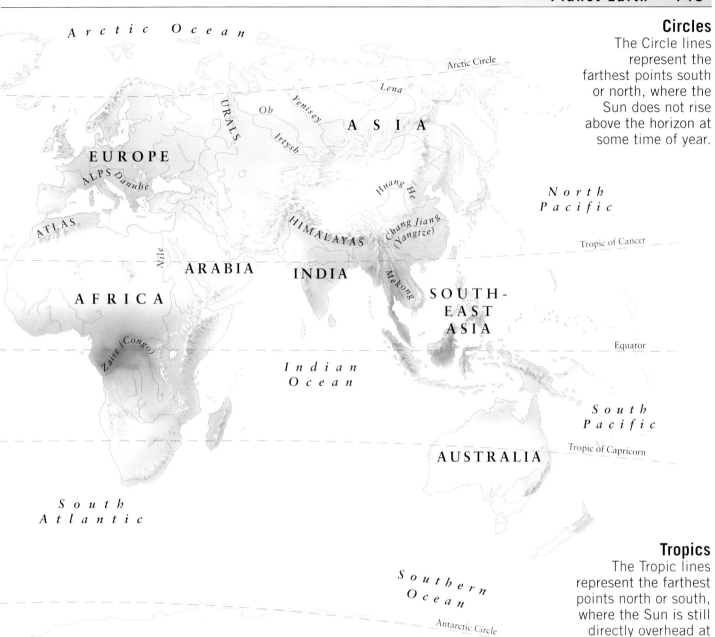

Arctic Ocean

Arctic Circle

Lena

URALS

Ob

Yenisey

A S I A

Irtysh

EUROPE

ALPS Danube

ATLAS

Huang He

*North
Pacific*

Nile

HIMALAYAS

Chang Jiang
(Yangtze)

Tropic of Cancer

ARABIA

INDIA

Mekong

AFRICA

**SOUTH-
EAST
ASIA**

Zaire (Congo)

*Indian
Ocean*

Equator

*South
Pacific*

*South
Atlantic*

AUSTRALIA

Tropic of Capricorn

*Southern
Ocean*

Antarctic Circle

Circles

The Circle lines represent the farthest points south or north, where the Sun does not rise above the horizon at some time of year.

Tropics

The Tropic lines represent the farthest points north or south, where the Sun is still directly overhead at some time of year.

Science discovery

James Hutton (1726-1797) was one of the first people to study geology as a proper science. He saw changes to the landscape happening very slowly around him, such as rivers wearing away their banks and cliffs collapsing. Hutton argued that the same processes much have been happening since Earth began. It had taken immense amounts of time, millions of years, to shape the planet we see today. This went against the ideas of his colleagues, but gradually Hutton's view was accepted.

Inside the Earth

THE EARTH SEEMS VAST AND SOLID. But inside, it is mostly molten or semi-molten, and is always on the move. The whole Earth is some 12,800 kilometres in diameter. But the hard outer layer, the crust, is only about 25-35 kilometres under the major land masses or continents, and even thinner, 5-10 kilometres, beneath the oceans. Below this is the thickest layer, the mantle, which is 2,900 kilometres deep. Within the mantle is the Earth's two-part core. The outer core, 2,200 kilometres thick, is composed of almost liquid iron-rich rocks. The solid inner core, 2,500 kilometres across, is also mainly iron and nickel. If you could travel down a drill hole into the Earth, the temperature would soon be unbearable even after a few dozen kilometres. At the core, it is nearly 5,000°C.

Layers

The bulk of the Earth's volume is the mantle. This is fairly firm in its upper region, but becomes semi-melted or plastic deeper down. The mantle is made of rocky minerals, rich in silicon, magnesium and iron. The fairly rigid upper 60-90 kilometres of mantle, plus the crust above, forms the lithosphere. This is cool and strong and is divided into huge lithospheric plates, as shown on the following page. In the crust, temperatures rise by about 2-3°C for every 90 metres of depth, but this rate soon becomes less.

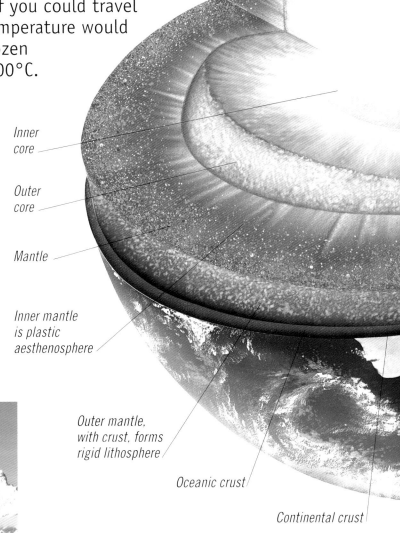

Inner core

Outer core

Mantle

Inner mantle is plastic aesthenosphere

Outer mantle, with crust, forms rigid lithosphere

Oceanic crust

Continental crust

Mountain roots

Mountains are vast lumps of rock that project higher than the normal surface level – and lower, too. Just as a thicker lump of wood floats higher and deeper in water than a thin lump, so the mountains of the Earth's crust "float" higher and deeper on the semi-molten rock beneath, than the much thinner oceanic crust floats.

See also: Planet earth page 142, Earth in space page 174

Oceanic crust is young, nowhere older than 200 million years

Some continental crust is over 3,000 million years old

Crust and mantle are separated by the "Moho" (Mohorovicic discontinuity)

Deep drilling

Most bores drilled for minerals, such as petroleum (crude oil), are a few hundred metres deep. The deepest drill into the sea bed, in the eastern Pacific Ocean, reached 2,111 metres down. On land, the deepest borehole went down about 12,260 metres in the Kola Peninsula, northern Russia. The temperature of the rocks at the bottom exceeded 200°C. Yet this is hardly halfway through the crust.

A mere pinprick

Projects such as the Channel Tunnel between France and England are huge engineering feats. The twin tunnels are almost 50 kilometres long, and go down many metres below the sea bed. But this is only the tiniest pinprick in the surface of the planet.

Restless Earth

ON A WORLD MAP, the east coastline of South America bears an uncanny likeness to the shape of the west coast of Africa. Look at the edges of the continental shelves of these two continents, a couple of hundred metres under the sea's surface, and the resemblance is even more striking. The two would fit together like pieces of a giant jigsaw. In fact, they once did. The idea of continental drift, once dismissed out of hand, is now well established in science. The major land masses or continents have changed less through time than the Earth's crust under the oceans. The oceanic crust has continually formed new patches from molten rocks welling up from below, while other patches melt back into the depths again. The continents have been carried around like giant rafts on these changing shapes of oceanic crust.

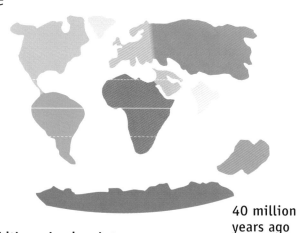

Part of the evidence

Evidence for continental drift comes from many areas, including fossils. Remains of the reptile *Lystrosaurus* have been found in South Africa, Antarctica, India and China, suggesting these lands were joined 230 million years ago.

40 million years ago

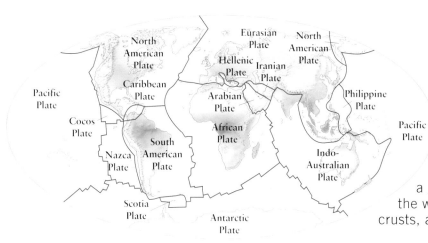

Lithospheric plates

The Earth's rigid crust and firm upper layer of mantle form the lithosphere, about 100 kilometres thick. This is not one continuous structure, like an unbroken egg shell. It is divided into about a dozen huge, curved pieces, called lithospheric plates, like parts of a giant ball-shaped jigsaw. The plates drift around the world, changing the shapes of their oceanic crusts, and carrying their continents with them.

Plate tectonics

The lithospheric plates move and change shape, driven by the incredible heat, pressure and movement in the mantle, according to the idea of plate tectonics. Molten rocks well up from the mantle and cool, joining onto some edges of oceanic crust and enlarging their plates. These are constructive plate boundaries. Meanwhile as the plates slide about, other plate edges are pushed down and melt back into the mantle. These are destructive plate boundaries.

Melting plate below causes volcanic activity

See also: Planet Earth page 142, The rock cycle page 148

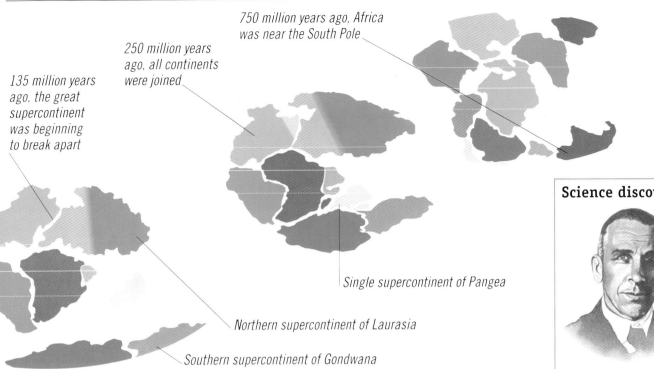

135 million years ago, the great supercontinent was beginning to break apart

250 million years ago, all continents were joined

750 million years ago, Africa was near the South Pole

Single supercontinent of Pangea

Northern supercontinent of Laurasia

Southern supercontinent of Gondwana

Seafloor spreading

Some of the most active regions for making new areas of oceanic plates, called constructive plate boundaries, are in the middle of the oceans. In the Atlantic, this happens at the chain of undersea peaks that runs along the middle of the ocean, the Mid Atlantic Ridge (left). Melted rocks from below cool and add to the plates, forcing them sideways (below). This process is pushing the Americas away from Europe and Africa, making the Atlantic Ocean wider at the rate of about 5 centimetres per year.

Science discovery

The idea of continental drift has been around for centuries. First to propose a scientific explanation was German weather expert Alfred Wegener (1880-1930), in 1912. But political problems, world wars and Wegener's background in meteorology meant his suggestions were not taken seriously until the 1960s.

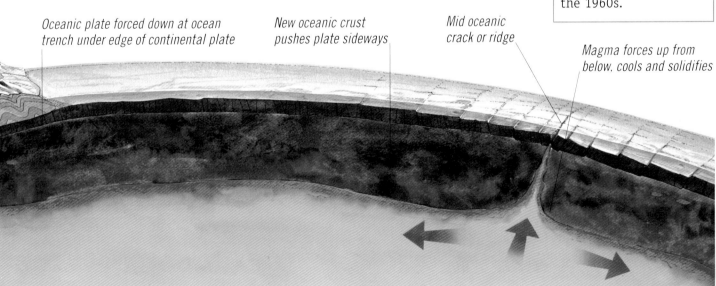

Oceanic plate forced down at ocean trench under edge of continental plate

New oceanic crust pushes plate sideways

Mid oceanic crack or ridge

Magma forces up from below, cools and solidifies

The rock cycle

THE ROCKS OF EARTH'S CRUST are made of various combinations of minerals, such as silica, olivine, pyroxene and hundreds of others. Minerals, like all substance and matter, are made of atoms, mostly joined into molecules. There is only a limited supply of such atoms, molecules and minerals on the planet. Rocks have been broken down by the forces of weathering and erosion, such as wind, rain, heat, ice and waves. They are then reformed into new rocks by heat, pressure and chemical changes. This means the same minerals go round and round, forming one type of rock and then another, over the millions of years of geological time. This process is known as the rock cycle.

Erosion
The forces of nature are especially harsh in desert regions. Windblown sand piles into crescent dunes, barchans. If harder rocks overlay softer ones, the soft rock is sand-blasted to leave a mushroom-like zeugen.

Rocks on the move

There are three main types of rocks. Igneous rocks form when rock minerals are so hot that they have melted, then they cool and go solid again. The rocks formed when lava from a volcano goes hard are igneous. Sedimentary rocks form when tiny particles are worn or eroded from other rocks and settle into layers, such as on the sea bed. They slowly get squashed and cemented – glued by chemical action – into hard rock again. Metamorphic rocks form when other kinds of rocks are subject to great pressure and temperature, such as in the roots of mountains. They change or metamorphose without melting into new rock types.

Igneous rocks form as lava cools

Great heat and pressure form metamorphic rocks

Particles washed into the sea settle as layers of sediments

See also: Planet Earth page 142, Restless Earth page 146

Settled particles are compacted and glued into sedimentary rocks

Layers of time

Sedimentary rocks form in horizontal layers, at the bottom of seas, in lakes and along rivers, and also in deserts, as sandstones. These layers represent the passage of time, covering millions of years. Only sedimentary rocks contain fossils. Any fossilized remains of plants or animals are destroyed when they are melted to make igneous rocks, or altered by pressure and temperature to form metamorphic rocks. Over time, sedimentary rocks may be bent and folded by earth movements, or worn away as particles that become future sedimentary rocks.

ROCK TYPES

There are hundreds of types of rocks. Many have special uses, especially in earlier times when people used more natural materials than we do today. Granites and basalts are igneous rocks. Sandstones, limestones and breccias are sedimentary rocks. Overall, sedimentary rocks cover two-thirds of the Earth's surface because they form on the ocean floor, overlaying the igneous rocks of seafloor spreading. Marbles, schists and gneisses are metamorphic.

Limestone cliffs (sedimentary)

Marble statue (metamorphic)

Granite blocks (igneous)

Volcanoes and earthquakes

FEW NATURAL EVENTS are more awesome than volcanic eruptions or earthquakes. A volcano is a place where red-hot liquid rock (magma) from the Earth's interior melts through the crust and erupts on the surface. Earthquakes are the shock waves from a sudden movement at a crack in the Earth's crust. Both volcanoes and earthquakes are terrifyingly unpredictable. But they do not happen anywhere. Most occur in zones that coincide with the cracks between the massive tectonic plates that make up the Earth's surface.

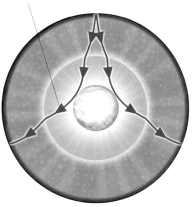

P waves pass deep into Earth and reflect off core

Fissures open

Plates slide sideways

How an earthquake happens

Most earthquakes start because tectonic plates sometimes snag or stick as they slide past each other. For a while, the rocks on either side of the crack bend and stretch. Then all of a sudden they snap or slip, sending shock waves called seismic waves shuddering through the ground.

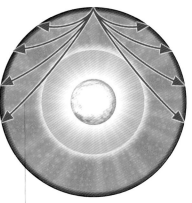

S-waves pass through mantle and curve to surface

HOW BIG IS AN EARTHQUAKE?

There are several ways of recording the size or power of an earthquake. Most widely used is the Richter scale, which depends on the height of the waves recorded on a seismometer – a device that detects vibrations of the ground. But a quake that measures 6 on the Richter scale has different effects depending on the type of ground. It causes more damage where buildings have their foundations in soil or soft rock than where they are built on hard bedrock. The Modified Mercalli scale (below) shows the severity of an earthquake by its effects.

Seismic waves recorded on seismometer

2 Felt by a few, slight effects

6 Felt by all, some damage

8 Large-scale structural damage

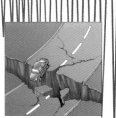

11 Broad cracks, buildings flattened

Seismic waves

Most seismic waves travel through the ground at 20 times the speed of sound. They are at their most powerful near the quake's focus or hypocentre – the place underground where it begins. The site on the surface above is the epicentre. Their power gradually dwindles as they move farther out.

See also: Planet Earth page 142, Restless Earth page 146

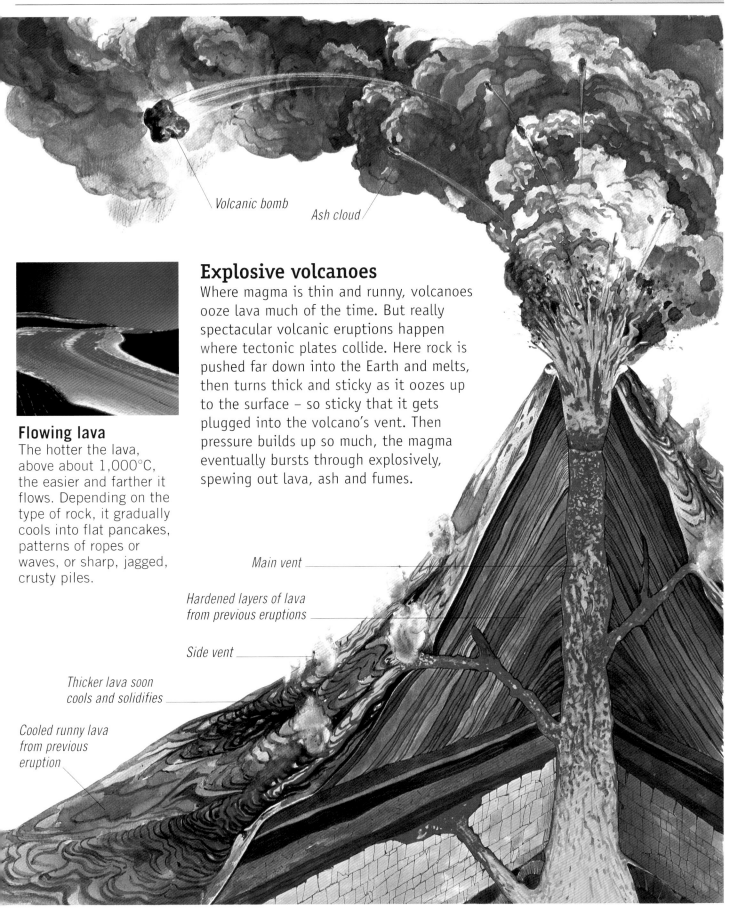

Volcanic bomb

Ash cloud

Flowing lava

The hotter the lava, above about 1,000°C, the easier and farther it flows. Depending on the type of rock, it gradually cools into flat pancakes, patterns of ropes or waves, or sharp, jagged, crusty piles.

Explosive volcanoes

Where magma is thin and runny, volcanoes ooze lava much of the time. But really spectacular volcanic eruptions happen where tectonic plates collide. Here rock is pushed far down into the Earth and melts, then turns thick and sticky as it oozes up to the surface – so sticky that it gets plugged into the volcano's vent. Then pressure builds up so much, the magma eventually bursts through explosively, spewing out lava, ash and fumes.

Main vent

Hardened layers of lava from previous eruptions

Side vent

Thicker lava soon cools and solidifies

Cooled runny lava from previous eruption

Atmosphere

WRAPPED AROUND OUR PLANET is a thin blanket of gases
called the atmosphere. It is barely thicker on the
Earth than the skin on an orange – about 1,000
kilometres high before it fades into the black
nothingness of space. Without the atmosphere, our
planet would be as lifeless as the Moon. It gives us
air to breathe and water to drink. It keeps us warm
by the natural greenhouse effect. And it shields us
from the Sun's harmful rays and from meteorites.

Layers in the air

Scientists divide the atmosphere into layers. We live in the
bottom layer, called the troposphere. Compared to the rest
of the atmosphere, the troposphere is a dense, thick soup,
and it contains three-quarters of its gases, even though it
only goes up 12 kilometres. The troposphere is warmed by
the Sun, but it gets most of this heat indirectly, reflected off
the ground. The air gets thinner and colder as you go higher.

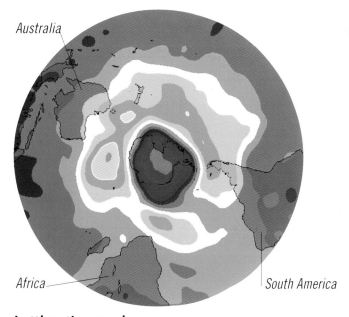

Australia

Africa   South America

Letting the sun in

There is a thin but vital layer of the gas ozone in the
stratosphere. So far, it has been enough to shield us
from dangerous ultra-violet rays from the Sun. But now it
is being attacked by chemical gases, such as the CFCs
(chlorofluorocarbons) once used in aerosol sprays and as
coolants in refrigerators. Now holes in the ozone appear
over the South Pole (colour-coded red above) and North
Pole every spring and are lasting longer each year.

**Aurorae
(Northern and
Southern lights)**

**Meteors (shooting
stars) burn up in
the mesosphere**

**Weather
balloon**

**The only clouds in the
stratosphere are very
rare 'nacreous' clouds
at 22-24 kilometres.**

**Most weather is in
the troposphere**

See also: Planet Earth page 142, Weather and climate page 154

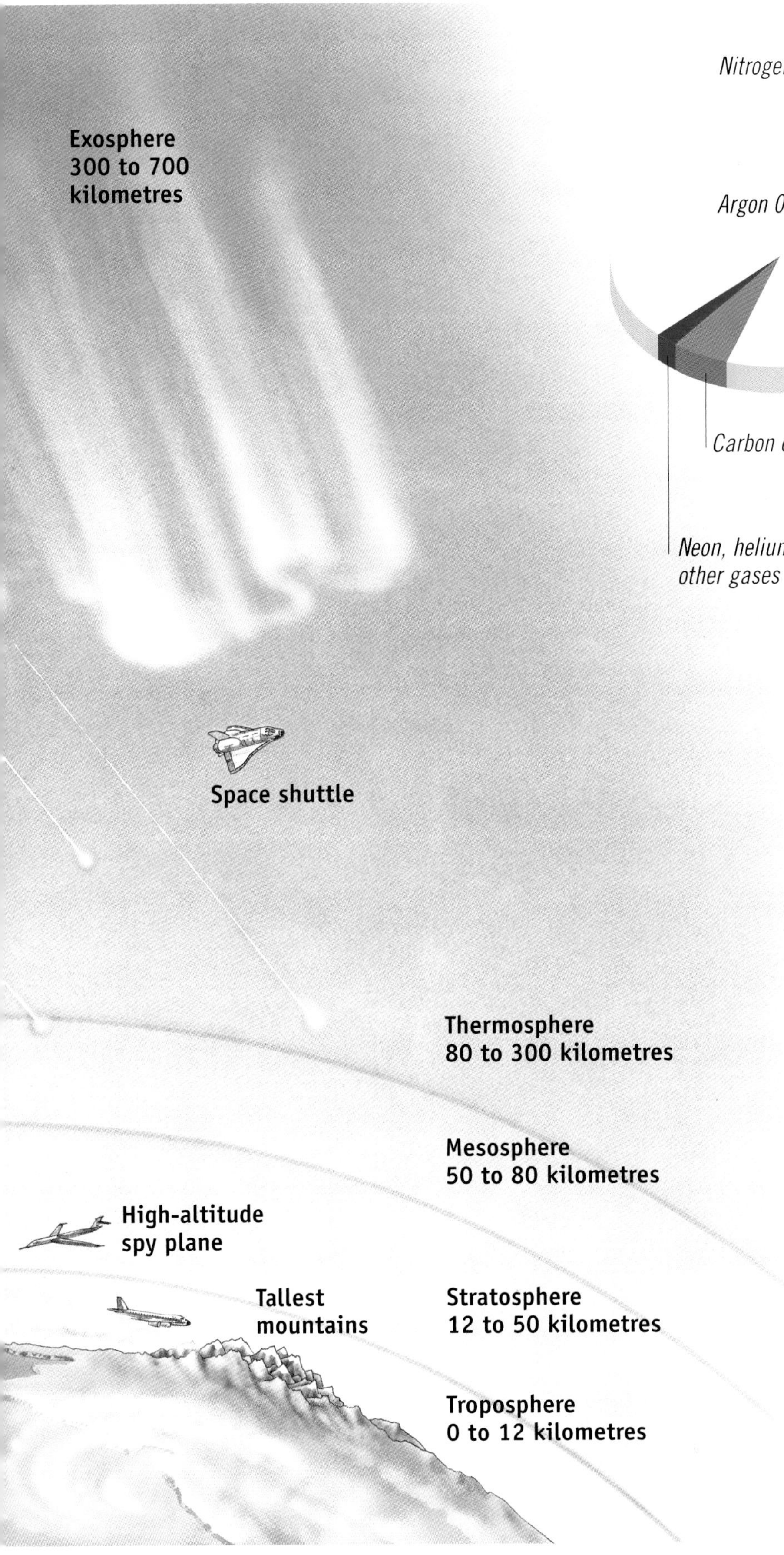

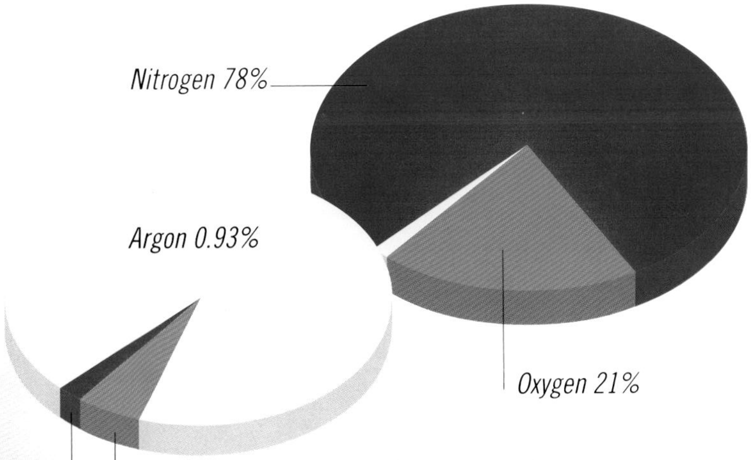

**Exosphere
300 to 700
kilometres**

Nitrogen 78%

Argon 0.93%

Oxygen 21%

Carbon dioxide 0.03%

Neon, helium, and
other gases 0.04%

Atmospheric gases

More than 99 per cent of
the atmosphere is just two
gases. These are nitrogen
(78 per cent) and oxygen
(21 per cent). The
remaining one per cent
includes argon, carbon
dioxide, water vapour and
minute traces of other gases
such as helium and ozone.

Space shuttle

**Thermosphere
80 to 300 kilometres**

**Mesosphere
50 to 80 kilometres**

**High-altitude
spy plane**

**Tallest
mountains**

**Stratosphere
12 to 50 kilometres**

**Troposphere
0 to 12 kilometres**

Taking the pressure

Because the air gets thinner with height,
so the air pressure becomes less. By the
time you get up into the stratosphere, the
air or atmospheric pressure is much too
low for us humans to survive. So if you go
this high – whether in a plane or a balloon
– you have to be inside a pressurized
cabin. Climbers scaling the world's
highest peaks usually need oxygen masks
to breathe. Even this short way up through
the atmosphere, just a few kilometres,
oxygen is getting very thin. The drop in
oxygen is only a few per cent, but this is
enough to make breathing very hard.

Weather and climate

WEATHER CONSISTS OF THE DAY-BY-DAY and week-by-week changes in the atmosphere. We notice it as sunshine, cloud cover, temperature, wind, rain or lack of it, frost, snow and ice. It affects our daily lives, whether we are planning a picnic or piloting a jetliner through a storm. Climate is patterns of weather over the longer term, years and decades and centuries. The climate determines which kinds of plants and animals live where, and the crops we grow in different seasons.

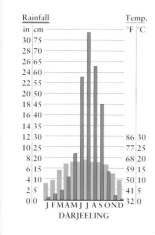

Global climate

The Sun's heat warms up different parts of the land and sea by varying amounts. Since the Sun is overhead in the Tropics, its rays have less atmosphere to pass through, so the heating effect is greater. Warm air rises and cool air flows along sideways to take its place. This large-scale air movement in the atmosphere is known as wind. The waters of the oceans also warm up in the Sun by different amounts and heat the air above them. And the Earth's spinning motion drags the atmosphere with it. The overall result is global patterns of winds in a regular yearly cycle, shown on the right. The main winds are named from the days when sailing ships, which needed the power of the wind, carried cargoes around the world.

WESTERLIES

NORTH EAST TRADES

DOLDRUMS

SOUTH EAST TRADES

WESTER

TEMPERATURE AND RAINFALL

These charts show the average rainfall (blue) and temperature (orange) for cities around the world. They show different types of climate and how these are affected by nearby oceans or land masses. Seattle on the west coast of North America has a temperate maritime climate with warm dry summers and cool damp winters. Darjeeling in India has a monsoon climate with a very rainy season. Manaus in Brazil has an equatorial wet climate, where the temperatures are much the same all through the year. Cape Town in South Africa and Melbourne in Australia have similar temperature ranges, but the rainfall in Melbourne is more regular each month, as it is in cooler London. Cape Zhelanlya in the Asian Arctic is frozen most of the year.

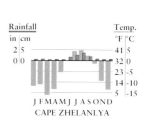
CAPE ZHELANLYA

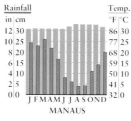
DARJEELING

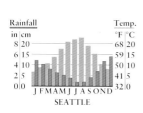
SEATTLE

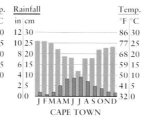
MANAUS

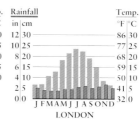
CAPE TOWN

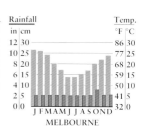
LONDON

MELBOURNE

See also: Planet Earth page 142, Atmosphere page 152

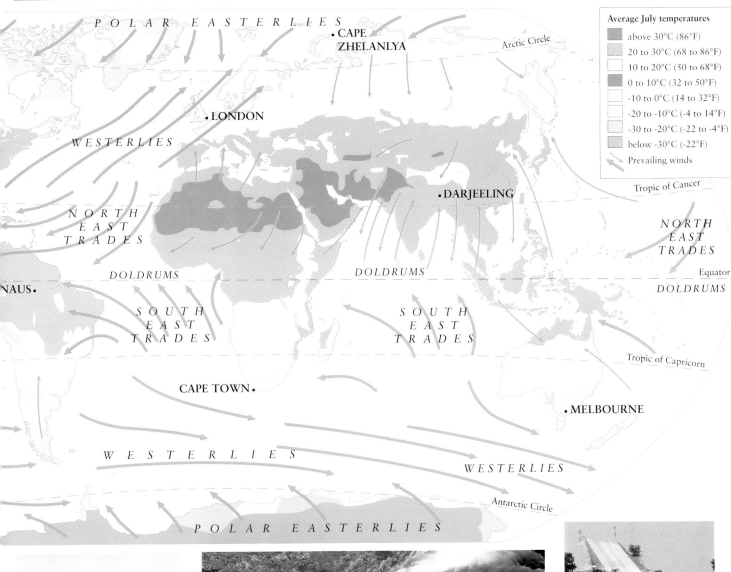

POLAR EASTERLIES

• CAPE ZHELANLYA

Arctic Circle

• LONDON

WESTERLIES

NORTH EAST TRADES

• DARJEELING

Tropic of Cancer

NORTH EAST TRADES

DOLDRUMS

DOLDRUMS

Equator

DOLDRUMS

NAUS •

SOUTH EAST TRADES

SOUTH EAST TRADES

Tropic of Capricorn

CAPE TOWN •

• MELBOURNE

WESTERLIES

WESTERLIES

Antarctic Circle

POLAR EASTERLIES

Average July temperatures	
	above 30°C (86°F)
	20 to 30°C (68 to 86°F)
	10 to 20°C (50 to 68°F)
	0 to 10°C (32 to 50°F)
	-10 to 0°C (14 to 32°F)
	-20 to -10°C (-4 to 14°F)
	-30 to -20°C (-22 to -4°F)
	below -30°C (-22°F)
	Prevailing winds

Drought

Desert regions receive less than 250 millimetres of precipitation each year. Precipitation includes all forms of water or frozen water reaching the ground, such as rain, mist, fog, hail, dew, snow and frost. Since all living things need water to survive, life is lacking in the desert.

Storm

Some weather systems are calm and move slowly. Others are not and do not. A hurricane is an area of rapidly moving winds, 112 kilometres per hour or faster, swirling around a central calm, the eye. This satellite photograph shows a hurricane approaching the coast of Florida, USA.

Flood

Most regions have land that is naturally adapted or eroded to the average rainfall. When excessive rain arrives, the streams and rivers cannot cope and burst their banks. Global warming may cause extra rainfall in some regions.

Mountains and valleys

A FEW OF THE WORLD'S high mountains are isolated volcanoes, like Mount Kilimanjaro in Africa, built up by eruption after eruption. But most mountains are in great ranges that stretch for hundreds or thousands of kilometres. All of these ranges have been thrown up by the enormous power of the Earth's crust moving. Some are huge slabs called fault blocks or "horst" thrown up by massive earthquakes. But most of the biggest ranges, like the Himalayas and the Andes, are fold mountains created by the buckling of rocks as the great tectonic plates squash together.

Valleys
As soon as land is raised above sea level, flowing rivers and moving ice in glaciers bite deep into the rock, etching out valleys. River valleys are typically V-shaped (above). But glaciers carve out huge, distinctive U-shaped troughs (top).

Snowfields at summit

Firn of compacted snow

Lateral moraine

Medial moraine

Crevasse

The glacier
A glacier is like a frozen river – a ribbon of ice that flows slowly downhill. Some glaciers move more than 1 metre each day, but most slide much more slowly. As the heavy ice rubs and grinds its way along, it scours the rock and picks up pieces of boulders and pebbles. These are carried along and are known as moraines. As the glacier flows around a bend the ice cracks, forming fissures called crevasses. Lower down, where the temperatures are higher, the ice eventually melts at the glacier's end, or snout. It forms meltwater streams that cut deep gorges or gouges before leaving the glacier.

See also: Restless Earth page 146, The rock cycle page 148

Young mountains
Mountain ranges like the European Alps and the Himalayas are young. Their jagged peaks have not yet been worn down by the eroding effects of ice, snow, wind and rain. In fact the Himalayas are still growing by about 2 centimetres yearly.

Old mountains
Older peaks, such as the Welsh or Cambrian ranges in Britain and the Appalachians in the eastern USA, have been worn rounder and smoother by erosion. The Appalachians are about 250 million years old and their tallest peak is Mount Mitchell, 2,037 metres.

FOLD MOUNTAINS
Whether they are made from sediments settling on the sea bed or from volcanic plateaux, most rocks tend to form in flat layers. But as tectonic plates move together, folds form as they are squeezed horizontally. Sometimes the folds are just tiny wrinkles only a few centimetres long. Sometimes the folds are gigantic, with hundreds of kilometres between the crests.

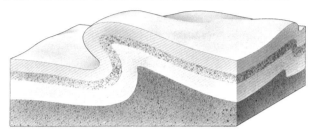

Recumbent fold forms

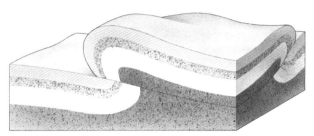

Fold breaks at thrust plane

Overthrust develops

Block-fault mountains
When the Earth's crust moves, the enormous forces generated can sometimes be enough to crack giant slabs of rock and thrust them upwards to create huge blocks of flat-topped mountains. The Black Forest in Germany formed this way.

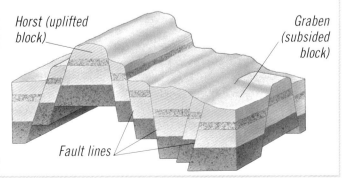

Horst (uplifted block)

Graben (subsided block)

Fault lines

Rivers and lakes

THE EARTH IS A VERY WET planet, with more than 1,300 million cubic kilometres of water on its surface. Yet over 97 per cent of this water is salty water in the seas and oceans. A further 2.2 per cent is frozen in the polar ice caps and glaciers. That leaves less than one per cent as non-salty or fresh water. But this one per cent plays a vital role in the life of the planet. It is actually never used up, but goes round and round in an endless cycle as it evaporates from the oceans and land, condenses into clouds, falls as rain, then runs back along rivers into the oceans again.

Dried up
Some rivers flow only after heavy seasonal rainstorms. For the rest of the year, they dry up, leaving baked river beds, called wadis or arroyos. Streams that flow all year – perennial streams – rely on water seeping through the ground to keep them going between rainstorms.

Deltas
Rivers often wash along huge quantities of sediment particles, such as sand and silt. But when they enter the sea or a lake, the water's speed suddenly slows down and loses its capacity for swishing along sediment. So the sand and silt fall to the floor and form a huge fan called a delta. In time, the river splits into several main branches as it flows across the delta.

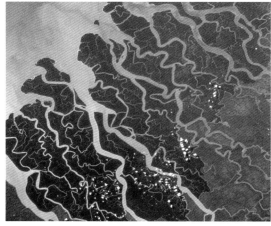

Water evaporates as invisible water vapour _____

Fresh water runs into sea at estuary _____

Bogs and swamps
In some flat or low-lying areas, water does not run away easily. Instead it sits on the surface in small lakes and pools, clogged by plants to form a wetland marsh or swamp. The Okavango delta in Botswana is where the Okavango River splits into dozens of small streams and slows down, dropping its sediment particles, such as mud and silt. Wetlands like these cover about one-sixth of the Earth's land surface and include some of the world's most precious wildlife habitats.

The water cycle
The water cycle begins as water evaporates in the Sun's warmth, mainly from oceans and seas, also from lakes and rivers. Water is also given off, or transpired, from trees, crops and other plants. All this produces water vapour which drifts up through the atmosphere. As the air cools, the water vapour condenses into droplets of water or ice crystals, forming clouds. Water falls from clouds as rain or snow, which either soaks into the ground and is taken up by plants, or runs off into rivers, and back into lakes, seas and oceans.

See also: Water page 32, The rock cycle page 148

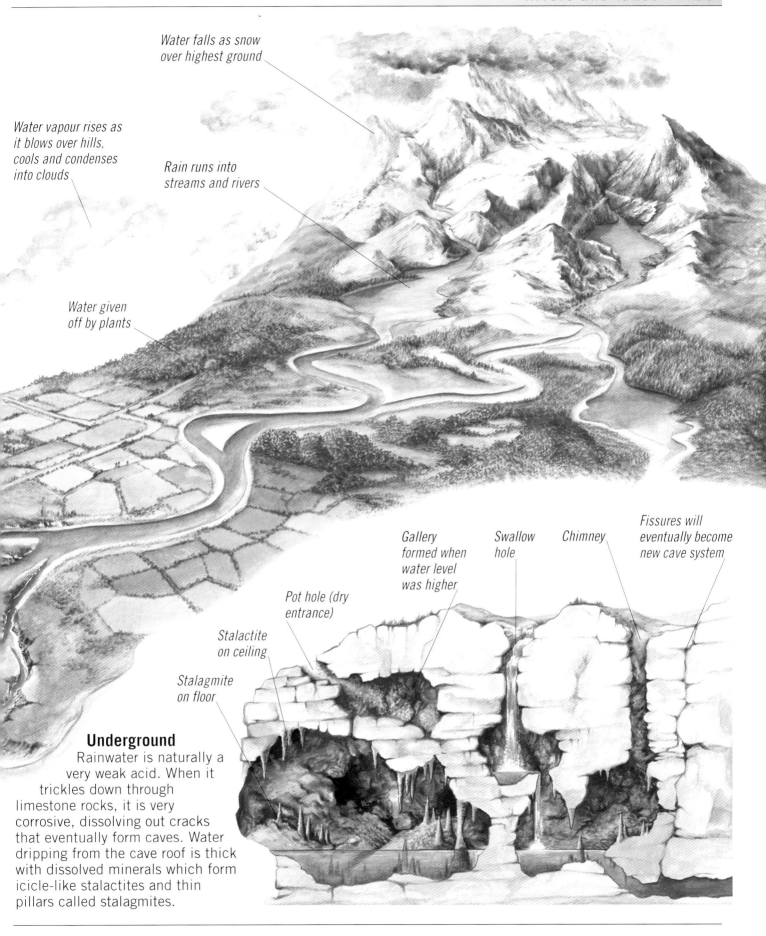

Water falls as snow over highest ground

Water vapour rises as it blows over hills, cools and condenses into clouds

Rain runs into streams and rivers

Water given off by plants

Gallery formed when water level was higher

Swallow hole

Chimney

Fissures will eventually become new cave system

Pot hole (dry entrance)

Stalactite on ceiling

Stalagmite on floor

Underground
Rainwater is naturally a very weak acid. When it trickles down through limestone rocks, it is very corrosive, dissolving out cracks that eventually form caves. Water dripping from the cave roof is thick with dissolved minerals which form icicle-like stalactites and thin pillars called stalagmites.

Coastlines

THE COASTLINE IS NEVER STILL. It changes by the second, as waves roll in and then fall back again. It changes by the hour as the sea rises and falls in tides. It changes by the month as constant battering by heat, cold, wind, rain and breakers shapes and reshapes it. On rocky coasts, steep cliffs and landslips and dangling fences all bear witness to the enormous erosive power of the sea as it batters the land. Hard rocks resist the wear better and stand proud as headlands, while softer rocks collapse to form bays and arches. On low coasts where the sea is shallow, beaches and banks of shingle, sand and mud – built up by the waves dropping their sediments – show that the sea can be constructive too. Everywhere, there is a mixture of advance and retreat.

Resistant rocks
Hard rocks such as granite can resist the waves for a time. Layers or strata of sedimentary rocks are worn into platforms.

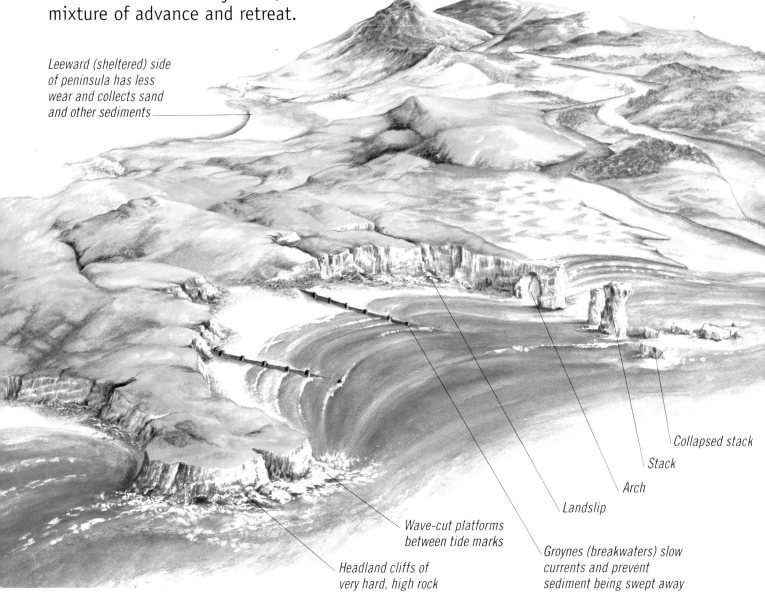

Leeward (sheltered) side of peninsula has less wear and collects sand and other sediments

Collapsed stack

Stack

Arch

Landslip

Wave-cut platforms between tide marks

Headland cliffs of very hard, high rock

Groynes (breakwaters) slow currents and prevent sediment being swept away

See also: Restless Earth page 146, The rock cycle page 148

A base for wildlife

A rocky shore forms a firm base for encrusting life-forms such as seaweeds, sponges, corals, barnacles, mussels and other shellfish. In turn these encrustations form shelter for small animals like crabs, sea-snails and marine worms. On a sandy shore, most life is buried below the surface, away from the rolling sand grains, until the tide comes in.

Sandy bay

Sand spit

Estuary forms where sea currents sweep sediment from left to right

Coastal landforms

Coasts vary tremendously in shape and character. But they are essentially of three kinds. Where massive rock structures abut the coast, there are generally rugged cliffs and headlands. As waves wear away the cliffs, they leave isolated stacks of resistant rock and carve out a broad platform at the cliff foot. Where the land is low and made of soft sediments, the sea creates sweeping beaches and sand bars. Where waves strike the coast at an angle, material is shifted sideways along the coast, creating features such as strips of sand across bays and estuaries, called spits.

UPS AND DOWNS

Every 12 hours or so, the sea falls in a low tide, then rises again in a high tide. Tides are caused by the way the Moon's gravity pulls the water in the oceans into an egg shape around the solid Earth, creating a bulge on each side of the world. As the Earth spins round, these bulges stay in the same place beneath the Moon. The effect is that the bulges move around the world, making the tide rise and fall as they pass.

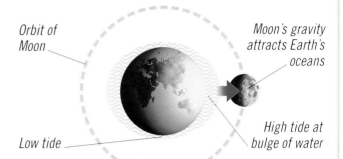

Orbit of Moon

Moon's gravity attracts Earth's oceans

Low tide

High tide at bulge of water

The Moon pulls the Earth's water towards it. The result is high tide on the side of the Earth nearest the Moon, and low tide on the opposite side.

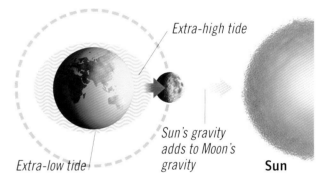

Extra-high tide

Extra-low tide

Sun's gravity adds to Moon's gravity

Sun

Spring tides are higher and lower than normal. The Sun and Moon line up, and their gravitational forces add together to make bigger bulges.

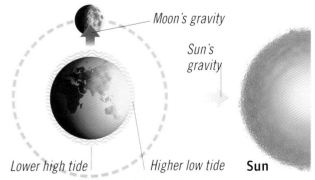

Moon's gravity

Sun's gravity

Lower high tide

Higher low tide

Sun

Neap tides are not so high or low as normal. The Sun and Moon are at right angles, and their gravitational forces pull against each other to make smaller bulges.

Seas and oceans

THREE-QUARTERS OF THE WORLD is underwater, submerged beneath five great oceans all linked together – the Pacific, Atlantic, Indian, Southern (around Antarctica) and Arctic. The water in the oceans is kept in constant motion by the wind, Sun and tides. The wind whips up the surface into waves and currents that flow for thousands of kilometres around the world. The heat of the Sun, aided by chemical differences in the ocean water, stirs up the ocean right to its very lowest depths.

Floating ice
Near the poles, glaciers and ice sheets float on the ocean. Often huge chunks, icebergs, snap off or "calve" as the ice is rocked up and down by waves. Only about one-ninth of a berg's volume shows above the water's surface.

North Atlantic Drift

Labrador Current

North Pacific Current

Arctic Circle

Oyashio Current

North Equatorial Current

Tropic of Cancer

Kuroshio Current

Equator

Monsoon Drift

Australian Current

Tropic of Capricorn

West Australian Current

Antarctic Circumpolar Current

Antarctic Circle

Rivers in the oceans
The world's biggest rivers are not the great rivers on land, but ocean currents. These are often scores of kilometres wide, hundreds of metres deep, and sweep along huge amounts of water through the relatively calm sea around them. They are driven along by a combination of the prevailing winds blowing over the oceans, the shape of the sea bed and the effect of the Earth's rotation. The main currents are split either side of the Equator into two giant rings called gyres that circulate continually around the edges of each ocean. In the Northern Hemisphere gyres flow clockwise; in the South, they flow anticlockwise. Branching from the gyres are many eddies and swirls.

Under an ocean
Around the edge of each ocean is a narrow shelf of shallow water rarely more than 130 metres deep, called the continental shelf. At the edge of this shelf, the sea bed plunges steeply down the continental slope into the deep, dark depths of the ocean basin, most of which is over 2,000 metres deep. In the middle of the Atlantic, molten rock oozes up from below and forms a chain of mountains, pushing the sea bed on either side. This is known as seafloor spreading.

Continental crust

See also: Restless Earth page 146, Weather and climate page 154

Science discovery

Few people have done more for our understanding of the oceans than Jacques Cousteau (1910-1997). In 1943, he helped to develop the scuba – Self-Contained Underwater Breathing Apparatus. With this breathing device, people can swim underwater for long periods without a heavy diving suit and a lifeline to the surface. Cousteau also brought amazing ocean creatures and sights to a wide audience with his many books and films.

Exploring the deep

Back in 1964, a remarkable little underwater craft called *Alvin* was built for the US Navy. Conventional submarines cannot dive much more than 300 metres without being crushed by the pressure of water. But with its thick titanium alloy hull, *Alvin* could go down over 4,000 metres. It opened up many secrets of the deep, and has been joined by several similar craft, such as *Deep Flight*.

Sea-cucumber (Holothuroidean)

Monsters of the deep

Many creatures from the ocean depths look extremely strange to our eyes. Sea-cucumbers as big as an arm plough their way through the ooze, filtering edible particles.

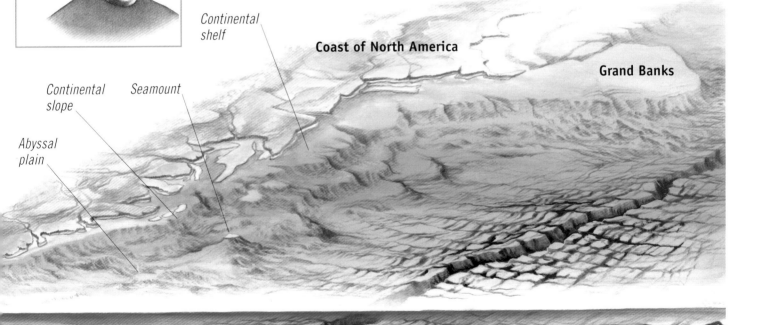

Continental shelf

Coast of North America

Grand Banks

Continental slope

Seamount

Abyssal plain

Oceanic crust   *Molten rock from below*   *Mid Atlantic Ridge*   *Sea floor is pushed sideways away from ridge*

Life on Earth

ON EARTH, LIFE IS CONFINED to a narrow zone between the lower layers of the atmosphere and the ocean bed. But within this zone is an amazing diversity of living things, or organisms. The total package of Earth's organisms – plants, animals, microbes and everything else – is called the biosphere. It is not separate from the non-living world, but linked intimately with it, with the soil, rocks, water and air.

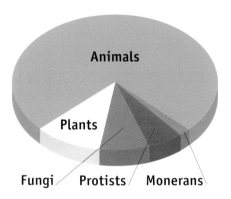

How many species?

There are five huge groups or kingdoms of living things. Each particular kind of living thing, such as a tiger or an oak tree, is called a species. There are many more species of animals, perhaps more than five million, than in any other kingdom. Only the major groups in each kingdom are shown here. In older classification schemes there were two kingdoms, plants and animals.

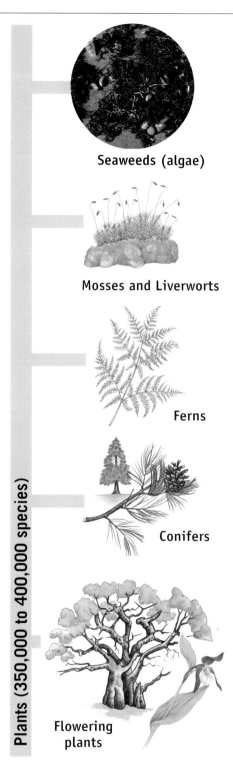

Seaweeds (algae)

Mosses and Liverworts

Ferns

Conifers

Flowering plants

Monerans (at least 10,000 species)

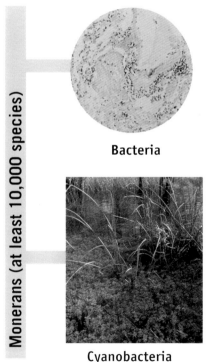

Bacteria

Cyanobacteria

Protists (about 70,000 species)

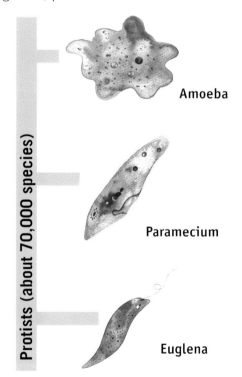

Amoeba

Paramecium

Euglena

Plants (350,000 to 400,000 species)

Monerans
These are microscopic living things, each made of a single cell which does not have a nucleus (control centre). Cyanobacteria (blue-green algae) form a "scum" on ponds.

Protists
These are also single-celled microscopic organisms. But each one has a nucleus inside. They include some animal-like types, such as amoebas, and plant-like ones such as euglenas.

Plants
A plant is a living thing that traps light energy from the Sun, by the process of photosynthesis, and uses it to live and grow. Flowering plants reproduce by flowers or blooms and include most non-conifer trees, as well as bushes, herbs, flowers and grasses.

See also: Evolution of life page 166, Prehistoric life page 168

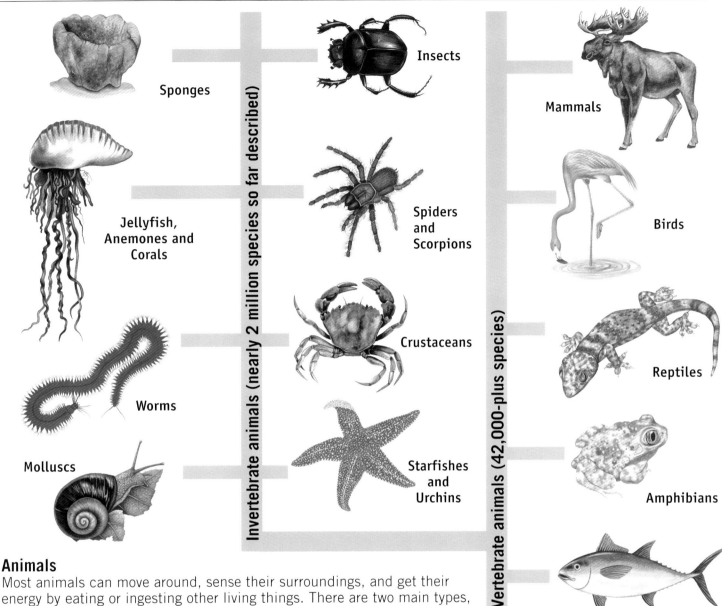

Sponges

Insects

Mammals

Jellyfish, Anemones and Corals

Spiders and Scorpions

Birds

Worms

Crustaceans

Reptiles

Molluscs

Starfishes and Urchins

Amphibians

Invertebrate animals (nearly 2 million species so far described)

Vertebrate animals (42,000-plus species)

Fish

Animals

Most animals can move around, sense their surroundings, and get their energy by eating or ingesting other living things. There are two main types, invertebrates, which lack a backbone, and vertebrates – such as ourselves.

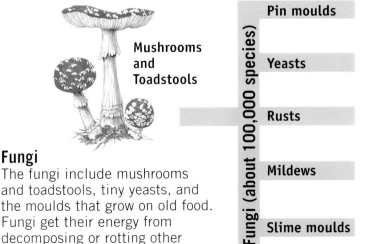

Mushrooms and Toadstools

Pin moulds

Yeasts

Rusts

Mildews

Slime moulds

Fungi (about 100,000 species)

Fungi

The fungi include mushrooms and toadstools, tiny yeasts, and the moulds that grow on old food. Fungi get their energy from decomposing or rotting other living things.

Science discovery

Aristotle (384-322 BC) of Ancient Greece was one of the first great naturalists, as well as being a philosopher and scientist. He spent much time observing animals and plants, especially along the shores of the Mediterranean Sea. He studied the insides of creatures such as starfish, and suggested the process of grouping or classifying organisms by their similarities. He was also teacher to the young Alexander the Great. Aristotle wondered if living things were fixed and unvarying for ever, or if they changed or evolved over time. Most scientists now hold the view that organisms evolve.

Evolution of life

THROUGH THE HISTORY of the Earth, conditions have changed. The climate stayed warm and dry for a time, then became cool and damp, to be followed by ice ages. Living things have changed or evolved too, to stay suited to their surroundings. Fossils show that millions of kinds of plants and animals once lived on Earth. Most died out or became extinct, as conditions altered and they could no longer survive in competition with better-adapted types. Other kinds, such as gingko trees, sharks and crocodiles, have survived almost unchanged for hundreds of millions of years.

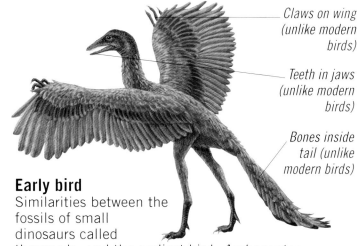

Claws on wing (unlike modern birds)

Teeth in jaws (unlike modern birds)

Bones inside tail (unlike modern birds)

Early bird
Similarities between the fossils of small dinosaurs called theropods, and the earliest bird, *Archaeopteryx*, make it likely that birds evolved from dinosaurs. But *Archaeopteryx* had features that modern birds lack. Whether it was an in-between version or an evolutionary side-line is not clear.

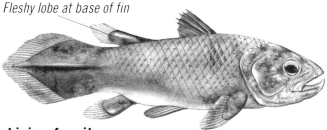

Fleshy lobe at base of fin

Living fossils
Lobe-finned fishes lived long ago, and the first large land creatures probably developed from them. It seemed that the lobe-fins had all died out around 100 million years ago. Then one was found alive and well near the Comoros Islands in the Indian Ocean, in 1938. This was the coelacanth. More have since been discovered and studied.

Homo erectus, **"Upright human"**

Relatively large brain

Made and used tools and fire

Early humans
Compared with other animals, humans have been around a very short time. The first human-like creatures, the hominids, appeared around four million years ago. They were small and looked like their ape ancestors. Gradually human types became taller, with much larger brains. "Fully modern" humans like us (*Homo sapiens*) probably evolved less than 200,000 years ago.

Upright posture

The horse's progress
Many fossils have been discovered that show the evolution of horses. Millions of years ago they were small woodland animals, like little deer. As vast open grasslands began to appear on Earth, they evolved longer legs for faster running across the plains. The modern horse *Equus* first appeared in North America.

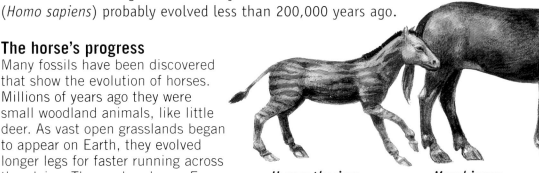

Hyracotherium **(40 million years ago)**

Mesohippus **(30 million years ago)**

See also: Planet Earth page 142, Life on Earth page 164

Science discovery

Charles Darwin (1809-1882) suggested the theory of evolution. Over millions of years, living species change or evolve to suit their surroundings, by the process of natural selection or "survival of the fittest". In each generation, some individuals have features that better adapt them to the surroundings. They are more likely to survive and pass these features onto their offspring.

FOSSILS AND HOW THEY ARE MADE

Fossils are the relics of dead plants, animals, bacteria and other once-living things, preserved for millions of years and usually turned to stone. They may be the living things themselves – usually hard parts like teeth, bones, shells and bark. Or they may be signs and traces, such as footprints or droppings. A fossil forms when a living thing dies and its soft parts rot away (1). On the sea bed, its bones and other hard parts are soon buried under sand and mud (2). Over millions of years, chemical changes and the pressure of mud above turn the mud into solid rock (3). Water trickling through the mud chemically alters the parts as well, turning them to stone, but preserving its shape. Later earth movements may expose the fossil at the surface (4).

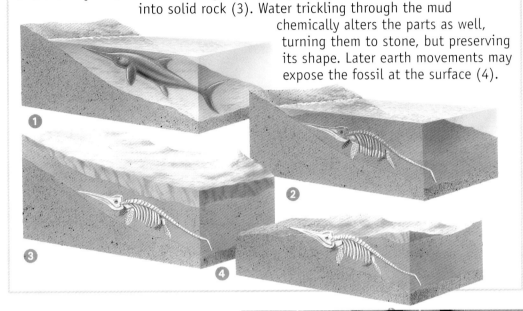

The Ice Man

Even in recent prehistoric times, preserved remains of plants, animals and people show how the world has changed. Some are entire human bodies, even with their clothes, tools and other items. An example is "Otzi the Ice Man". He died on a glacier in the European Alps about 5,000 years ago. His body was frozen into the ice, as though in a deep freeze. His clothing and travelling items show how his people crafted cloaks, tunics, shoes and hats, and weapons such as spears and arrows, from natural materials such as grass, leather and stone.

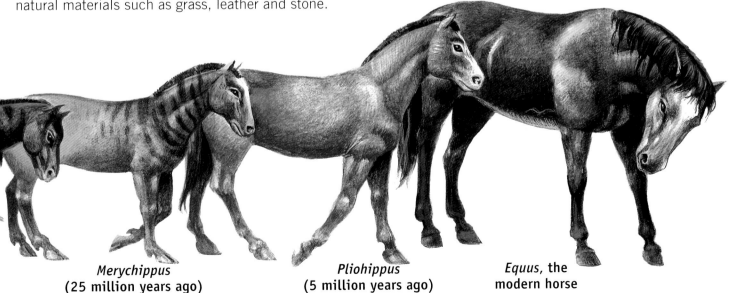

Merychippus
(25 million years ago)

Pliohippus
(5 million years ago)

Equus, the
modern horse

Prehistoric Life

FOR BILLIONS OF YEARS ON EARTH, the only living things were microscopic, single-celled organisms. Then about 700 million years ago, the first real animals, such as jellyfish and sponges, appeared in the sea. They were entirely soft-bodied, but rare fossils give us a glimpse of how they looked. Over the next 200 million years, creatures with hard parts (shells and bones) appeared. From this time on, the beginning of the Cambrian Period, the fossil record becomes much more detailed. Some kinds of animals, like sharks and crocodiles, have survived for long periods. Others died out rapidly as conditions changed. Still others have gradually changed or evolved from prehistoric into modern forms.

Geological time

The Earth is about 4.6 billion years old. Just as time on a clock is divided into hours, minutes and seconds, so Earth's history is divided into four huge chunks called eons. The first three of these, lasting four billion years, are often grouped together as Precambrian time because very few fossils survive to tell us much about it. The last one, called the Phanerozoic eon, began about 540 million years ago, and is divided into four eras. The eras, in turn, are divided into periods, lasting from 2 to 80 million years.

Fossils
These are mostly the hard parts of living things, like teeth, claws, shells, cones and wood, turned to stone and preserved in rocks.

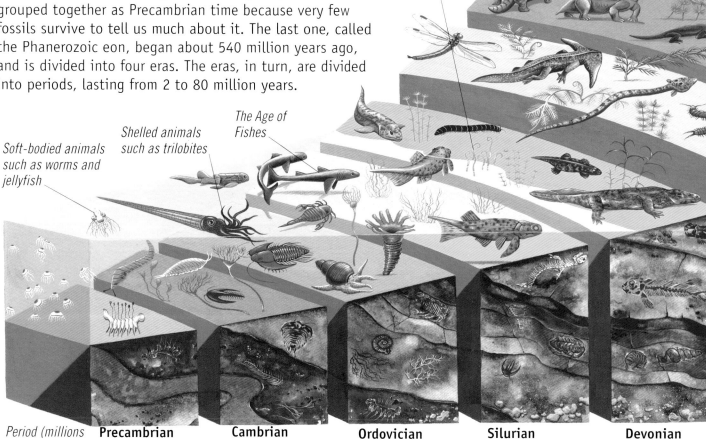

Humans begin about 2 million years ago

Dinosaurs and many other animals and plants die out 65 million years ago

The Age of Dinosaurs

Life comes onto land, first plants, then insect-like animals

The Age of Fishes

Shelled animals such as trilobites

Soft-bodied animals such as worms and jellyfish

| Period (millions of years ago) | Precambrian Long ago to 540 | Cambrian 540 to 505 | Ordovician 505 to 433 | Silurian 433 to 410 | Devonian 410 to 360 |

See also: The rock cycle page 148, Evolution of life page 166

Mass extinctions

Fossils show that several times during Earth's history, there have been mass extinctions where many kinds of living things die out very quickly. The end-of-Cretaceous extinction involved dinosaurs, pterosaurs (flying reptiles) and many others. The end-of-Permian extinction was even more drastic. Fossil evidence suggests that almost four-fifths of life-forms were wiped out.

Ichthyostega, an early land animal

The Age of Mammals and Birds

Giant birds ruled for a time

Woolly animals thrived during the ice ages

Carboniferous
360 to 286

Permian
286 to 245

Triassic
245 to 202

Jurassic
202 to 144

Cretaceous
144 to 65

Tertiary
65 to present

Earth in trouble

HUMANS NOW DOMINATE the Earth, and our activities are in grave danger of doing the planet irreparable damage. Our demands on its fragile resources are threatening everything, from the atmosphere to plant and animal life. Car exhausts and factory chimneys choke the air. Rivers are poisoned by agricultural chemicals. Forests are felled as countryside disappears under concrete.

Flooded away?
Global warming due to the increased greenhouse effect may make the world 4°C warmer by the middle of the 21st century. This would melt much of the ice at the poles, raising sea levels and bringing devastating floods to low-lying areas, including many ports and coastal lands.

Atmospheric harm

Two main processes are damaging the atmosphere. One is the thinning of the ozone layer, which absorbs much of the Sun's harmful ultra-violet radiation and so protects us from it. The other is the greenhouse effect, which has always been present but is now becoming more severe.

Sun sends out waves of light, heat and other forms of energy, known as solar radiation

Healthy ozone layer traps and reflects most ultra-violet rays

Thinned ozone layer in atmosphere allows through more harmful ultra-violet rays

See also: Atmosphere page 152, Weather and climate page 154

Poisoned waters

Gold is a precious metal that can make prospectors rich quick. In parts of the Amazon region, there are tiny particles of gold in the water. These can be obtained by combining them with the metal mercury. But the unwanted or used mercury is extremely poisonous and washes away, killing fish and other water life for hundreds of kilometres downstream.

GLOBAL CONTRASTS

▶ The average person in the US uses 34 million kilojoules of energy per day; in India this figure is 0.6 million.

▶ The developed world consumes three-quarters of the world's energy for one-quarter of the people.

▶ Barely five per cent of the world's energy comes from renewable sources such as water, wind and sunlight.

▶ 20 million hectares (an area the size of Wales) of tropical rainforest is felled every year.

▶ Up to 7 million hectares of farmland are lost yearly to soil erosion through overcropping.

Soil erosion

As soil is farmed too intensively, its minerals and nutrients are used up. The roots of trees and other natural plants no longer hold the soil particles together. The soil becomes loose and blows away in the wind or is washed by rain into rivers.

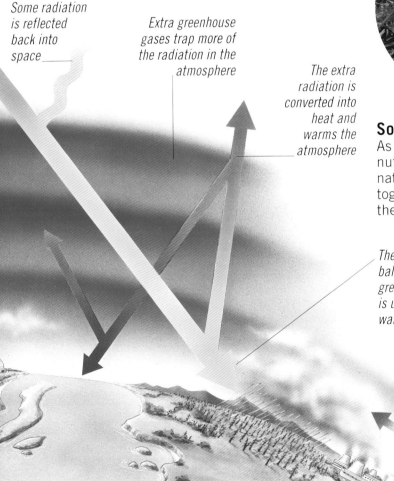

Some radiation is reflected back into space

Extra greenhouse gases trap more of the radiation in the atmosphere

The extra radiation is converted into heat and warms the atmosphere

The natural balance of the greenhouse effect is upset and global warming happens

The greenhouse effect

The atmosphere receives many kinds of rays and waves from the Sun. Some of these bounce and reflect within it, and are changed into warmth. Without this natural effect, which has been happening for millions of years, Earth would be 10-15°C cooler. However gases from human activities, such as carbon dioxide and methane, are increasing the greenhouse effect.

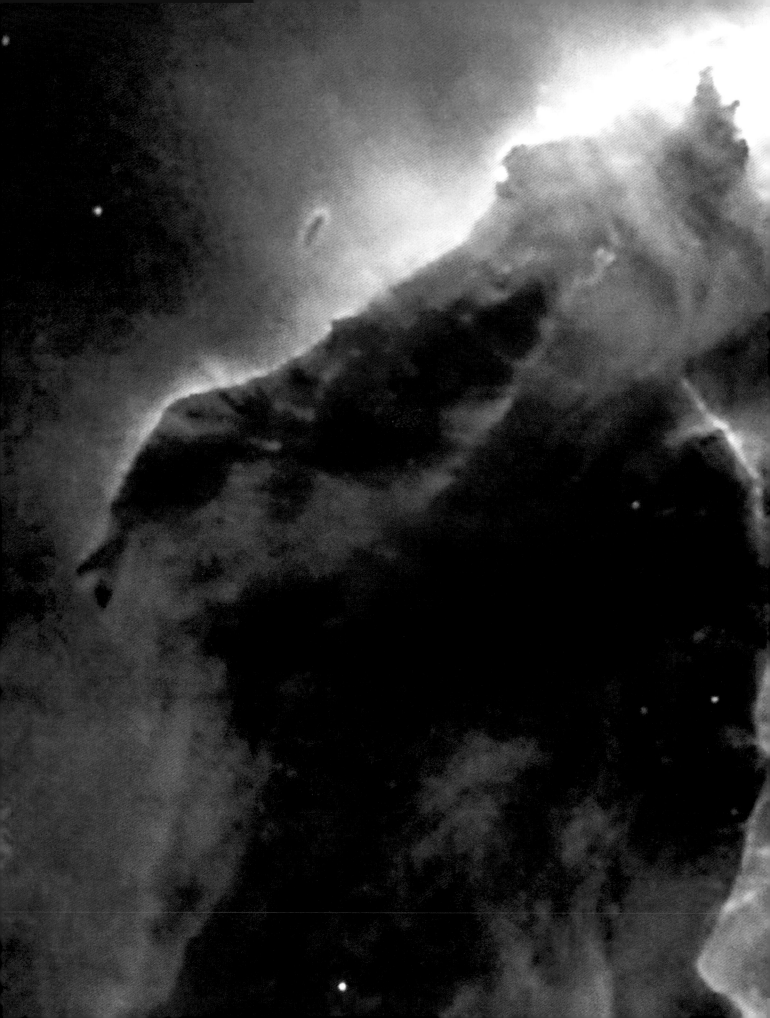

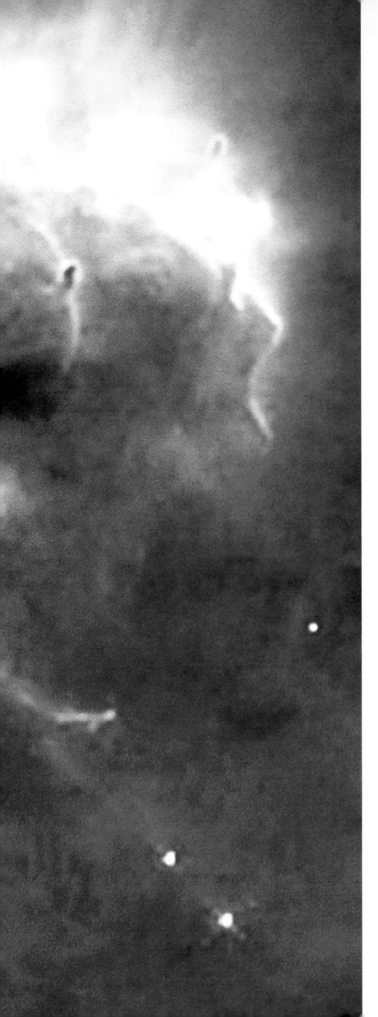

6

Space and Time

Away from daily life here on Earth, the Universe is a weird and truly wonderful place. Stars are born and explode. Star clusters, called galaxies, fly away from each other. Straight lines are really bent, and time goes faster or slower. Modern science explains some of these mind-boggling events – but not all.

Earth in space

IN ANCIENT TIMES, people believed that the Earth was flat and the centre of everything. Gradually, scientific study and exploration showed that Earth was not flat, but ball-shaped, and that Earth's place in space is really just a small planet going around our local star, the Sun. From our planet the Sun, Moon and stars seem to travel across the sky. True, the Moon does orbit the Earth. But the apparent orbit by the Sun and stars is an illusion caused by the movements of the Earth.

Science discovery

Nicolaus Copernicus (1473-1543) studied arts, medicine and law before becoming a church canon in Poland. Then he turned his attention to astronomy. He suggested that the geocentric idea of the Earth as the centre of everything, believed since ancient times, did not fit with astronomical observation. He proposed the heliocentric theory where the Earth and other planets went around the Sun. This caused great debate but also began a new phase of science.

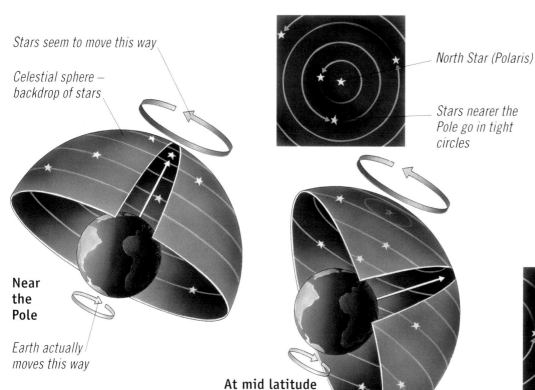

Stars seem to move this way

Celestial sphere – backdrop of stars

North Star (Polaris)

Stars nearer the Pole go in tight circles

Near the Pole

Earth actually moves this way

At mid latitude

Stars nearer the Pole go in tight circles

Stars nearer the Equator go in wide arcs

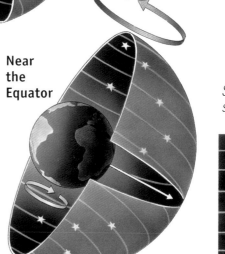

Near the Equator

Stars seem to move straight across sky

Why stars move

The stars seem to move in different ways across the night sky, depending on where you are on the Earth. In the far north or south, near the geographic pole, they trace circular paths around the sky. In the north the North Star, Polaris, is directly in line with the Earth's axis of spin. So it appears to stay still as the other stars twirl around it. At mid latitudes, the stars nearer the Pole (farther north or south) look as though they travel in tight circles, while those towards the Equator move in wider arcs. At the Equator, you see the stars "side-on". They seem to move almost straight across the sky, in parallel lines. Of course, the stars hardly move at all. It is the Earth turning on its axis that makes them appear to move.

See also: Planet Earth page 142, Exploring space page 176

FACTS ABOUT THE PLANETS

Planet	Distance from Sun (millions of kilometres)	Diameter (thousands of kilometres)	Length of day (Earth hours or days)	Length of year (Earth days or years)	Number of moons
Mercury	58	4,880	58.6 days	88 days	0
Venus	108	12,104	243 days	224.7 days	0
Earth	149.6	12,756	24 hours	365.3 days	1
Mars	228	6,787	25 hours	687 days	2

Asteroid Belt between Mars and Jupiter

Planet	Distance from Sun	Diameter	Length of day	Length of year	Number of moons
Jupiter	778	143,000	10 hours	11.9 years	16
Saturn	1,427	120,000	10 hours	29.5 years	20-plus
Uranus	2,875	51,100	23 hours	84 years	16-plus
Neptune	4,497	49,500	16 hours	165 years	8
Pluto	5,900	2,200	6 days	248 years	1

Science discovery

Robert Goddard (1882-1945) was a physicist and engineer who designed and launched the first liquid-fuel rocket, in 1926. It rose only about 56 metres, but Goddard followed it with bigger, more powerful versions. His work laid the basis for later space rockets.

STATION IN SPACE

The former Soviet Union launched the central part of the *Mir* space station in February 1986. Its name means "peace" and "world" in Russian. The main core of the station is about 17 metres long and 4 metres wide. It was similar to the preceding *Salyut* spacecraft, but with four extra ports where visiting craft could dock, and two private compartments for long-term living in space. The *Kvant 1* science module was added to the core in 1987. Many people have lived and worked in *Mir*, some for more than one year. It is serviced by crew-less *Progress* ferry craft. In the 1990s the space station suffered several problems, including damage by a visiting craft and power failure.

Earth-rise

The astronauts of the Apollo 10 space mission in May 1969 were the first to see planet Earth from another world. As they orbited the Moon, on their preparatory mission before the Apollo 11 landing, Earth rose above the horizon. Like the Moon, the Earth does not produce its own light. It shines with reflected sunlight.

Exploring space

THE SPACE AGE BEGAN on 4 October, 1957, with the launch of the satellite *Sputnik 1* by the former Soviet Union. This was a simple metal ball about 58 centimetres across and 84 kilograms in weight, containing a radio transmitter and a thermometer. The world was stunned. Today there is about one space mission each week, as a launch vehicle blasts free of our planet's gravity and delivers its payload into Earth orbit – or beyond.

Launch vehicles

The launcher is the most powerful type of engine available, the rocket engine. It must escape the pull of Earth's gravity, which means achieving orbital velocity – a speed of 27,350 kilometres per hour at a height of some 160 kilometres. Following this path, a spacecraft's tendency to go in a straight line, according to the third law of motion, is balanced by the tendency of Earth's gravity to pull it downwards. So the craft follows a curved path, falling endlessly to the surface as the surface curves endlessly away.

8 mins 50 secs
The huge fuel tank is empty, and released. The main engines shut down and the smaller orbit-adjust engines give the orbiter its final push into Low Earth Orbit, about 120 kilometres high.

8 mins
The shuttle is close to orbital velocity, pushed by its main engines.

2 mins 12 secs
The boosters burn out and fall back into the sea for recovery.

See also: Planet Earth page 142

Ready for work

The orbiter's cargo bay doors open to reveal the contents, such as satellites. The shuttle can carry 30 tonnes of cargo or payload into space. On some missions the crew manoeuvre near to a satellite which is already in orbit. The satellite is captured and brought back to Earth for modifications or repairs.

MOON LANDINGS

The Apollo missions planned to land people on the Moon. First to set foot on the lunar surface was Neil Armstrong of Apollo 11, on 20 July, 1969. Five further missions followed, carrying out experiments and taking measurements and bringing back samples of Moon rocks for analysis. The last mission was Apollo 17, in December 1972. The next space missions taking people to another world may be to Mars, around 2020. The journey would take about nine months each way.

Ascent stage blasted off from Moon

Apollo Lunar Module

Descent stage stayed on Moon

US astronauts on the Moon

The space shuttle

The US space shuttle has four main parts. These are the plane-like orbiter with its three rocket engines at the rear, a giant tank containing extra liquid fuel for the launch, and two solid-fuel rocket boosters. The boosters provide extra thrust at blast-off, when the pull of gravity is greatest, and the entire shuttle weighs 2,000 tonnes.

EVA

Extra-vehicular activity is a "space walk". Inside the pressurized space suit, the astronaut has air to breathe, and is protected from the intense rays, extreme temperatures and small dust particles of the space environment.

MMU (Manned Manoeuvring Unit) backpack

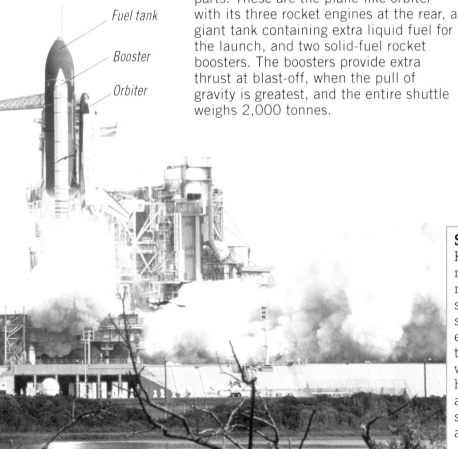

Fuel tank

Booster

Orbiter

Science discovery

Konstantin Tsiolkovsky (1857-1935) was a maths teacher who foresaw many developments in space exploration. He suggested that a rocket engine would work in the vacuum of space, which many people of his time doubted. He also predicted space suits, space stations and artificial satellites.

Earth's orbit

A SATELLITE IS AN OBJECT that goes around, or orbits, another object. The Moon is a natural satellite of the Earth. We have also launched many artificial satellites, usually simply called "satellites", for purposes such as surveying the land, telecommunications, tracking the weather and spying on possible enemies. But the Earth itself is also a satellite – of the Sun. The Earth's spinning on its own axis produces day and night, and its elongated or elliptical orbit around the Sun gives us the seasons.

Autumn in North, spring in South

Sun

The yearly journey

The Earth spins like a top around its axis, which is an imaginary line passing through the North and South Geographic Poles. It turns around once every 24 hours. From the surface, it seems as if the Sun is passing across the sky during the day, and then disappearing below the horizon at night. As the Earth spins, it also whirls through space at 30 kilometres every second, on its year-long journey or orbit around the Sun. The axis of spin is not at right angles to the level or plane of the orbit. This means, for part of the year, that the upper half or Northern Hemisphere of the Earth is tilted nearer the sun, giving the warmer temperatures of summer.

Winter in North, summer in South   *Earth's orbit around Sun*

Science discovery

Mathematician and astronomer Johannes Kepler (1571-1630) supported the ideas of Copernicus. The Earth was not the centre of the Universe, with everything going around it. Earth and the other planets went around the Sun. Kepler worked out the orbits of Earth and other planets known at the time, in mathematical detail – Kepler's three laws of planetary motion.

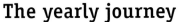

Seasons in the Sun

The tilt of the Earth's axis, at 23.5° to its orbit around the Sun, produces seasonal changes on Earth. At the Equator, the Sun is directly overhead at midday on the spring (vernal) and autumnal equinoxes, in the calendar months of March and September. At the summer solstice (midsummer) in June, it is highest in the sky as seen from the Northern Hemisphere, but lowest as seen from the Southern Hemisphere, where it is midwinter. The Antarctic Circle is tilted away from the Sun, so the Sun does not rise in the sky. Meanwhile the Arctic Circle is facing the Sun and so the Sun never sets. Six months later, the situation is reversed.

Low and cold

During winter, the Sun is above the horizon for less time compared to summer. Also it does not rise so high in the sky, so its rays pass at a slanting angle through the Earth's atmosphere. The result is that less of the Sun's warmth reaches the ground, so temperatures are lower. Meanwhile in the opposite hemisphere, the Sun is higher in the sky for longer each day. Its rays pass almost vertically down through the atmosphere. This gives higher temperatures.

See also: Planet Earth page 142, Atmosphere page 152

Axis of spin of Earth

Summer in North, winter in South

Night-time on side of Earth away from Sun

Daytime on side of Earth facing Sun

Spring in North, Autumn in South

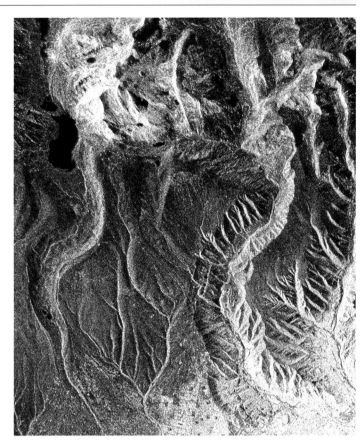

Phases of the Moon

The Moon goes around or orbits the Earth at an average distance of 384,400 kilometres. But the orbit is elliptical, so this distance varies from 356,000 to 407,000 kilometres. One orbit takes about one month. More accurately, it takes 27.3 days for the Moon to orbit the Earth, with respect to the hardly changing background of the stars. This is a sidereal month. But the Moon takes 29.5 days to orbit the Earth with respect to the Sun, because during this time the Earth has moved on in its own orbit around the Sun. This is a synodic month. The Moon does not make its own light. It shines with reflected sunlight. The portion of the sunlit part of the Moon that we can see from Earth gives the phases of the Moon, and the phases repeat every synodic month.

Scenes from space

Satellite orbits vary according to their purpose. A survey satellite that takes photographs of the surface, like the image above, has a low earth orbit of around 500 to 1,000 kilometres. However this may be elliptical, so for part of the orbit the satellite is less than 100 kilometres high, for a close-up view. A telecommunications satellite may orbit 35,800 kilometres high, directly above the Equator. At this distance, each orbit takes 24 hours. The Earth below also spins around once in this time. So from the surface, the satellite seems to "hang" in the same place in the sky. This is a geostationary orbit. It means satellite dishes here on Earth do not have to tilt or swivel to track the satellite across the sky.

New crescent   First quarter   Waxing gibbous Moon   Full Moon   Waning gibbous Moon   Third quarter   Old crescent

Magnetic Earth

THE EARTH IS ACTUALLY a giant magnet. Its magnetic power affects any magnetic material that comes within range. In some ways, it is like a huge steel bar magnet inside the globe. Like a bar magnet, it has two ends or magnetic poles. These are not at the planet's North and South Geographic Poles, around which the Earth spins, but nearby, as shown opposite. The magnetic poles are where all the Earth's magnetic power is focused. Any object that can swivel freely, from an ordinary bar magnet to the tiny electrically charged particles that make up atoms, swings around so that one end points towards the Earth's magnetic North Pole and the other to the magnetic South Pole. The needle of a magnetic compass is a thin magnet that does this, to point north and south.

Aurorae are spectacular, shimmering curtains of colours that ripple in the night sky

High lights
The northern and southern lights, aurorae borealis and australis, are thought to be created by high-energy particles streaming from the Sun into the clefts in the Earth's magnetic field above the poles.

Science discovery
James van Allen (1914-) discovered the Earth's outer magnetic field or magnetosphere, using information from early rockets and satellites. He found doughnut-shaped belts of radiation encircling the Earth, created by charged particles from the Sun trapped by the Earth's magnetic field. On the side of the Earth facing the Sun, this extends 60,000 kilometres into space. On the far side it is blown out into a tail by the solar wind.

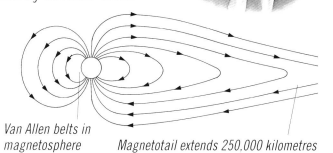

Van Allen belts in magnetosphere   *Magnetotail extends 250,000 kilometres*

NAVIGATING BY MAGNETS
In ancient times, seafarers relied on magnetic compasses to find their way across the oceans. The compass is reasonably accurate, but it is affected by local variations in the Earth's magnetic field, called magnetic anomalies. These are caused by huge lumps of iron-containing rocks in the crust and similar features. Also, as you reach the far north or far south, the magnetic lines of force pass into the Earth almost vertically. This makes the compass needle swing wildly as it tries to align itself with the magnetic field.

See also: Mysterious Magnetism page 92, Planet Earth page 142

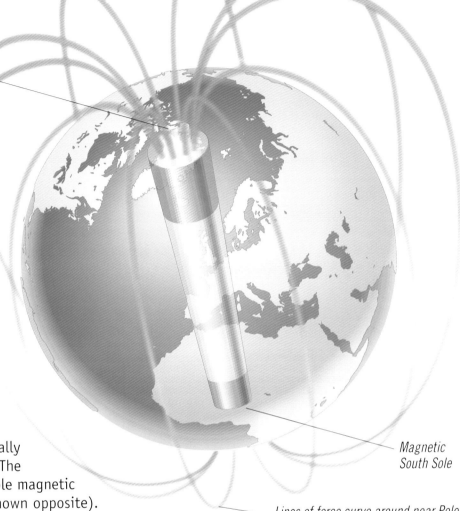

Magnetic lines of force pass vertically into the ground at the magnetic North Pole

Invisible magnetic lines of force

Magnetic field extends out into space

Magnetic lines of force are parallel with the surface at the Equator

Magnetic South Sole

Lines of force curve around near Pole

The magnetic field

The Earth's magnetic field curves around the planet, as though a giant bar magnet was inside the globe. This magnetic field is by no means limited to magnets and other materials on the Earth's surface. It extends into the atmosphere and even affects electrically charged particles far out into space. The Earth is surrounded by a huge invisible magnetic cocoon called the magnetosphere (shown opposite).

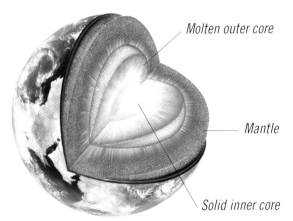

Molten outer core

Mantle

Solid inner core

The geodynamo

The Earth's metal core is like a giant dynamo, sometimes called the geodynamo. The combination of heat and the Earth's rotation makes the molten outer core swirl around, creating massive electrical currents that generate the magnetic field by the electromagnetic effect.

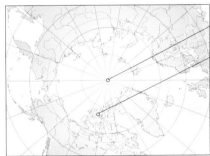

Geographic North Pole

Magnetic North Pole is at 70° N 100° W, Prince of Wales Island, Canada

Magnetic poles

The Earth's magnetic North Pole is several hundred kilometres away on Prince of Wales Island, in Canada – at the moment. Like the South Magnetic Pole, it actually moves or wanders with time. And every 200,000 years or so, it swaps with the South Pole, a process called magnetic reversal.

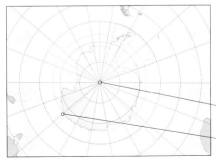

Geographic South Pole

Magnetic South Pole is at 68° S 143 °E, South Victoria Land, Antarctica

Inner planets

EARTH IS ONE OF FOUR planets that orbit relatively close to the Sun. The others are Mercury, Venus and Mars. These inner planets can all get quite warm – although Mercury and Mars also get very cold on the side away from the Sun, because they have too little atmosphere to hold in the heat. The four inner planets are rocky or terrestrial, unlike the large outer planets, which are balls of gas.

EARTH'S MOON

Most planets have moons. Earth has one, the Moon. It orbits at an average distance of 384,000 kilometres. The Moon is about one-quarter of the diameter of the Earth and weighs one-eightieth as much. It has a similar internal structure to Earth, and its surface is covered with meteorite craters.

Mantle

Inner core   Outer core

Lunar craters

Polar white cap enlarges in winter

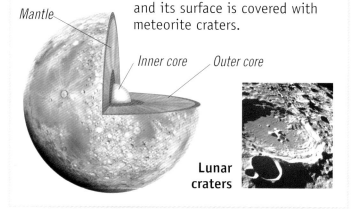

Earth

From space, our home would show some of the most exciting changes of any planet, as white clouds swirl in ever-changing daily patterns over the deep blue oceans and the green and brown land. Earth is, as far as we know, the only planet in the Solar System with life. However some of the moons of outer planets, like Saturn's Titan, are Earth-sized and may possibly have an atmosphere and water that could support life – at least, as we know it.

Mars

Mars is known as the Red Planet because of the reddish dust scattered over its surface. This dust is made of iron oxides – which on Earth we call rust. The landscape is broken by craters, chasms and old volcanoes, including the largest mountain in the Solar System, Olympus Mons, which is 25 kilometres high. Mars is the only planet to have an atmosphere and daytime temperatures remotely like the Earth's. But the atmosphere is so thin that night temperatures plunge below minus 130°C. Recent meteorite evidence from Mars could suggest that microscopic life once lived at or below the surface, and there may still be water underground.

See also: Planet Earth page 142, Earth in space page 174

Venus

Venus is our nearest neighbour, sometimes coming as close as 42 million kilometres! It is wrapped in a thick atmosphere of carbon dioxide and other gases, with clouds of sulphuric acid. The atmosphere is so thick that the pressure on the planet's surface is 90 times that of the Earth – enough to crush a house flat. The gases trap the Sun's heat so effectively that Venus has a runaway greenhouse effect, boosting temperatures to more than 470°C – the hottest of any planet. Venus is almost the same size as Earth, and about four-fifths of Earth's mass.

Seas and oceans are mostly deep blue

Dense atmosphere of gases, fumes, vapours and acid droplets

Surface features are hidden by clouds

Very thin atmosphere of sodium vapours

Craters from meteorite impact

Mercury

The *Mariner 10* space probe revealed Mercury as a barren, dusty planet. It is too small to hold onto an appreciable atmosphere, so there is nothing to protect it from meteors. Its surface is pitted with craters, like the Moon. Surface temperatures can soar to 430°C or plummet to minus 180°C, the most extreme of any planet.

PLANET SIZES

The inner planets are all quite similar in size, compared to the variation between the outer planets. Mercury is smallest, at 4,880 kilometres, and is about one-eighteenth the mass of the Earth.

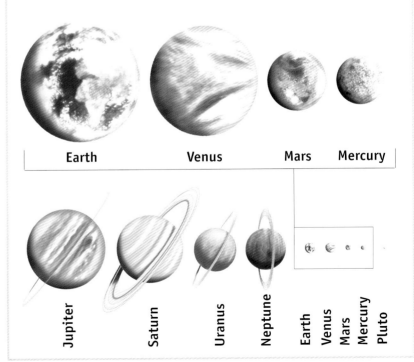

Earth   Venus   Mars   Mercury

Jupiter   Saturn   Uranus   Neptune   Earth   Venus   Mars   Mercury   Pluto

Solar wanderers

ALONG WITH THE PLANETS and their moons, thousands of smaller bits of rock and ice circle the Sun. They range from tiny dust particles to mini-planets hundreds of kilometres across. These are asteroids, the leftover debris of the solar system – fragments too scattered to gather together to form a proper planet. Most lie in a wide band between Mars and Jupiter, called the asteroid belt. But some spin near the Earth and occasionally smash into it. Fortunately, most are so small they burn up as they hit the atmosphere, glowing in the night sky as meteors or shooting stars.

Comet Hale-Bopp
Most comets are too small to see with the naked eye. But in 1995, an unusually large and bright comet was spotted beyond Jupiter, by Alan Hale and Thomas Bopp in the USA. Named Hale-Bopp in the traditional way, after its discoverers, its view from Earth was best in 1997. Hubble Space Telescope pictures showed its nucleus was gigantic, 40 kilometres across.

Nucleus inside head

Head

Tail

Inside a comet
The central part or nucleus of a comet is a large "dirty snowball" – a lumpy, potato-like block of ice covered in dust, usually a few hundred metres across. But as it nears the Sun, this dirty snowball starts to melt in the heat. Dust, vapours and gases are blown out in a huge tail millions of kilometres long. Because the tail is blown by the solar wind, it always faces away from the Sun. As the comet passes the Sun and heads out into deep space again, its tail faces the direction in which it is moving.

BAD OMENS

People used to think comets must be a warning of some terrible event.

▶ A Chinese book 2,400 years old catalogues 27 types of comet and the kind of disaster they create.

▶ When the comet now known as Halley's Comet appeared in 66 AD, people believed it foretold the fall of Jerusalem.

▶ In 1835, Halley's Comet was blamed for a fire in New York, the massacre at the Alamo, and wars in Cuba and Latin America.

See also: Earth in space page 174, Inner planets page 182

Comets and craters

Comets follow long, oval or elliptical orbits around the Sun. They come in from deep space, swing around the Sun and head off again, to return years or centuries later. If Earth passes through a comet's tail, the particles of dust become meteoroids that burn up in our atmosphere, as a spectacular meteor shower. Occasionally larger chunks of space rock do not burn up completely. They smash into the Earth's surface at incredible speed, creating a huge hole called a crater. The chunks that get through the atmosphere to hit the Earth are called meteorites.

Science discovery

American astronomer Fred Whipple (1906-) was the first to suggest, in 1949, that comets had a tiny nucleus of ice and dust, along with frozen carbon dioxide, methane and ammonia. This idea was known as the "dirty snowball". The dust and melting gases account for a comet's huge glowing tail. Whipple's ideas were confirmed in 1986.

Some asteroids are as small as a house

SIGNS OF LIFE?

In 1997, scientists announced Mars could harbour life. Yet there were no spacecraft anywhere near Mars at the time. What happened was a meteorite found on Earth was identified as a fragment of Martian rock, knocked from the planet by a previous meteorite. Microscopic study showed minute structures in the rock which could be fossils of tiny life-forms. Might these organisms still live on the Red Planet?

Some asteroids are many kilometres across

Danger zone

A spacecraft voyaging between Mars and Jupiter has to negotiate the asteroid belt. Most asteroids are far apart, but they also occur in dense groups called swarms.

Outer planets

THE OUTER PLANETS of the Solar System – Jupiter, Saturn, Uranus, Neptune and Pluto – are very different from the inner planets. Apart from Pluto, they are much bigger. Jupiter is nearly 1,500 times the size of the Earth. They all have small cores of iron and rock, but they are made mostly of gases. This means they are all quite light for their size. If you could find a bathtub of water big enough, Saturn would actually float in it. Because the outer planets are so large and so far from the Sun, they are very cold and the gases are turned to liquid or even solid.

Rings are only 1-2 kilometres deep

Thin ring system   *Great Red Spot*   *One of Jupiter's moons*

Jupiter
Jupiter is the largest planet, and twice as heavy as all the rest put together. It spins so rapidly, once in less than 10 hours, that it bulges at its equator. Although Jupiter is made mostly of hydrogen and helium gas, it is so massive that its own gravity squeezes these substances into liquid near the centre, with a small solid core. On the surface is a giant storm, the Great Red Spot, which is three times bigger than Earth.

Jupiter's equator bulges with its speed of rotation

Space probes
Several deep-space probes have visited the outer planets. *Voyager 2* flew past Saturn, Uranus and Neptune, The *Cassini-Huygens* probe is due to reach Saturn in July 2004. The *Cassini orbiter* will go around Saturn while the *Huygens lander* will touch down on its moon Titan.

Charon

Pluto

Pluto
Pluto is the smallest planet, even smaller than Mercury. It is so far away that from its surface, the Sun would look only slightly bigger than any other star in the sky. Pluto has a moon called Charon, which is over half its size. They form a twin-planet system, like our Earth and Moon, orbiting around each other like a set of spinning dumbbells. Pluto is so small that it is often called a minor planet, rather than having full planetary status.

See also: Earth in space page 174, Inner planets page 182

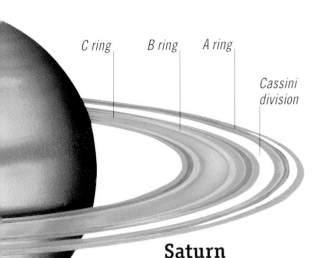

C ring   B ring   A ring

Cassini division

Faint ring system   Great Dark Spot

Saturn

Saturn is almost as big as Jupiter and also made largely of liquid and solid "metallic" hydrogen and helium. It is surrounded by a shimmering halo of rings – countless billions of tiny blocks of ice and dust, most no bigger than a tennis ball, circling endlessly around the planet.

Neptune

Neptune is very slightly smaller than Uranus and equally as cold. Like Uranus, it has an ocean of water, methane and ammonia thousands of kilometres deep around its rocky core. Above that is a deep atmosphere of hydrogen and helium, through which winds roar at over 2,000 kilometres per hour. From afar the planet looks blue with wispy white clouds. Like Jupiter, Neptune has a giant storm area, called the Great Dark Spot.

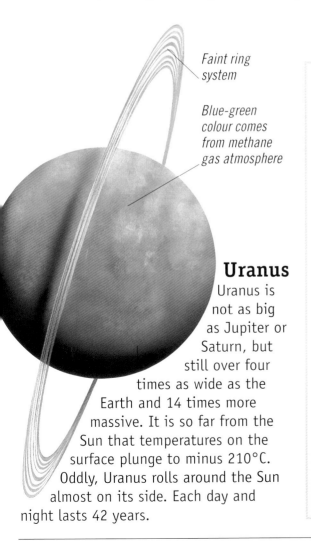

Faint ring system

Blue-green colour comes from methane gas atmosphere

Uranus

Uranus is not as big as Jupiter or Saturn, but still over four times as wide as the Earth and 14 times more massive. It is so far from the Sun that temperatures on the surface plunge to minus 210°C. Oddly, Uranus rolls around the Sun almost on its side. Each day and night lasts 42 years.

PLANET SIZES

All the outer planets except Pluto have ring systems, although none is as spectacular as Saturn's. Also, all but Pluto have not just one moon, but a whole swarm. Jupiter's moon Ganymede and Saturn's moon Titan are both substantially bigger than the planet Mercury.

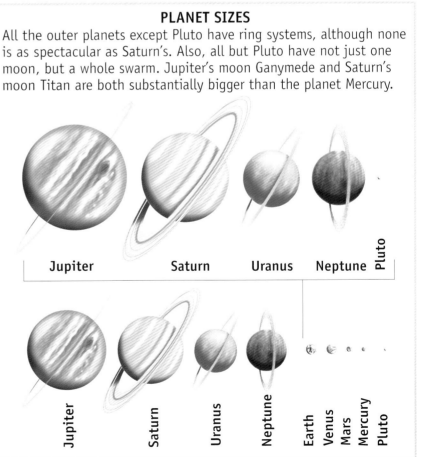

Jupiter   Saturn   Uranus   Neptune   Pluto

Jupiter   Saturn   Uranus   Neptune   Earth   Venus   Mars   Mercury   Pluto

The Sun

THE SUN IS OUR LOCAL STAR, a vast fiery spinning ball of burning gases – three-quarters hydrogen and a quarter helium. It is so big, over 1.3 million times the volume of Earth and 333,420 times as heavy – that the pressures in its centre are gigantic. Such immense pressure is enough to turn the Sun into a huge nuclear power plant by fusing together hydrogen atoms, releasing so much energy that temperatures are boosted to 15 million°C. All this incredible heat turns the Sun's surface into a raging inferno.

Corona

Chromosphere

Inside the Sun

The surface or photosphere glows at over 5,500°C – enough to melt almost any substance. It is mottled with bright spots called granules, where heat from the core erupts through the radiation and convection zones onto the surface. Above the photosphere is the Sun's atmosphere, with the chromosphere below and the corona on top. Huge flame-like tongues of hot hydrogen called solar prominences shoot out over 100,000 kilometres.

Solar prominence

Core

Sun power

The light and other forms of radiation streaming from the Sun provide us with warmth and light directly, and light energy for plants to use. Fuels like oil and coal were once tiny organisms and plants which got their store of energy from the Sun.

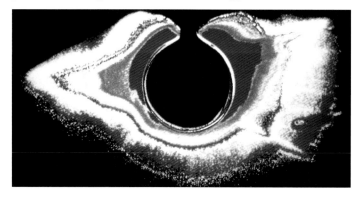

Science discovery

Galileo Galilei (1564-1642) was one of the greatest scientists who ever lived. He made many discoveries about gravity and acceleration. But he is especially famous because he was the first to use a telescope to scan the heavens and make many important discoveries, described in his book *The Starry Messenger* (1610). He was the first to see mountains on the Moon, the moons of Jupiter, and sunspots – though looking at the Sun badly damaged his eyesight.

See also: Earth in space page 174, Stars page 190

Photosphere

Convection zone

Radiation zone

SOHO

Even though the Sun is fairly nearby for an astronomical object, and also very large, there is still a great deal about it that scientists do not understand. So on 2 December, 1995, NASA launched SOHO, the Solar and Heliospheric Observatory. This now orbits the Sun, balanced between the pull of the gravity of Earth and the gravity of the Sun. It monitors the Sun continually and should supply streams of information, coming back to Earth from its radio antenna, for many years.

Solar panels

Radio antenna (dish)

Sunspot   Solar prominence   Granules

Sunspots

Around the middle of the Sun are cooler, darker sunspots. Typically, they appear in groups and move across the face of the Sun as it turns. Their numbers vary, and seems to reach a maximum every 11 years. Some scientists believe they are linked to cooler, stormy weather on Earth.

Moon between Sun and Earth

Moon's orbit around Earth

Day-time on light side of Earth

Moon glows with reflected sunlight

Night-time on dark side of Earth

Fully eclipsed Moon when Earth is between Sun and Moon

Shadow of Moon on Earth

Sun blocks

Every now and then, the Earth and the Moon get in between each other and the Sun. This is called an eclipse, because one eclipses the Sun from the other. A lunar eclipse is when the Moon goes round behind the Earth into its shadow. A solar eclipse is when the Moon comes in between the Sun and the Earth, casting a shadow a few kilometres wide on the Earth. Other planets are eclipsed by their moons too. From Earth, we can see the moon and also its shadow passing across the planet's surface.

Dark side of Moon

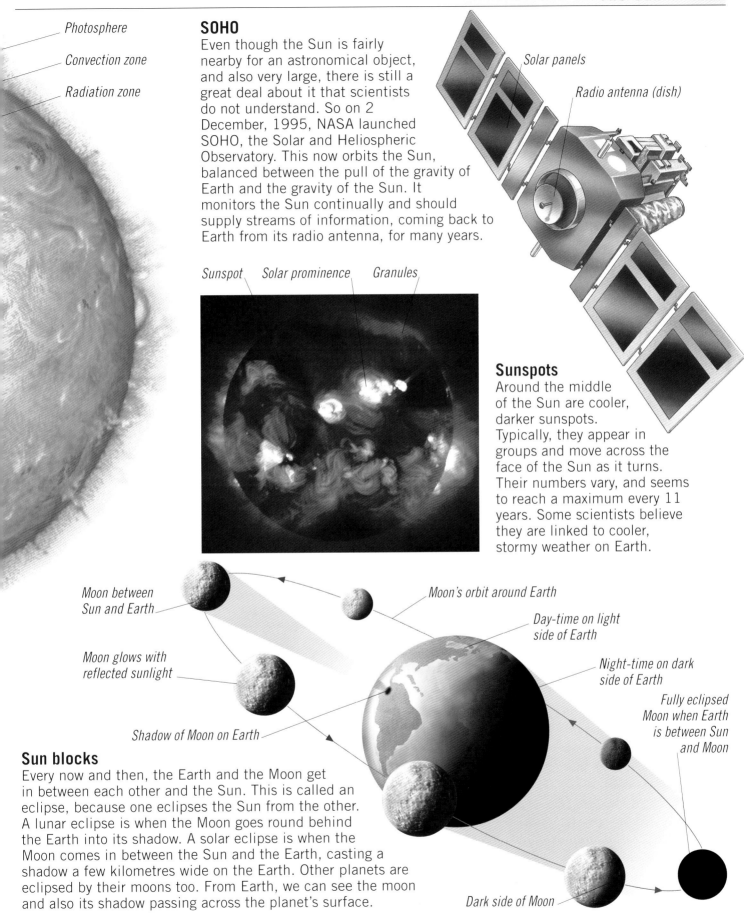

Stars

THE FEW HUNDRED OR THOUSAND STARS you see twinkling in the night sky are just a tiny fraction of the stars scattered throughout the Universe. There are countless billions of them and, like our Sun, they are all huge, fiery balls of gas. Our Sun is, in fact, average or even slightly small for a star. There are red giant stars 100 times as big, and supergiant stars 500 times larger! There are also white dwarf stars smaller than the Earth, neutron stars or pulsars just a few kilometres across, and many other amazing deep-space objects.

COLOURS OF STARS

Although stars are very far away, we can tell a lot about them from their colours.

▶ The whiter and hotter stars are, the brighter they glow.

▶ The redder and cooler they are, the dimmer they glow.

▶ So cool red stars that are bright must be relatively nearby, while hot white stars that are dim must be relatively far away.

▶ Bluish white stars are more than 25,000°C at the surface.

▶ Yellowish stars are about 6,000°C.

▶ Orange-red stars are below 3,500°C.

Science discovery

Edmond Halley (1656-1742) made major discoveries in all fields of science. He made the first map of the world's wind patterns, estimated the size of an atom, worked out that the aurorae were magnetic, and made the first accurate map of the stars in the southern sky. Later he worked out that comets return at regular intervals – including the comet that now bears his name.

Star birth
Stars are born in clouds of dust and gas called nebulae. Clumps are pulled together by their own gravity.

Ready to shine
As each clump pulls itself tighter it begins to get hot, but not hot enough to glow.

Glowing at last
Smaller clumps fizzle out as "brown dwarves". If the clump reaches 10 million °C, nuclear fusion begins and the clump condenses and becomes a glowing star.

Steady shine
In a medium-sized star the heat tries to make the star bigger, but this is balanced by gravity which tries to shrink it. So the star stays the same size and glows steadily for billions of years.

The lives of stars

Stars are being formed or born, and fading away or dying, all over the Universe. Looking at different types of stars, we are in effect seeing stars at different stages in their lives. Astronomers have been able to piece together the life history of typical star types. Big stars usually have short, spectacular lives, burning ferociously for no more than ten million years before collapsing into a black hole. Medium stars like our Sun last for about ten billion years before exploding or dwindling to a white dwarf. Small stars go on glowing faintly for much, much longer.

Nuclear fusion makes the star shine

The core of the star burns hydrogen into helium, then burns helium

See also: The Sun page 188, Galaxies page 192, Deep space page 194

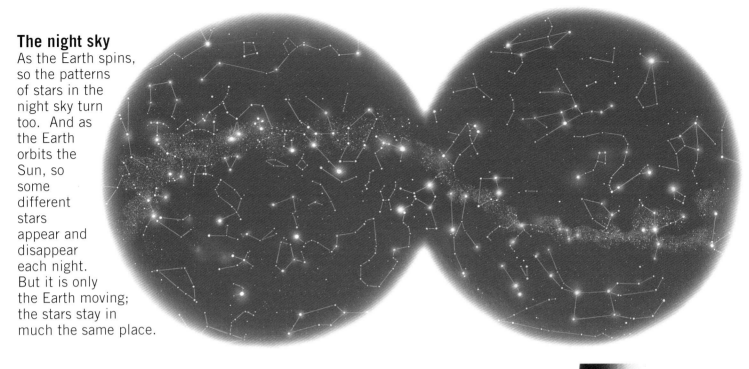

The night sky
As the Earth spins, so the patterns of stars in the night sky turn too. And as the Earth orbits the Sun, so some different stars appear and disappear each night. But it is only the Earth moving; the stars stay in much the same place.

Bigger and redder
When the hydrogen is burned up, the core of the star shrinks and begins to fuse helium atoms together instead. The outer layers of gas cool and swell, and it becomes a red giant.

Collapse
In the biggest stars, more changes take place in the core, and the star suddenly takes in energy instead of giving it out. It collapses in seconds.

The remains of an exploding star or supernova collapse to become a pulsar

White dwarf

Black hole

At the death
The remains of a supernova may condense into a pulsar, a rapidly spinning star made mainly from atomic particles called neutrons. A small star (smaller than our Sun) gradually cools and shrinks into a white dwarf. It may continue to shrink until all its matter is compacted into a single point of infinite density – a black hole.

Supernova
The collapse of a huge star is like a giant nuclear explosion called a supernova. For a few weeks it shines with the brightness of millions of Suns. Astronomers' records of supernovae go back to the time of Ancient China and Egypt.

A big star becomes a supergiant, with immense pressure in the centre

As the chemical changes begin to make iron in the core, the star suddenly collapses

Galaxies

UNTIL ABOUT 1918, astronomers thought that all stars were clumped together in a big disc, with our Sun in the middle. The hazy band of light you can sometimes see stretching across the sky on a dark night is our edge-on view of this disc, the Milky Way or Galaxy. It is a vast collection of 100 billion stars, over a million trillion kilometres across. But soon, in the 1930s, ideas were revised again – and then again. In fact, our Galaxy is just one of countless millions of galaxies scattered throughout the Universe. Each galaxy contains billions of stars.

The Milky Way
Our Galaxy is the pale streak of light you can sometimes see stretching across the night sky. You can distinguish very few stars within it. It almost seems like someone has spilled milk across the sky, which is why it is called the Milky Way. The word *galaxy* is Ancient Greek for "milky".

Our Galaxy
Galaxies are not spread evenly through the Universe. They are clumped together in clusters of anything from half a dozen to several thousand. Our Galaxy is part of a neighbourhood cluster of 3,000 galaxies called the Local Group. All the other clusters are so far away that we see them as nothing more than pinpoints of light. But within the Local Group we can identify several different shapes of galaxies, shown opposite. Our galaxy is of the spiral type, like the Andromeda galaxy.

Our Sun and Solar System are about here

Arms get thinner at their ends

See also: The Sun page 188, Stars page 190, Deep space page 194

Science discovery

William Herschel (1738-1822) trained as an organist but was so keen on astronomy that he built his own giant telescope in the cellar of his house in Bath, England. In 1781, he added to the five planets known since ancient times – Mercury, Venus, Mars, Jupiter and Saturn – when he spotted another planet. He wanted to call it George, after King George III of England, but it is now known as Uranus.

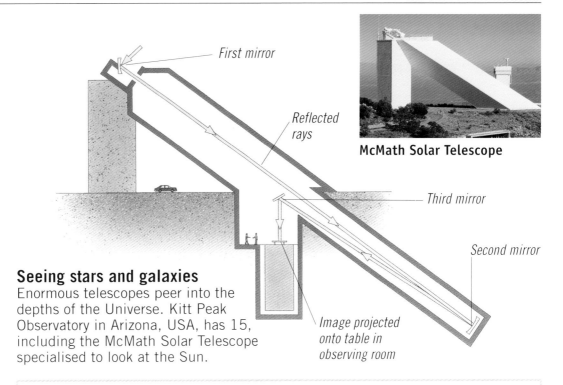

First mirror

Reflected rays

McMath Solar Telescope

Third mirror

Second mirror

Image projected onto table in observing room

Seeing stars and galaxies
Enormous telescopes peer into the depths of the Universe. Kitt Peak Observatory in Arizona, USA, has 15, including the McMath Solar Telescope specialised to look at the Sun.

Empty regions between galaxies

TYPES OF GALAXIES
There are several main types of galaxies, grouped by their shapes. They are not still, but moving through space at incredible speed. Sometimes they actually crash into each other. As this happens over hundreds of millions of years, each galaxy's gravity rips long trails of stars and gas from the other. There are also radio galaxies, which send out little light, but emit vast amounts of radio and other electromagnetic waves.

Central disc or hub

Arm

Spiral galaxy

Barred spiral galaxy

Central region

Irregular galaxy

Elliptical galaxy

Deep space

STARS AND GALAXIES beam out huge amounts of waves or radiation all the time. Some is light. But most is invisible radiation, with wavelengths too long or short for our eyes to register. Astronomers use specialised telescopes to detect this invisible radiation – including X-rays, gamma rays and radio waves. This had led to the discovery of some of the Universe's most amazing objects in deep space. They include pulsars, quasars and black holes, which challenge the normal principles and laws of science and require new ways of thinking.

Radio telescopes
The dish or wires of a radio telescope pick up faint natural radio waves from space. The signals are so weak, the bigger the dish, the better. The biggest single dish is the Arecibo telescope in Puerto Rico, South America. It is set into a valley in the hills and its dish is 305 metres across.

The birthplace of stars and galaxies
A nebula is a vast cloud of hydrogen and other gases, dust and bits of interstellar matter, that glows with light and many kinds of radiation. The Eagle nebula shows "fingers" of gas throwing out EGGs – evaporating gaseous globules. They are stellar nurseries and in billions of years they will have condensed to form stars. This image of the Eagle nebula, which is about 7,000 light-years away, was taken by the Hubble Space Telescope.

Centre of black hole

Matter and energy swirl down a "funnel" towards the central black hole

Matter and energy being sucked into the black hole

Black holes
Black holes are places where the gravity is so strong that it sucks in everything – including light, which is why the hole is so black. No-one has actually seen a black hole, but they are thought to form when a star or galaxy gets so amazingly dense that it collapses under the pull of its own gravity. It shrinks to an unimaginably small point called a singularity.

See also: Galaxies page 192, The Universe page 196

Searchlights of space

Quasars are space's most intense sources of energy. They are as bright as 100 galaxies, yet no larger than our Solar System. Possibly powered by a black hole, they beam out immense amounts of radio waves and other energy. They are the oldest, most distant things we can detect. The farthest quasars may be 12 billion light-years away, at the edge of space, time and the Universe.

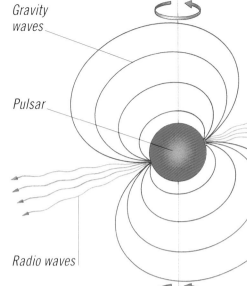

Gravity waves

Pulsar

Radio waves

Axis of spin

Pulsars

These are tiny stars that send out powerful radio signals as regular pulses, like a flashing beacon. When they were first detected, astronomers suggested jokingly that the signals came from aliens and called them LGMs (little green men). In fact, pulsars are neutron stars – supergiant stars that have collapsed under their own gravity. They are only a few kilometres across and spin around every minute or so. Their matter is mainly neutrons and is packed so densely that a teaspoon of a neutron star would weigh ten billion tonnes.

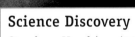

Science Discovery

Stephen Hawking (1942-) is unable to move or speak normally because he is affected by motor neurone disease. But this has not stopped him becoming famous for his brilliant ideas about space and time. His computerised voice is often heard on television and radio. He convinced astronomers that black holes, which had already been suggested, could really exist. His book *A Brief History of Time* is one of the world's best-sellers. Hawking also suggests that our Universe is not alone. There could be many others, making up a "Super-Universe".

The Universe

No-one really knows how big the Universe is. It may have an end which is too far away to detect. It may have no end and go on for ever. It may even curve around on itself, so it is endless like a circle. It may have links to other universes. But we do know that the Universe is getting bigger all the time. Galaxies are speeding away from us in every direction. In the past, the Universe used to be thought of as everything that exists. But in recent years, cosmologists (scientists who study the nature of the Universe) have narrowed it down to everything – all space and time and matter – that we can ever know about.

Universal scale

We can imagine size and distance in our local area, such as the size of a sports ground in square metres, or the distance to school in kilometres. But sizes and distances in space are too great to understand fully. The numbers of kilometres are so enormous, scientists use the light-year as a measure of distance. One light-year is how far light (or other electromagnetic waves) travels in one year – 9,460,000,000,000 kilometres. Even then, distances to distant quasars are measured in billions of light-years.

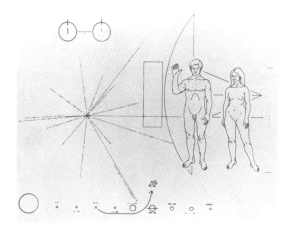

Pioneering craft

Although humans have still only travelled as far as the Moon, robot spacecraft are probing deeper into space, and finding out more about our neighbouring planets. In 1989, the *Voyager 2* probe reached Neptune – it was launched in 1977 – and discovered six new moons. It is now speeding way beyond the Solar System, into the vastness. Like its companion *Voyager 1*, it carries a gold-coated plaque showing likenesses of human figures, Earth and our nearby planets and stars, and even recordings of speech and music. Will it ever be found?

Planet Earth is about 12,800 kilometres across

The Solar System is about 7,000 million kilometres across

Light from the nearest bright star Alpha Centauri takes 4.3 years to reach us, so it is 4.3 light-years away

See also: Deep space page 194, About time page 196

Old Universes

We are so familiar with our understanding of the Universe, and the Earth's tiny globe spinning in the vastness of space, that it is hard to imagine how people ever thought differently. But it has taken thousands of years of scientific study and thought to build up this idea. The Ancient Egyptians thought of the Universe as a pyramid, with the Earth as the base and the heavens as the four sides. The early Hindus believed the world was a plate resting on the backs of four elephants standing on a giant floating turtle.

The end of the Universe?

Radiation from some quasars takes 12 billion years to reach us. This is near the time when the Universe began, and so the beginning, rather than the end.

A typical spiral galaxy is 100,000 light-years across

Science discovery

Edwin Hubble (1889-1953) was one of the great astronomers of the 20th century. Trained as a lawyer and also successful as a boxer, he turned to astronomy in the 1920s. Working with the giant telescope at Mount Wilson in the USA, he showed that there are many galaxies apart from our own. Hubble also used red shift (right) to show that these other galaxies are zooming away from us, and so the Universe must be getting bigger.

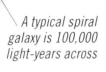

Red shift

Study of the light waves that galaxies send out show that they are red-shifted. That is, the waves are slightly longer, and so redder in colour, than we would expect. (This is a result of the Doppler effect that also happens with sound waves.) The farther away that galaxies are, the more their light is red-shifted, so the faster they are going. The most distant galaxies have such massive red-shifts they must be zooming away at nearly the speed of light. The conclusion is that the Universe is expanding, and the expansion is getting faster!

About time

TIME SEEMS TO BE the single constant feature of our world. The clock ticks steadily. Seconds, minutes and hours pass. You cannot rush time, or make it go backwards. But is this true? Modern ideas in science say: No. Time is not constant. It varies. The faster you move, the slower time passes. There are even theories which say that it could be possible to make time stand still – or even go backwards.

Time going faster?

In the dim and distant past, not much seemed to happen, very slowly. Humans evolved from ape-like ancestors over thousands of years. Then people began to farm and live in towns. Our experiences today are that time seems to fly by, as new inventions change the world almost weekly.

4,000 years ago

People began to live in small huts, then settle in towns. The Civilization Revolution began, with large cities, magnificent temples and other great buildings.

400 years ago

The Renaissance Period allowed science to flourish. New ideas and experiments abounded. The Industrial Revolution that followed, beginning in the 18th century, speeded up the arrival of new gadgets and inventions.

FASTER MEANS SLOWER

Einstein's theory of relativity predicts time is relative to motion. The faster you move, the slower time passes. Astronauts who spend months orbiting Earth in the *Mir* space station come back one or two seconds younger than if they had stayed on the surface.

40 years ago

In a few hours, airliners could carry passengers on long-distance journeys that once took days. Skyscrapers rose in cities around the world. Radio and then television came into people's homes, fuelling the Communications Revolution.

See also: Changing times page 200, Past and future page 202

MEASURING TIME

Our years, months and days are worked out from the way the Earth and Moon revolve in space and journey around the Sun. Timekeeping devices such as candle-clocks and sundials meant that days could be divided into hours. Mechanical clocks were invented in the 17th century, and gradually improved to the accuracy of tenths of a second. Today's electronic and atomic clocks are accurate to millionths of a second.

Hours
The nearest hour or two can be near enough, if time is not of the essence for traditional events.

Minutes
As timekeeping devices became more accurate, minutes counted, as when catching a coach or train.

Fractions of a second
With electronic timing, one or two hundredths of a second can now mean a new world record.

4 billion years ago

Earth formed from a ball of gases and dust that gathered together in space, got very hot and then slowly cooled.

4 years ago

Space missions were launching many new telecommunications satellites, to cope with the Information Revolution and its boom in mobile phones, computer data transfer and the Internet.

Today

The orbiting International Space Station is being assembled piece by piece, over 20 years.

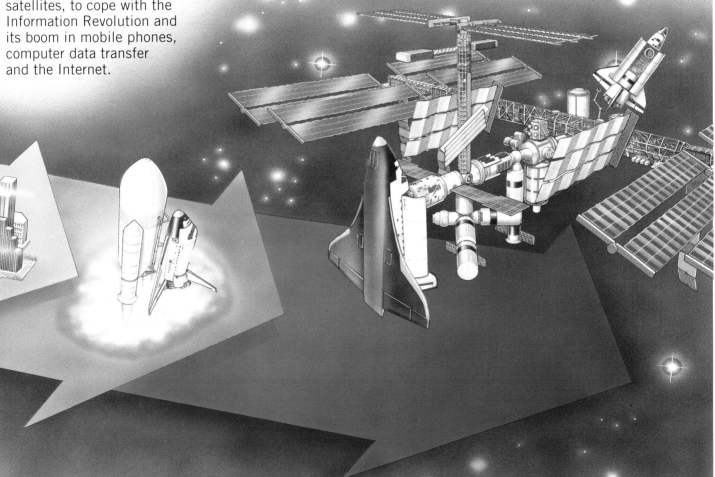

Changing times

EVERYONE KNOWS ABOUT TIME. Yet scientists find it hard to pin down exactly what time is. In our common-sense view, it goes only in one direction, from past to future. But most of science's main laws do not require this to happen. For example, the laws of motion work just as well whether time goes backwards or forwards. Scientists now think of time, not as running backwards or forwards, but as another dimension. We experience three dimensions daily. These are the spatial dimensions of length, width and height. Time is added to these, as a fourth dimension, to make the space-time continuum – what we call "space-time".

Relative time

What time is it? If you sent a "live" picture of your watch, as radio waves, to a friend on a distant planet, the friend would not see it until minutes later. Who would have the right time, you or your friend? You can only tell the time in relation to something else, like the position of the Sun in the sky. This is why time is said to be relative.

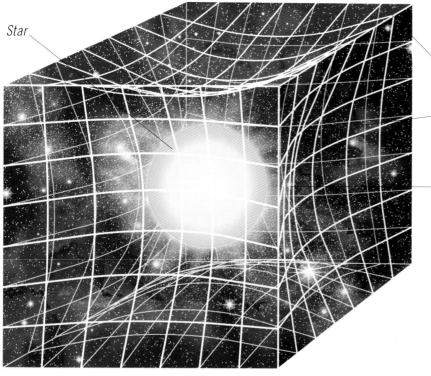

Star

Three dimensions of space

Space distorted or bent by pull of star's gravity

Distortion is greater, nearer to star

Early, simple life-forms (like bacteria and blue-green algae) produced oxygen, making the atmosphere more like today's

Warped space-time

The theory of general relativity says that gravity does not just pull on atoms of matter. It pulls on everything. The immense gravitational pull of a star can even stretch and bend space-time. When this happens, a light ray that travels in a straight line through space, bends as it passes the star. It is still going straight through space, but the space itself is bent. Imagine a two-dimensional rubber sheet. A strong gravitational pull is like a heavy ball dumped in the middle of the sheet, to stretch and distort it. Extend this idea to three dimensions of space, and then to four dimensions with time, and this is how gravity distorts space-time.

See also: About time page 198, Past and future page 202

The times of the Earth

It's believed that the Earth formed around 4.6 billion (4,600 million) years ago. Like the other planets in the Solar System, it began as a cloud of gas and dust spinning around the Sun. As the cloud swirled, it began to condense or clump together under the pull of its own gravity. Its temperature rose as it finally gathered into a ball of molten rock, then started to cool. As the rocks became more solid they gave off water vapour, which condensed into clouds and fell as massive rainstorms lasting tens of thousands of years. Meteorites which have reached Earth are other bits of rock from elsewhere in the Solar System. They have also been dated to an age of 4,600 million years. So have the Moon rocks brought back by the Apollo missions.

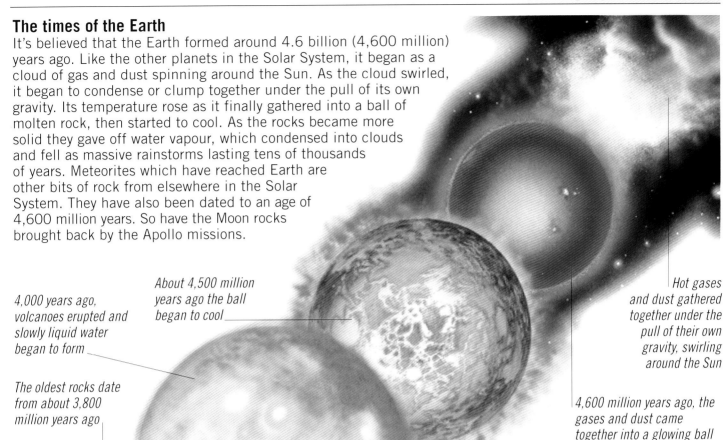

4,000 years ago, volcanoes erupted and slowly liquid water began to form

About 4,500 million years ago the ball began to cool

Hot gases and dust gathered together under the pull of their own gravity, swirling around the Sun

The oldest rocks date from about 3,800 million years ago

4,600 million years ago, the gases and dust came together into a glowing ball

At first the atmosphere was made up of poisonous gases such as methane, carbon dioxide and sulphur dioxide

WHEN TIME BEGAN

If the Universe began at the event called the Big Bang, then this may be when time itself began. Perhaps there was nothing before, at all. If there was no space, there could be no time either.

▶ **0 seconds** The Universe began as a tiny, hot, dense ball which grew as big as a pumpkin, as it cooled to 10 billion billion billion°C.

▶ **10^{-35} secs** A split second later, space swelled a thousand billion billion billion times in a fraction of a second. This period of inflation gave the infant Universe the room to grow.

▶ **10^{-32} secs** As the Universe mushroomed out, it flooded with energy and matter. Basic forces like gravity and electromagnetism were made. There were no atoms, but a soup of tiny particles such as quarks.

▶ **10^{-8} secs** Everything was divided into matter and its mirror image, anti-matter. Matter and anti-matter cannot exist together, and they destroyed each other. There was just slightly more matter than anti-matter, and this matter survived. The matter-anti-matter annihilation left the empty space that makes up most of the Universe.

▶ **3 mins** Quarks began to join up to form the smallest atoms, hydrogen. Then hydrogen atoms joined to make helium atoms. Soon the Universe filled with clouds of hydrogen and helium.

▶ **1 million years** The gas clouds curdled into long strands called filaments.

▶ **300 million years** Filaments clumped into clouds, and clouds began to clump together to form galaxies and stars.

Past and future

GRADUALLY SCIENTISTS ARE LEARNING more about our world and Universe. In only the past few years, we have come to understand more about how the Universe began, how stars form, how the Earth has changed and how life has evolved. We have learned how all matter is made of tiny particles held together by four basic forces. Science progresses ever faster, especially in areas such as genetics, computing, communications and space exploration.

But there is still much to find out. One day, scientists hope to develop a "grand theory of everything" – a simple, elegant idea that will make sense of all forces, matter and energy, everywhere and for all time.

Science discovery

Pierre de Fermat (1601-1665) was a spare-time mathematician who worked on complex ideas in geometry, probability, number theory and physics. In 1637 he devised a problem known as Fermat's Last Theorem, which he said that he had solved. But he did not say how. It has puzzled scientists ever since, until 1994, when it was at last solved by Andrew Wiles.

Future telecommunications-web

Two linked technologies will play important roles in the future – computers and telecommunications. Already, computer scientists talk about manipulating atoms to build powerful computers so small that they could fit in a button. Linked by tiny radio systems, they would have instant satellite access to a worldwide web of total information.

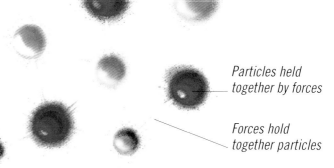

Particles held together by forces

Forces hold together particles

Fundamental science

What are the most basic, fundamental parts of our Universe? There seem to be two main divisions – matter or substance, and forces. In terms of matter, there do not appear to be any particles smaller than quarks, and a similar group of particles known as leptons. In terms of forces, there seem to be four. These are gravity, electromagnetism, and the strong and weak nuclear forces. We presume that these have been in existence since space and time began, when the Universe formed over 12 billion years ago.

See also: Atoms page 14, The Universe page 196

Bang to Crunch?

What is the ultimate fate of the Universe? Will it expand for ever? The answer depends partly on how much matter there is. Most of the Universe may be made up of mysterious "dark matter" which we have not even detected yet. If there is not very much, the Universe may go on getting bigger. If there is lots of dark matter, its gravity will put a brake on the expansion and begin to pull it together again. It will then shrink faster and faster, like the Big Bang in reverse, to end with a Big Crunch. Will that mark the end of time?

Genetic engineering

After unlocking the structure of the genetic molecule DNA and cracking its genetic code, scientists are now able to modify genes in living things. Genetic instructions have been transferred between widely differing organisms. For example, an "anti-freeze" gene that makes the blood of a certain Arctic fish resistant to freezing, has been put into a tomato to make it frost-resistant. Also, researchers hope to carry out gene therapy to cure inherited diseases. But the long-term effects of swapping and transferring genes are not known. One fear is that genes could transfer into germs, and allow a race of super-bugs to cause devastating worldwide epidemics.

OTHER WORLDS

In 1976, two Viking space probes soft-landed on Mars. They sent back pictures of the surface and tested samples of Martian dust for signs of life, with negative results. In 1997 another probe, *Pathfinder*, visited the planet with a small remote-controlled buggy, *Sojourner*. As our space exploration becomes increasingly complex and sophisticated, we discover more about our Solar System. But visits to other galaxies would require faster-than-light travel, which is still very much science fiction.

Viking probe to Mars

View of Martian surface from *Viking* probe

7

Science Projects

The scientific method involves devising an idea or theory, making a prediction from it, and carrying out experiments to test it. By trial and error we discount old theories and develop new ones, gradually moving toward greater understanding. The practical work of projects, tests, and experiments is central to scientific progress.

Light for growth

Plants use the energy in light to make their food. Find out what happens if plants are kept in the dark!

SEE: LIFE ON EARTH PAGE 164

You will need

Cress seeds

Potting compost

A shallow tray for growing seeds

Cardboard and scissors

1 Fill the tray with potting compost. Sprinkle cress seeds on the surface and water them gently.

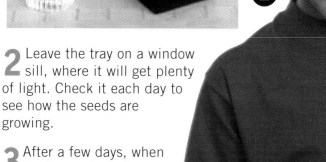

2 Leave the tray on a window sill, where it will get plenty of light. Check it each day to see how the seeds are growing.

3 After a few days, when the leaves have formed, cut a piece of cardboard big enough to cover the tray. Cut out a shape in the cardboard, and put it over the tray. Again, check it each day. What happens to the shoots under the cardboard? How can you tell from this project that plants need light to grow?

Phototropism

Plants try to grow towards bright light so that their leaves get all the light they can. This is known as phototropism.

SEE: LIGHT PAGE 124

You will need

Cress seeds

Potting compost

Small shallow tray for seeds

Cardboard box and scissors

1 Fill the tray with potting compost. Sprinkle the cress seeds on top and water them gently.

2 Cut a hole about 10 centimetres long in the side of a cardboard box. Put the tray inside the box and put the lid on the box. Leave the box near a window so that light comes in through the hole.

WARNING!
Be careful with mould. If you touch it, wash your hands afterwards. Wash the container it was in when the project is over.

3 Watch the seeds as they sprout. Do they grow straight upward, as they would normally, or towards the hole?

Like molds, ferns reproduce from spores. But they do so in a different way. First the spore grows into a small heart-shaped leaf, a prothallus. This then develops into the main fern plant.

Mould

Mould is a kind of fungus. It grows on old and dead living things, including old food.

SEE: LIFE ON
EARTH PAGE 164

You will need

A small, shallow dish
Cling film
Some bread
A magnifying glass

1 Put some small pieces of bread into the container. Leave it in the open air for a few hours. Add a few drops of water to the bread to make it damp. Cover the container with the film and leave it in a warm place.

2 After a few days, there should be plenty of mould on the bread. Look at the mould through the cling film. Study it with a magnifying glass. Can you see thin threads spreading across the bread, and tiny black spheres growing upward? This type of mould is called pin mould. The black "pin heads" release minute spores, small as grains of dust. These spores grow into more mould.

Minibeasts in the soil

Garden soil has many tiny creatures living in it.
Find and study some of them.

SEE: LIFE ON EARTH
PAGE 164

You will need

Rubber gloves

A trowel

A jar

A sheet of plain paper

An old pencil

A magnifying glass

1 Collect a sample of loose garden soil in a jar. Spread it out on a sheet of paper. Wear your rubber gloves, and break the soil apart with the pencil. Look out for any small creatures you might see.

WARNING!

Beware of dangerous germs in soil and water. Only use soil or pond water from your garden or the school. Always wear gloves when you work with soil or water, and wash your hands afterwards.

2 Look at the creatures with a magnifying glass. Try to make sketches of them. Animals in the soil do an important job. They help rot dead pieces of plants such as leaves. This turns them into nutrients that other plants need to grow. Some animals, such as worms, break up the soil and help get air into it. After you have studied the creatures, return them and the soil to where you found them.

Life in water

Tiny creatures live in streams and ponds. Have a look at a sample of water and mud to see if you can find any of them.

SEE: RIVERS AND LAKES PAGE 158

You will need

Rubber gloves
Empty jars and string
A shallow glass dish
Plain white paper
A magnifying glass
A microscope
(if you can obtain one)

1 Wearing your rubber gloves, use a jar on a string to collect some water from a garden pond. If you can, collect some mud from the pond's bottom, too. **Make sure an adult is with you when you do this.**

2 Put the glass dish on the plain white paper. Pour a little of the water into it. Now look at the water through a magnifying glass. Can you see any small creatures in it? Spread out a small lump of mud in the dish, and study this too. If you have a microscope, use it to look at a drop of pond water.

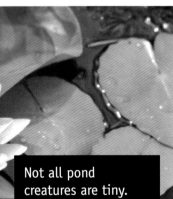

Not all pond creatures are tiny. You may find a young dragonfly, or nymph. It lives under water and only leaves after several months. It creeps up a stem and sheds its skin to reveal wings, like the adult in this picture.

Reaction times

Animals react when things happen. This project tests your own reaction time.

SEE: ABOUT TIME PAGE 198

You will need

A ruler
A pencil and paper

1 Work with a friend. Hold your hands with the palms facing each other, a few inches apart.

2 Ask a friend to hold a ruler so that the zero on the scale is level with your thumbs, as shown.

3 When your friend drops the ruler, try to catch it by clapping your hands together. Write down the position of your thumbs on the scale where they grabbed the ruler. The lower your score, the faster your reaction!

Seeing is believing?

Eyes can play tricks, or optical illusions.

SEE: DETECTING LIGHT PAGE 130

You will need

A small ball (golfball)
A large ball (basketball)

1 Place the small ball in front of the large one, so that they both seem about the same size.

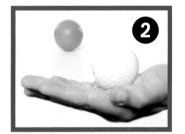

2 Close one eye. Now the balls really do look the same size! Using only one eye makes it harder for your brain to work out distances. But you still know the basketball is farther away, because you know from memory it is larger.

Optical illusion 2

You will need

The picture below

1 Stare at the cubes in the picture. Do the white pieces seem to be on top of the dark cubes? Or do they seem to be the undersides of the tops on the cubes? Like animals, we use our eyes and brains together, to judge shapes and positions of objects. But sometimes the eyes cannot give the brain enough information. The picture below does not have enough information to show where the white pieces are.

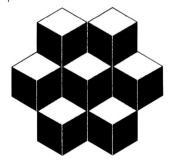

Mixing and diffusion

As liquids mix together, the particles in them gradually spread out and mingle. This is known as diffusion.

SEE: LIQUIDS
PAGE 26

You will need

2 same-sized jars
Petroleum jelly
Food colouring
Kitchen cooking foil
Tray

1 Remove the lids from the jars. Smear some petroleum jelly around the rim of each one.

2 Fill one jar right to the brim with tap water. Put a piece of cooking foil over the jar. Make sure the petroleum jelly keeps it in place.

3 Fill the other jar with tap water. Add a few drops of food colouring to it. Put it on the tray (in case of spills).

4 Carefully, turn over the jar with the foil and put it on top of the first jar.

5 Wait a few moments then, very carefully, slide out the foil.

6 Look at the jar every 15 minutes. What happens to the colour?

The tiny particles of food colouring are too small to see individually. But you can see how they mix together, even without stirring. This is diffusion taking place.

Making solutions

A solution forms when one substance dissolves in another.

SEE: DISSOLVING PAGE 34

You will need

Salt or sugar
Water in jar

1 Three-quarters fill the jar with cold water. Make a mark on the outside of the jar level with the water surface. Add salt or sugar to the water, one level teaspoon at a time. Stir the water until the salt or sugar dissolves and disappears. Keep going until no more salt or sugar dissolves. Note the number of teaspoons.

2 Do the experiment again, but this time use warm water, up to the same mark on the jar. Does more or less salt or sugar dissolve in the warmer water?

When a substance dissolves in a liquid, it breaks down into tiny particles. These mix with the particles that make up the liquid to form a solution.

Growing crystals

Some solids have their atoms or molecules arranged in a neat pattern or framework.

SEE: CRYSTALS PAGE 30

These amazing rocks in Northern Ireland formed millions of years ago when hot, molten rock cooled, slowly. Tall, hexagonal (six-sided) crystals were made as the rock particles formed regular patterns. The rocks are called the Giant's Causeway.

You will need

Alum powder (from a pharmacist)

Medium-sized jars

Cotton thread, scissors

A drinking straw

A rubber band

1 Ask an adult to fill a jar with warm water from a kettle. Add alum powder, a teaspoon at a time, and stir it. Allow the excess crystals to settle and carefully pour the liquid into another jar.

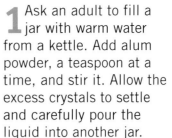

2 Tie a piece of cotton thread to the centre of a drinking straw. Cut the thread so that when the straw rests on the rim of the jar, it hangs down about three-quarters of the way into the jar. Bend

down the ends of the straw and secure them over the jar with the rubber band.

2 After a few days you should be able to see some alum crystals growing on the thread. Try to draw their shape.

Alum crystals (see page 30)

DID YOU KNOW? You can smell things, such as baking bread, because particles from them diffuse quickly through the air. Your nose senses the particles when you breathe the air.

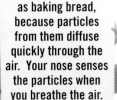

Separating colours

Most inks and dyes are a mixture of different pigments (coloured substances) in a solvent. The process of chromatography separates these different pigments.

SEE: LIGHT PAGE 124

You will need

Filter or blotting paper

Scissors

Small canes

String

Pegs or paperclips

A shallow tray or similar shallow container

A large rubber band

Samples of coloured liquids such as food colourings, pen inks, or poster paints.

1 Put the large rubber band around the small tray. Push small canes through the band to make two uprights. Fill the tray with water.

2 Tie the string between the uprights. Cut strips of filter paper long enough to reach from the string into the water in the tray.

3 To test a sample, put a blob of it near one end of a strip of filter paper. Peg the strip to the string so that only the very bottom of it hangs in the water.

4 The water will move up the paper very gradually, carrying the colours from your sample with it, but by different amounts. You can tell from this how many colours are mixed together to make up your sample.

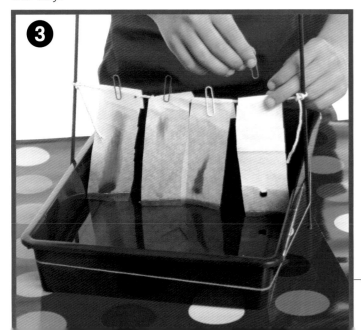

Chemical reactions

In this chemical change, vinegar and baking powder react and give off a gas.

SEE: CHEMICAL CHANGES PAGE 36

You will need

A small strong plastic bottle (fizzy drink bottle)

A balloon

Vinegar

Baking powder

A funnel

1 Pour vinegar into a small bottle until it is about one centimetre deep. Using a funnel, pour two teaspoons of baking powder into the neck of a balloon.

2 Stretch the neck of the balloon over the neck of the bottle, being careful not to let the baking powder out of the balloon.

Now lift up the balloon so that the powder runs into the vinegar. Shake the bottle. What happens?

When two substances react together, they form new chemicals, or products. One of the products here is carbon dioxide, as bubbles of gas, which inflate the balloon.

Baking powder makes cakes and buns rise. It does this because it gives off bubbles of carbon dioxide gas when it heats up. This makes the cake mixture rise. As the cake cooks the carbon dioxide bubbles are trapped in the mixture, making it spongy.

Electrolysis

Electrolysis is a way of separating chemicals from each other, using electricity.

SEE: USING ELECTRICITY PAGE 88

You will need
Pencil leads (as used in propelling pencils)
A 9-volt battery
A length of bell wire
A magnetic compass
A jar
Some salt

1 Use a piece of bell wire about a metre long and bare the ends. Wind the middle part of the wire around a compass about 12 times.

2 Attach one end of the wire to one battery terminal. Wrap the other end around a pencil lead. Do the same with the other battery terminal, another pencil lead and more wire.

3 Fill a jar with tap water and stir in a few

teaspoons of salt. Dip the two pencil leads into the salt water. The compass needle should twitch, showing there is a current in the wire.

Can you see gas bubbles forming on the leads?

One gas, chlorine, has the smell of bleach or swimming pools. It comes from the salt, which is made up of chlorine and sodium, NaCl. Chlorine is given off from one of the electrodes (pencil leads). The gas given off from the other electrode is hydrogen, from water, H_2O.

What does fire do to air?

Fire needs air to burn. More accurately, it needs one of the gases in air – oxygen. This project with a candle shows how much of the air is used before a fire goes out. (Ask an adult to help you with this project.)

WARNING!
Be careful when you strike the match to light the candle, and don't put your fingers too close to the candle flame. Ask an adult to help you.

SEE: ATMOSPHERE
PAGE 152

You will need
A small safety candle
Modelling clay
A shallow dish
A jar
Water

1 Stand the candle in the centre of the dish. To keep it upright, hold it in place with three or four blobs of modelling clay. Make sure the top of the candle is above the level of the edge of the dish.

2 Put three or four small blobs of clay in the dish, each one the same distance from the candle. You are going to rest the neck of the jar on these.

3 Fill the dish with water. Carefully light the candle and then, very quickly, put the jar upside down over it. Balance the jar's rim on the blobs of clay, with the rim under the surface.

4 What happens? Wait until the candle goes out, then look at the jar. What has happened to the water level?

1

3

2

4

Firefighters sometimes spray special foam on to a fire. This stops oxygen reaching the fire, so it can no longer burn.

Water floods into the jar, but only fills part of it. This shows that part of the air has been used in burning. The water has filled the space where it used to be. The part of the air that was used is the gas oxygen. It is used in breathing, as well as burning. The rest of the air that is not used in burning is made up of other gases. Most is nitrogen, which forms four-fifths of normal air.

A weather map on television shows where there is high and low atmospheric pressure. High pressure normally means fine weather. Low pressure suggests rain is on the way.

The air and the weather

Air presses down on the Earth all the time. You cannot feel it, but the pressure is always there. There is more pressure if the air is dry, and less if it is damp and rainy. We use a barometer to measure this air or atmospheric pressure. You can make your own simple barometer and use it to help forecast the weather.

SEE: WEATHER PAGE 154

A barometer measures air pressure in inches and millibars (mb). Air pressure varies from place to place and can change even in a few minutes.

You will need

A jar
A balloon with the neck cut off
A strong rubber band
A drinking straw
A piece of thick cardboard
Tape
Glue (suitable for paper)
A pen

1 Stretch the balloon over the top of the jar. Put the rubber band around the neck of the jar to stop the balloon slipping off.

2 Glue one end of the straw to the balloon. Use tape to fix a piece of cardboard to the jar, behind the straw. The card should be a taller than the jar, wider than the straw, and not touch the straw.

3 Mark the cardboard to show where the end of the straw is pointing. Label the mark with the date. Do this at the same time each day. Why does the straw move? As the surrounding air pressure goes down, the higher air pressure in the jar makes the balloon bulge up, so the straw tilts down.

DID YOU KNOW?

The Namib Desert runs along the coast of Namibia, in southwest Africa. It has a very strange climate. The air is full of moisture, and thick fogs drift in from the sea. Yet it hardly ever rains on land. It is one of the world's driest places.

Hot-air balloon

A hot-air balloon contains air that is warmer and less dense than the air around it. This is why the balloon floats upward.

SEE: HEAT AND COLD PAGE 58

You will need

Plenty of tissue paper
A piece of cardboard about 45 x 5 centimetres
Scissors
Glue
A hairdryer

1 Carefully cut out five squares of tissue paper. Also cut out four pieces that are more wedge-shaped, as shown below. The diagram shows the sizes of these pieces.

2 Glue the pieces together. Make a cross shape, as below, then glue together the cross's edges.

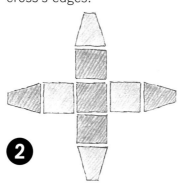

❷

3 Glue a cardboard ring around the balloon's neck.

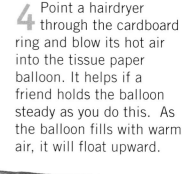

❸

4 Point a hairdryer through the cardboard ring and blow its hot air into the tissue paper balloon. It helps if a friend holds the balloon steady as you do this. As the balloon fills with warm air, it will float upward.

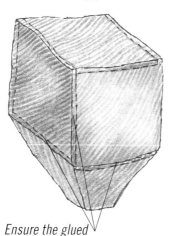

❶

Ensure the glued edges are airtight

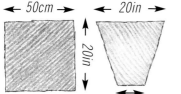

← 50cm →   ← 20in →

20in   20in

10in

Some sheets of tissue paper are 50 centimetres wide when you buy them.

Making the balloon can be tricky. You may need an adult to help. Take your time, to avoid tearing the tissue paper.

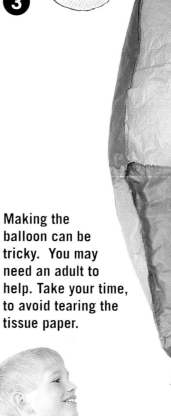

❹

Aircraft wing

This project shows how an aircraft's wing works. The wing is an airfoil, with a special shape. As the wing moves, air passing over the top travels faster than air underneath. This lifts the wing into the air.

SEE: WATER PAGE 32

You will need:

2 drinking straws
Modelling clay
Thin cardboard
Thicker, stiff cardboard
Paper
A hole punch
Scissors, glue

1 Cut a piece of thin card about 25 centimetres long and 10 centimetres wide. Choose one long side to be the front and make a hole near each end. This card is your aircraft wing.

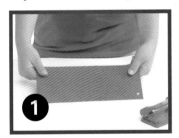

2 Cut out a baseboard from stiff cardboard, about 30 x 10 centimetres. Using modelling clay, fix two straws to the baseboard, so they stick through the holes in the wing.

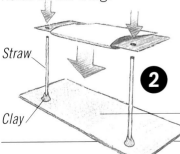

Straw

Clay

Thick cardboard baseboard

3 Aim a hairdryer at the wing from about 1 metre away. Can you get the wing to rise upward? (As you aim the hairdryer, the straws may tilt backward and the baseboard may even slide back. This is because a force called drag pushes the wing backward as air rushes over it.)

4 Now make the flat wing shape into an airfoil. To do this, cut out a piece of paper almost the same size as the cardboard wing, but slightly shorter, and slightly wider.

5 Glue the paper over the wing as the photograph below shows, to make the top curved.

6 Aim the hairdryer at the wing again. What happens? This time, the wing lifts up more easily. Can you see how the shape of an aircraft's wing helps it to fly?

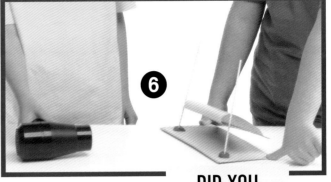

DID YOU KNOW?

The aircraft wing lifts because of the Bernoulli principle. This works with moving gases—and flowing liquids too. Try the project below to find out more about this.

Bernoulli's principle

Moving air or water creates less pressure than still air or water. This was discovered by Swiss scientist Daniel Bernoulli, so the principle or law is named for him.

You will need

Paper
A cardboard tube
Scissors
Tape

SEE: WATER PAGE 32

Air moving fast between the strips exerts less pressure than normal, still air. So by blowing sharply down the tube, the strips are pushed together.

1 Cut two strips of paper 20 x 3 centimetres.

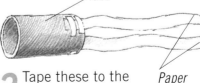

Tube

Paper strips

2 Tape these to the outside of a short cardboard tube.

3 Blow sharply down the tube. What happens?

Autogyro

An autogyro is an aircraft with an unpowered rotor on top. The rotor spins as air passes over it and helps to lift the craft.

SEE: ATMOSPHERE PAGE 152

You will need

Thin cardboard or stiff paper
Pencil
Ruler
Scissors
2 paperclips

1 Cut a piece of cardboard 40 by 3 centimetres. Fold it in half. Lay it flat and fold one end over, 10 centimetres from the end. Make the fold at a slight angle as in the picture.

2 Turn the cardboard over and fold the other end in the same way.

3 Unfold the ends to make two wings. Fix two paperclips to the bottom of your autogyro.

4 Drop your autogyro from a high place. Watch it twirl as it falls. The air pushes against the angled blades and makes them spin.

What a drag!

Anything that moves through air has to push the air in front of it out of the way. This creates a force called air resistance–friction or drag–that tries to slow down the object. Some shapes let air pass around them more easily than others. These sleek, streamlined shapes create less drag.

SEE: FRICTION PAGE 70

You will need

Thin cardboard
Stiff cardboard
Tape
Scissors

1 Make three cardboard shapes, each 10 centimetres high and 5 centimetres across. Make one a rectangle (box), another a tube and the third a fish shape. Tape each end-on, to a square of thick card, as shown. Put the shapes in a line. Using a hairdryer on a low setting, point it at the shapes.

2 Start with the dryer about one metre away. Gradually bring it closer. Which shape moves most? This is the

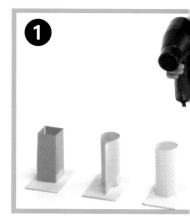

one with the most air resistance, and it soon topples over or blows away! Which shape has the least air resistance, creates the least drag, and stays standing longest?

This is a real-life autogyro. It looks like a helicopter, but it works in a different way. Instead of having a motor to turn the big rotor on top, the autogyro has a propeller at the back to push it along. It is this forward movement that makes the rotors turn.

Wind generator

A wind generator uses the wind to turn its blades or sails and drive a generator, to make electricity. Make blades that also turn in the wind, like those of a wind generator.

SEE: ENERGY FOR THE WORLD PAGE 72

You will need

A large plastic drinks bottle
A piece of thin garden cane
Round-headed map pins
A stapler
Scissors
Tape

1 Ask an adult to help you cut the top and bottom off the bottle to make a tube. Take care when you are cutting plastic as the edges can be sharp. Cut the tube in half

lengthwise to make two curved C-shaped vanes.

2 Overlap the edges of the vanes by 7-8 centimetres to make an S-shape. Staple them together along the edges only, as shown in the photographs. Leave an open slot along the middle of the overlap.

3 Slide the garden cane along the slot. Tape it in place at each end.

4 Put a round-headed map pin in each end of the cane. Now rest the cane on one hand or finger so that it is vertical (upright). Hold it gently in place with your other hand, as the picture shows. If you take your generator to a windy place and hold it in this way, you will see how it spins around. It may even spin around if you blow gently on it.

WARNING!
Cutting plastic can be difficult. Ask an adult to make the first cut, with a craft knife or safe scissors. Be very careful of the cut edges—it's safest to cover them with tape.

This windmill is not really a mill. The wind turns the blades, or sails, which work a pump that stops the field from flooding.

Vanishing water

Rain puddles gradually dry up after the rain stops. The water seems to disappear. In fact, it turns into invisible water vapour.

SEE: WATER PAGE 32, DISSOLVING PAGE 34

You will need

2 saucers of water

1 Put a saucer in a warm place and pour a little water into it. Put another saucer in a cool place, with the same amount of water in it. What happens?

2 When water is warmed, it evaporates. It turns into a gas, water vapour, and floats away in the air. This happens faster in a hotter place.

What happens when water freezes?

Most things get smaller, or contract, when they change from liquid to solid. But not water.

SEE: SOLIDS, LIQUIDS AND GASES PAGE 26

You will need

A yogurt pot

A saucer

A jug of water

1 Fill up the yogurt pot to the brim with water. Carefully put it on the saucer in the freezer, where it will not spill, overnight.

2 The next day, the water will be frozen into solid ice. Does the ice take up more or less room than the original liquid water? As it became frozen, it got bigger or expanded. The weight is the same, so ice is less dense than water.

Water gets bigger, or expands, when it freezes. This makes rocks crack and fall apart. These jagged mountaintops were formed by rain seeping into the rocks, then expanding and making the rocks break. This process is called erosion by frost-wedging.

❶

Water in the air

There is always water vapour in the air. You can make it condense, or change back into water.

SEE: RIVERS AND LAKES PAGE 158

You will need

A glass

Ice-cold water

1 Pour the iced water into the glass. Watch the outside of the glass. Can you see a cloudy film or drops of water on the glass? Water vapour from the air is condensing and becoming liquid water.

Invisible water vapour in the air is a gas. It turns back into a liquid when the air is cooled. The icy water cools the air around the glass, and the water vapour condenses.

DID YOU KNOW?

As the Earth's climate gets hotter, with global warming, ice in the Arctic and Antarctic may start to melt. Sea levels will rise, and many low-lying places could be flooded.

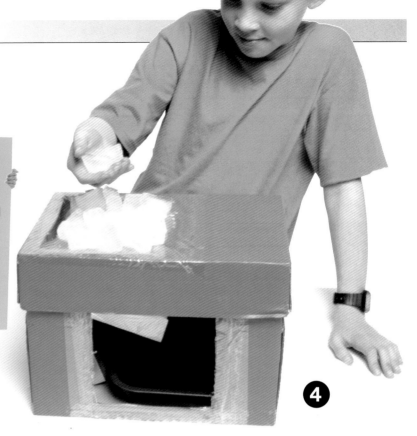

4

Rain and rivers

This project shows how water falls from the sky as rain, then returns to the air.

SEE: ATMOSPHERE PAGE 152

You will need

A large cardboard box with a removable lid

A deep roasting tray or cake pan that fits in the box

A small box or other support, taller than the tray

Scissors

Ice cubes

A piece of stiff cardboard about 15 centimetres across

Cling film, tape

Hot water

1 Cut a hole about 10 centimetres across at one end of the box lid. Use tape to fix the film over it. Cut a window hole in the side of the box. Tape over this, too.

2 Put the roasting tray in the box, at the other end from the lid hole.

3 Cover the cardboard with sandwich film. Fold up its sides to make a U-shaped channel. Using the small box as a support, tape the channel so that it slopes down toward the tray. Ask an adult to fill the tray with hot water.

4 Put the lid on the box and cover the cling film on the lid with ice. Water vapour from the hot water condenses on the film under the ice. This is how clouds form. It drips, like rain, into the channel. Then it flows, like a river, into the tray–the sea.

WARNING!

Take care! You have to use hot water for this—so get an adult to help you. The hotter the water, the better the project will work.

3

Water pressure fountain

Water is heavy and presses on everything in and around it. This is water pressure.

SEE: ENERGY PAGE 46, FORCES PAGE 52

You will need

A plastic drinks bottle
A craft knife
A large tray, basin, or sink
Pitchers of water

1 **Ask an adult** to help you cut a small hole in the bottle, using the craft knife. It should be about 10 centimetres from the base of the bottle.

2 Put the bottle in the large tray or basin. Fill it with water. The water escapes from the bottle as a sideways fountain. The more water in the bottle, the more powerful the fountain. This happens because water presses in all directions and forces itself out through the hole. The more water there is in the bottle, above the level of the hole, the greater the pressure. So the jet of water spurts further.

Simple siphon

How can you get water from one bowl to another, without moving either bowl?

SEE: WATER PAGE 32

You will need

2 bowls, clean tap water
Clean thin plastic tubing
A box
Food colouring

1 Fill a bowl with water and put it on top of the box. Add some drops of food colouring to the water to see it more easily.

2 Put the empty bowl on the table next to the box. Put one end of the tubing into the coloured water in the upper bowl.

3 Suck the free end of the tube so that water travels along it, almost to your mouth. Take the end of the tube out of your mouth and put your finger over it. Lower this end into the empty bowl and take your finger away. Water flows from the upper to the lower bowl. This is called a siphon.

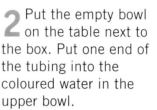

Floating and sinking

Density is the weight of an object for its volume. Floating or sinking depend on it.

SEE: MEASURING FORCES PAGE 54

You will need

Corks

Marbles

Pieces of wood and plastic

Coins

Balls filled with air, such as table tennis balls

A bowl of water

1 Test different objects to see how well they float. Put each one into the bowl of water. Light objects float. Heavy ones sink.

2 Push a table tennis ball under the water. Feel the water pushing upward. This upward force is called "upthrust". If it is greater than the weight of the object, the object floats.

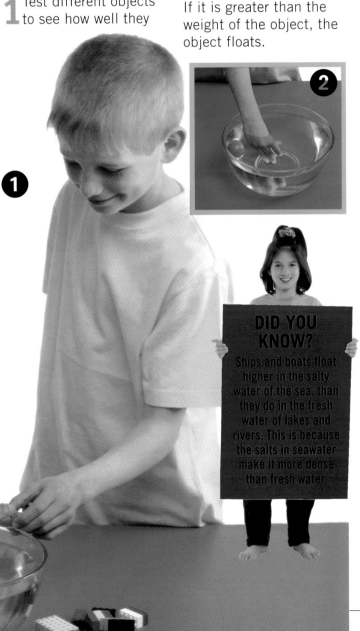

DID YOU KNOW?

Ships and boats float higher in the salty water of the sea, than they do in the fresh water of lakes and rivers. This is because the salts in seawater make it more dense than fresh water.

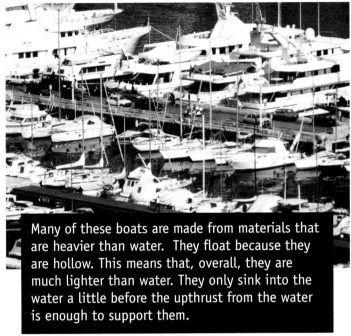

Many of these boats are made from materials that are heavier than water. They float because they are hollow. This means that, overall, they are much lighter than water. They only sink into the water a little before the upthrust from the water is enough to support them.

Model boats

Boats are heavy, but they float because they are hollow and contain very light air.

SEE: WATER PAGE 32, OCEANS PAGE 162

You will need

Bowl of water

Modelling clay

1 Put a blob of the clay in a bowl of water. It sinks—it is denser than water.

2 Now make the blob into a hollow boat shape. Can you make it float? The weight of the clay plus the air in it make the whole boat shape less dense than water.

Capillary action

Water molecules pull themselves into tiny spaces and make water creep or flow.

SEE: LIQUIDS PAGE 26

You will need

Water and food colouring
Clear plastic rulers
Blotting paper
Tape, scissors

Pond skaters can run across the pond without falling through the surface of the water. The weight of their light bodies is spread between the middle and back legs and is not enough to break the surface tension of the water.

Surface tension

Molecules of water are strongly attracted to each other. This creates surface tension, which is like a stretchy skin on water.

SEE: MOLECULES PAGE 22, WATER PAGE 32

You will need

Some paperclips
A small bowl of water

1 Put a paperclip on the tip of your finger and place it very carefully on top of the water. Can you get the paperclip to rest on the surface of the water and not sink?

2 Look carefully at the water around the clip. See how the water surface dips down around the clip.

1 Put some water with food colouring into a glass. Look through the glass from the side. Can you see how the water rises slightly up the sides of the glass? This is called the meniscus.

2 Use one ruler to measure the depth of the water.

3 Tape a strip of blotting paper to one ruler about 1 centimetre above where the water reached. Tape the two rulers together, sandwiching the blotting paper between them. Put the rulers in the water. Hold them straight, so the blotting paper does not touch the water.

4 The water should rise up between the rulers and reach the blotting paper. This "creeping" of a liquid along a narrow space is called capillary action. Water molecules cling to the ruler, and to each other, rising upward between the rulers–then through the blotting paper's tiny fibres.

Waterwheel

Make a water turbine–as used in giant hydroelectric power stations!

SEE: ENERGY FOR THE WORLD PAGE 72

You will need

6 screw-type plastic bottle tops

Some bendy plastic, like a margarine container

Waterproof glue, scissors

Stiff wire (as from a coat hanger)

Plastic bottle used for the fountain project (page 222)

Two thick rubber bands or some strong tape such as insulating tape

1 Cut two disks of plastic, both 7.5 centimetres across. Make a small hole in the middle of each. **Ask an adult to help with this.**

3 Push the wire through the wheel and bend it as the diagram shows.

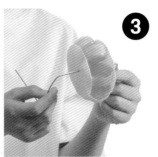

3

4

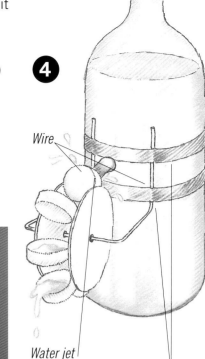

Wire

Water jet

Rubber bands or tape

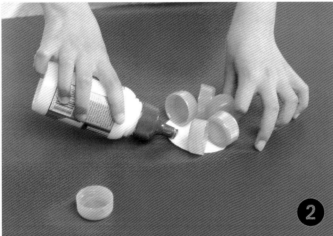

2

2 Glue the bottle tops around the edge of one disk. Fix them so that they will act as cups to catch the water as the wheel turns. Glue the other disk on top.

4 Fix the wheel to the bottle, using either the rubber bands or tape, or both.

5 Fill the bottle with water. As water flows out of the hole, it will turn the wheel.

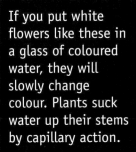

If you put white flowers like these in a glass of coloured water, they will slowly change colour. Plants suck water up their stems by capillary action.

DID YOU KNOW?

Flowers and plants give off water vapour into the air. They suck up more water through their roots and stems, to replace it. This water flow is called transpiration.

Spreading vibrations

Sound makes things vibrate. This project shows the vibrations.

SEE: SOUND WAVES PAGE 112

You will need
A balloon
Strong cardboard tube about 10 centimetres long
A rubber band
Sugar or salt
Scissors

1 Cut the neck off the balloon. Stretch the balloon over the tube end to make a tight drum.

2 Put the rubber band around the tube to keep the balloon in place. Sprinkle a few grains of salt or sugar on the balloon. With your mouth near the balloon, hum or sing a low note. The grains should jump about. If they don't, try singing louder, or try different notes, higher or lower

3 Try other noises too, such as beating a drum. Which sounds make the grains jump about the most?

DID YOU KNOW?
Sound travels at different speeds through different substances, or media. It goes more than ten times faster through wood than through air.

Waves in a tray

Sound travels as waves, similar to waves of water.

SEE: ABOUT WAVES PAGE 110

You will need
A large high-sided tray
Water

1 Carefully fill the tray with water until the surface is about a centimetre from the top.

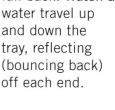

2 Put a finger tip into the water in the centre of the tray and let the water settle. Now pull your finger out quickly and watch how waves spread out in a circle–like sound waves in air.

3 Let the water settle again. When it is still, lift one end of the tray very slightly, and let it fall back. Watch as waves of water travel up and down the tray, reflecting (bouncing back) off each end.

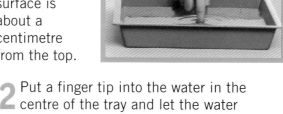

Two-ear hearing

Having two ears helps to locate the direction of a sound.

SEE: SOFT AND LOUD
PAGE 116

You will need
A blindfold
Several friends

1 Listening to sounds with two ears is called stereo (stereophonic) hearing. Ask your friends to stand around you in a circle, about 3 metres away from you. Put on the blindfold.

2 Cover one ear, so that you can only hear with the other. Ask your friends to clap lightly, each in turn.

3 Try pointing to where each clapping comes from. Your friends can move around the circle to confuse you!

4 Try again, but leave both ears uncovered. You should be able to point much more accurately each time you hear a clap.

Bats send out high-pitched sounds as they fly in the dark. The echoes help them to detect objects to avoid or insects to eat.

Waves in the sea travel along the surface of the water in a rippling up-and-down movement, until they crash on the shore. Sound also travels in waves, though you cannot see them. A wave is a way of carrying energy, such as sound or light, from one place to another.

Sound from a record

Make a simple vinyl record player to reproduce sounds from the wavy groove.

SEE: STORING SOUNDS PAGE 120

You will need

An unwanted vinyl record
Paper
Stiff cardboard
Round-headed map pins
Drawing pins
Sheet of thick cardboard
Scissors
Glue, tape

1 Tape a drawing pin point-down into the record's central hole, and another pin point-up near it.

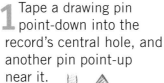
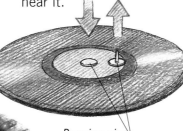
Drawing pins

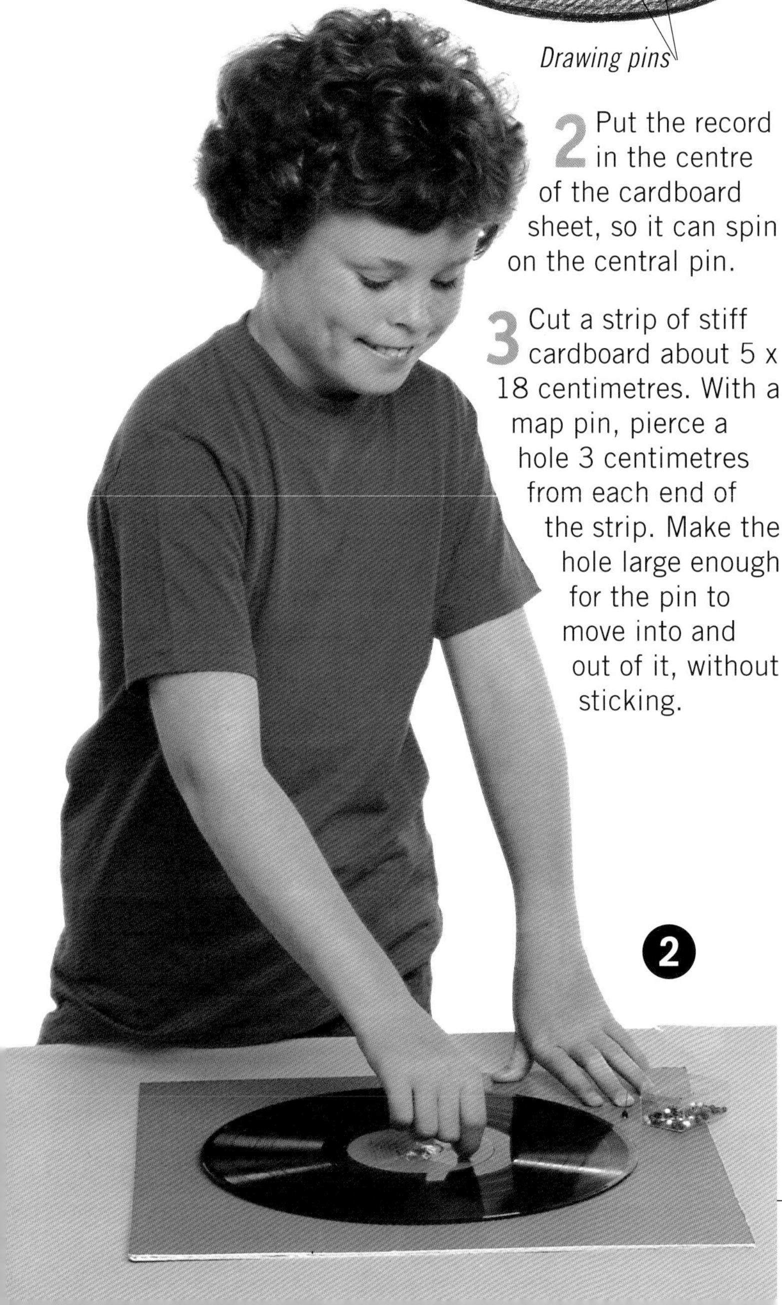

2 Put the record in the centre of the cardboard sheet, so it can spin on the central pin.

3 Cut a strip of stiff cardboard about 5 x 18 centimetres. With a map pin, pierce a hole 3 centimetres from each end of the strip. Make the hole large enough for the pin to move into and out of it, without sticking.

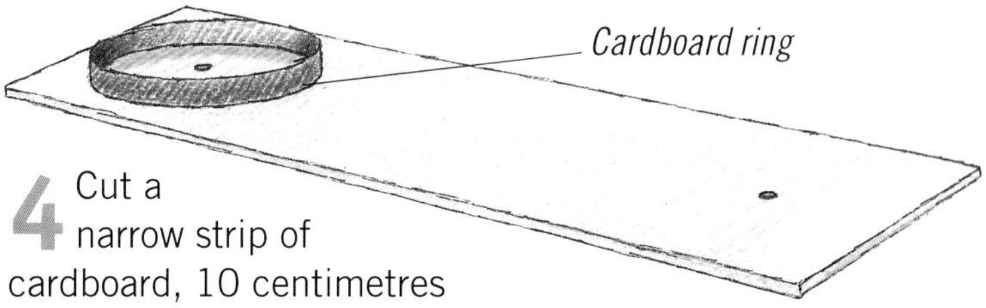

4 Cut a narrow strip of cardboard, 10 centimetres long. Glue it on its edge around one hole to make a ring, as shown.

Cardboard ring

5 Cut a paper disk large enough to cover the cardboard ring. Glue the head of a map pin to its centre, as shown below. When dry, glue the disk to the ring so that the pin sticks through the hole in the cardboard strip. This is the playing needle.

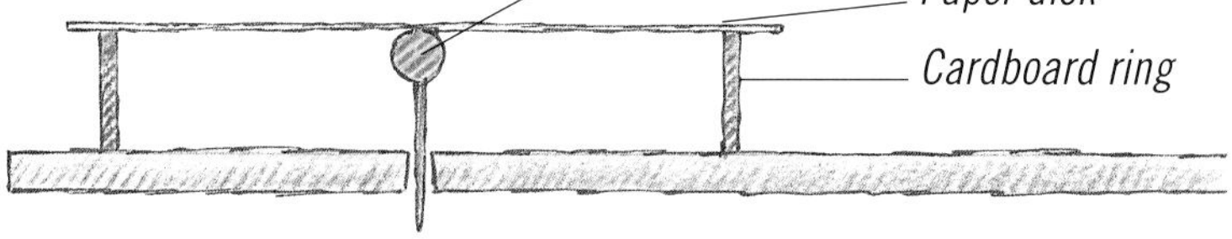

6 Make a paper cone from a sheet of paper, as shown on the right. The narrow end of the cone must fit over the cardboard ring. Tape it in place.

7 Stick a map pin onto the sheet of thick cardboard, about 2 centimetres beyond the edge of the record, with the point sticking upward.

8 Place the cardboard strip so that the playing needle is on the outer edge of the record and the other hole in the cardboard strip is over this pin. Use the upside-down drawing pin near the centre of the record as a handle to turn it. Listen carefully, and you will hear sounds!

Round headed map pin
Paper disk
Cardboard ring

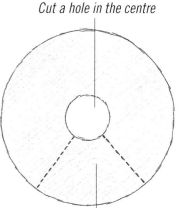

Cut a hole in the centre

Cut out this section

String instrument

The sounds of this instrument come from its shaking string.

SEE: HIGH, LOW
SOUNDS PAGE 114

You will need

A large cardboard box
A long, large rubber band
Pens
Tape
A craft knife

1 Ask an adult to cut a large hole in one end of the top of the box.

2 Wrap the band over the hole and around the box. Tape pens under it near each end of the top.

3 Pluck the band and listen to the note. Put a thicker pen under the band as shown, and try again. The note is higher because the part of the band that vibrates is shorter and so moves faster.

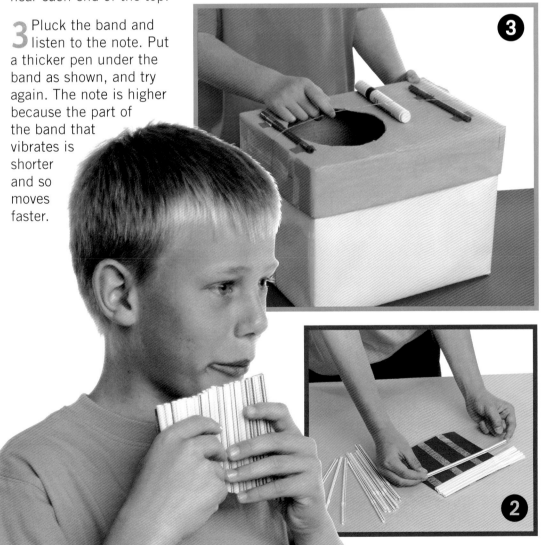

As the strings of a guitar vibrate, they make the air and guitar body near them vibrate, causing sounds. The thicker strings vibrate more slowly than the thinner ones, making deeper notes.

Wind instrument

The sounds come from air vibrating inside tubes.

SEE: MAKING
SOUNDS PAGE 118

You will need

About 20 drinking straws
Stiff cardboard
Scissors
Double-sided tape

1 Cut a piece of card 15 x 15 centimetres. Stick strips of double-sided tape to it.

2 Stick 20 straws to the tape on the cardboard, in a row. Trim bases from long to short, as shown.

3 Hold the top of a straw near your bottom lip and blow across it. A note! Longer straws have deeper notes.

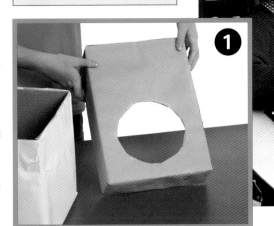

Shadow-clock sundial

Before clocks, people kept time by the moving shadow made by the Sun on a dial.

SEE: EARTH IN SPACE PAGE 174

You will need

Some stiff cardboard
Scissors
A geographic atlas
A protractor, tape
A pair of compasses–for drawing circles
A magnetic compass

1 Cut two rectangles of thick card about 15 x 30 centimetres.

2 In an atlas, look up the latitude where you live. Lines of latitude, in degrees (°), go across the map.

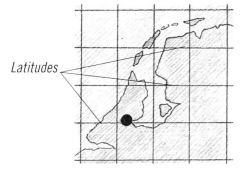

Latitudes

3 Measure an angle equal to this latitude, with the protractor. Mark it on the bottom corner of the card. Cut along the line.

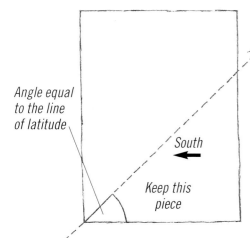

Angle equal to the line of latitude

South

Keep this piece

4 Draw a half-circle on the other card, with its centre halfway along one of the long edges.

5 Fix the cardboard triangle to this base. Use small pieces of cardboard and tape to hold it upright.

6 On a sunny day, take your sundial outside. Using the magnetic compass, position it so the lower end of the triangle points south. Then, every hour, make a mark on the card to show where the shadow of the triangle falls across the semicircle on the base. Label each mark with the time in hours.

Now you can use your sundial to tell the time. On a sunny day, with the triangle pointing south, the shadow shows the hour.

Some sundials were beautifully made, and are valuable as sculptures and works of art. One problem is that the times become less accurate as the seasons change. Many sundials have several sets of numbers for different times of year.

Reflecting light

This project shows how light reflects, or bounces back, from a mirror or similar smooth, shiny surface.

SEE: BOUNCING LIGHT PAGE 128

You will need

Cardboard
A flashlight
A small mirror
Scissors
Modelling clay

1 Cut a piece of cardboard 15 x 10 centimetres. Cut a narrow slot 5 centimetres long in one longer edge.

2 Stand it upright using modelling clay.

4 Reflect the beam with the mirror. Swivel it from side to side and the direction of the beam changes. But the angles at which the beam hits the mirror, then leaves it, are the same as each other.

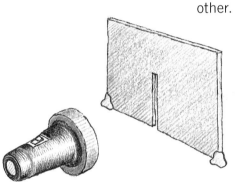

3 In a darkened room, shine a flashlight through the slot to make a narrow beam of light that shows on the tabletop.

Optical fibres

Optical fibres carry flashes of laser light, even around corners. A jet of water works in a similar way and shows the principle.

SEE: LASER LIGHT PAGE 134

You will need

A plastic drinks bottle
A craft knife
A flashlight

1 Ask an adult to cut a hole in the plastic bottle, as for the fountain project on page 222.

2 Fill the bottle with water, keeping your finger over the hole. Shine a flashlight through the bottle, opposite the hole.

3 Move your finger. The beam shines along the watery spout, even as it curves down.

Water spout

How deep?

When light passes from air into water, it is refracted (it changes direction).

SEE: BENDING LIGHT
PAGE 128

You will need

A glass tumbler of water
A coin

1 Put a coin in the bottom of the tumbler.

2 Look down through the water. Move your finger up and down outside the tumbler until it seems to be level with the coin. The look from the side. Is it level with the coin? In fact, the

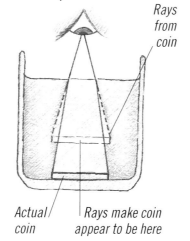

Rays from coin

Actual coin

Rays make coin appear to be here

coin will seem to be less deep in the water than it really is.

Camera in a box

Try making a camera obscura–a camera with no film. It collects light from a scene and creates an image on a screen.

SEE: DETECTING LIGHT PAGE 131

You will need

A small cardboard box
A magnifying glass
Tracing paper
Scissors, tape

1 First, you need to find the focal length of the lens in your magnifying glass. In a big room, hold the lens about 3 centimetres from a window.

2 Move your hand until the lens makes a clear image of the scene outside on your palm. The distance between the lens and the palm of your hand is the focal length of the lens.

3 The cardboard box should be a few inches longer than the focal length of the lens.

Cut around the centre of the box to make two halves.

3 Cut along the edges of one side so that it slides into the other half. Fix the new edges together with tape, as below.

4 Cut a large hole in the end of the other box half. Cover it with tracing paper.

Hole in end of box

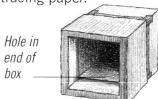

Slits along edges

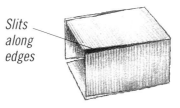

Taped end of box half

One half of box slides into other half

5 Cut a hole slightly smaller than the magnifying glass in the end of the other box half. Tape the magnifying glass into it.

6 Aim the camera at a bright object. Move the two box halves together or apart until you get a clear image of the object on the tracing paper screen. This is called focusing the camera.

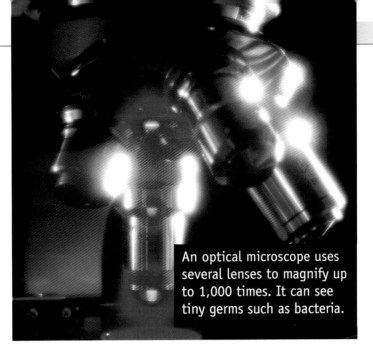

An optical microscope uses several lenses to magnify up to 1,000 times. It can see tiny germs such as bacteria.

Water-drop microscope

Lenses make objects look bigger or nearer than they really are. You can make a simple microscope from a drop of water!

SEE: USING LIGHT PAGE 132

You will need

A plastic drinks bottle
A small box, such as a paper tissues box
A hole punch
Scissors, tape
Water

1 Ask an adult to help you cut a narrow strip of thin plastic, about 10 x 3 centimetres, from the bottle. Using a hole punch, make a hole close to one end of the strip. Next, tape the strip firmly to a small box so that the end with the hole is hanging over the side of the box.

2 Use your finger to put a drop or blob of water into the hole. It should form a curved lens shape in the hole.

3 To use the microscope, put your eye close to the water lens. Hold an object under it. Move the object up and down (focusing) until you can see the object clearly.

Making a spectrum

Light seems colourless or white, but it is really a mixture of colours. You can separate the colours to form a spectrum.

SEE: LIGHT PAGE 124

You will need

A shallow roasting tray
or cake tray
White cardboard, scissors
A small mirror
Scissors

1 Carefully cut a piece of cardboard about 20 x 15 centimetres. Cut a narrow slot in the top of the cardboard, as shown on the right.

2 Fill the shallow tray with water. Stand the tray in direct sunlight. Prop up the cardboard against it, so that light shines through the slot into the water.

3 Hold the mirror at an angle in the water. Move the mirror until a spectrum, like a rainbow, appears opposite, on the card below the slot. The meniscus (curved water surface) against the mirror acts as a lens to split white light into its colours.

Sunlight

Spectrum

Slot

Mirror

When sunlight shines through drops of rain water, the drops work as prisms and split the light to form a spectrum – the rainbow.

See double

An image of what we see forms in our eyes. But the eye goes on seeing an image for a short time after it has gone. This is the after-image effect.

SEE: DETECTING LIGHT PAGE 130

You will need

A large paperclip
Cardboard, pens, or pencils
Tracing paper
Scissors
Glue

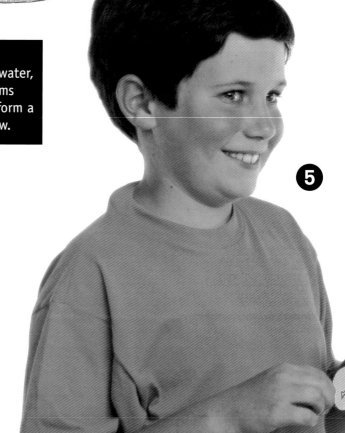

5

1 Draw a picture. It must fit into a circle about 7 centimetres across–and be in two parts, one to go on top of the other. You could draw a bird and a cage, a head and a hat, or a fish and a bowl.

2 Cut two cardboard circles the same size. Trace one part of the picture onto one circle, and the other half onto the other.

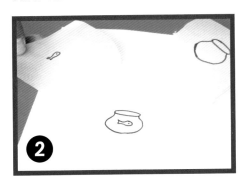

3 Unbend a paperclip to make a straight piece of wire.

4 Glue the two cardboard circles back to back, pictures the same way up and facing outward, the wire trapped between them.

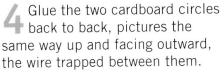

Card spins

Paperclip

5 Hold each end of the wire between a thumb and finger. Spin it around fast to twirl the cards. Do the two parts of your picture merge and make one picture? The image of one part of the picture lingers in your eye. As the card twirls, this *after-image* joins with the other part so that you see just one picture.

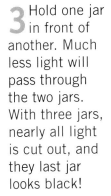

Colour filters

A colour filter lets some colours of light through, and not others. This project shows how they work.

SEE: LIGHT PAGE 124, THE EMS PAGE 136

You will need

3 jars
Red, green, and blue food colourings

1 Fill the three jars with water. Add about six drops of food colouring to each jar.

2 Put the jars near a window so light comes through. The coloured water acts as a filter, cutting out all the colours of white light except the colour of the water. For example, red water cuts out all colours except red, which passes through.

3 Hold one jar in front of another. Much less light will pass through the two jars. With three jars, nearly all light is cut out, and they last jar looks black!

DID YOU KNOW?

Stare at a patch of bright red or green for 30 seconds, then close your eyes. You still see a patch of colour, but it is the opposite or complementary colour.

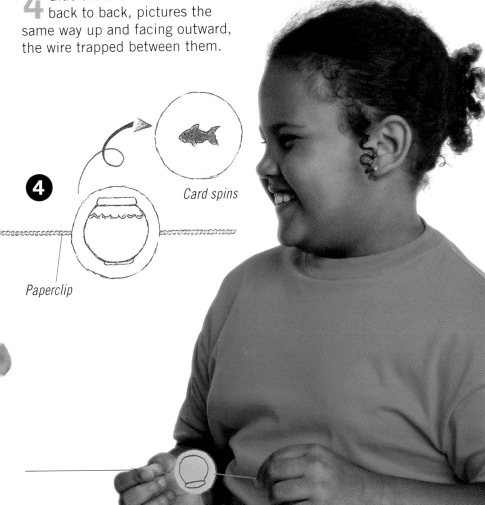

Changes of energy

Energy makes things happen. There are many different kinds of energy, and one kind can change or convert to another. This project shows some types of energy conversion–simply by lifting up a book and then dropping it on the floor!

SEE: CONVERTING ENERGY PAGE 48

You will need

An old book

1 Make sure the book is unwanted, because you will have to drop it, and it might get damaged!

2 Start by putting the book on the floor. Then lift it slowly to shoulder height. As you do this, you are giving the book potential energy because you are lifting it up against the force of gravity, which is pulling it downward. The energy to make it fall is there, but it is not being used. Potential means something that has not happened, but could. The energy used to raise the book is made by chemicals inside your body working your muscles.

3 Now drop the book. The potential energy of book changes to movement energy as the book falls. The energy of movement or motion is called kinetic energy.

4 Where does the energy go to when the book hits the floor? When it does so, most of the potential energy you gave it has turned into movement energy. A small amount has been lost as heat as it falls, due to air resistance or friction.

5 When the book hits the floor, the rest of its energy changes into heat and also into sound energy, which you hear as a thud. In the whole process of picking up the book and dropping it, no energy is lost–only converted into other forms.

Convected heat

Heat energy can travel from place to place in moving air currents. This is convection.

SEE: HEAT AND COLD PAGE 58

You will need

A mug and warm water
Cardboard
Modelling clay
A long pin
Tape, scissors

1 Cut a triangle of cardboard slightly wider than the mug you are going to use in this project.

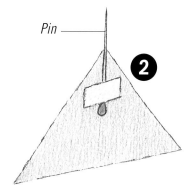

2 Tape the pin to the top corner so that it points upward.

3 Fill the mug with warm water. Rest the triangle on the top of the mug and fix it in place with modelling clay.

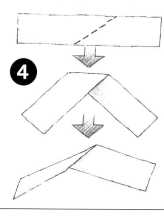

4 Cut a long paper strip. Fold it at an angle to make an L shape. Open it again to make a propeller.

5 Balance your propeller on top of the pin. See how it spins in the rising warm air currents from the mug below.

In hot, sunny places, the houses are often painted white. This helps to reflect the heat of the Sun and keep the houses cool.

Radiated heat

The Sun's heat and light reach us by radiation. Colour affects how objects absorb radiation.

SEE: BEYOND LIGHT PAGE 136

You will need
White and black cardboard
A box, scissors

1 Cut equal-sized pieces of white and black cardboard.

2 On a sunny day, lean both pieces against a box, so that they directly face the Sun. After five minutes, put your hand on each piece. Which feels warmer?

Conducted heat

Heat can travel through objects by thermal conduction. Find out which substances are good thermal conductors.

SEE: METALS PAGE 40, COMPOSITES PAGE 42

You will need
Long, slim items such as cutlery or strips made of different substances—metal, wood, porcelain, plastic
A mug
Hot water
Butter or margarine
Plastic beads

1 Stand the various pieces of cutlery or similar items in the empty mug. Smear blobs of butter on their upper ends. Stick a small bead onto each blob.

2 Ask an adult to pour hot water carefully into the mug. Watch the butter and beads. As each substance conducts the heat upward, its butter melts and the bead falls off. The first bead to fall shows which substance is the best thermal conductor.

The effects of forces

Find out what happens when you apply forces in different directions and places.

SEE: FORCES PAGE 52

You will need
A large sponge

1 Put the sponge on a smooth tabletop. Use a finger to push it in the middle of one side. Does it slide in a straight line?

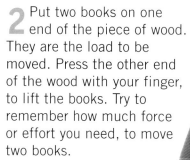

2 Now push the end of one side of the sponge. What happens? With the other hand, push on the other side of the sponge. Can you make the sponge spin on the spot?

3 Press opposite sides of the sponge at the same time. It does not slide along because the two forces cancel each other out–but they squash it!

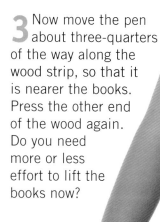

Levers

Levers are simple machines that are used in hundreds of devices and gadgets.

SEE: SIMPLE MACHINES PAGE 62

You will need
A piece of wood about as wide as a ruler, but thicker, and 50 centimetres long
Some small books
A thick pen

1 Put the pen on a flat surface. Lay the strip of wood on top of it, with the middle of the strip over the pen. The pen is now the pivot, or fulcrum. If you apply a force to one end of the wood, it will move or tilt at the pivot.

2 Put two books on one end of the piece of wood. They are the load to be moved. Press the other end of the wood with your finger, to lift the books. Try to remember how much force or effort you need, to move two books.

3 Now move the pen about three-quarters of the way along the wood strip, so that it is nearer the books. Press the other end of the wood again. Do you need more or less effort to lift the books now?

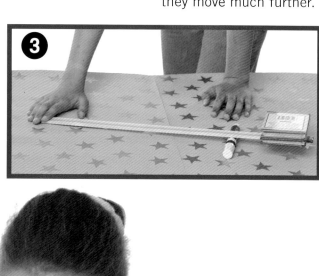

4 Move the pen to about three-quarters of the way along the wood, towards your hand. Press again. You need much more effort to raise the books. But see how they move much further.

Pen is halfway between effort and load

High and low pressure

The pressure produced by a force depends on the area it presses on. Try pushing different objects into clay. The same push exerts more or less pressure, depending on the shape of the object.

SEE: FORCES PAGE 124, GRAVITY PAGE 56

You will need
Modelling clay
Different shaped objects

1 Shape blobs of the clay into thick, flat sheets.

2 Press different objects into the surface of the clay. Try to use the same force each time. Objects with sharp edges sink in most easily. The force of your push is concentrated into a smaller area, creating a greater pressure.

Each swing of the pendulum in this grandfather clock takes the same time. The pendulum keeps the clock running accurately

Pendulum swings

Investigate how to make a pendulum and how it swings from side to side.

SEE: GRAVITY PAGE 56, EARTH PAGE 142

You will need
A piece of string at least 1 metre long
Modelling clay, tape
A watch with seconds

DID YOU KNOW?
The scientist Galileo studied pendulums. In church, when he was bored, he watched candle-holders swinging on long ropes from the ceiling.

1 Tie a blob of modelling clay to the string. Tape the other end of the string to a support, such as the top of a door frame, so the weight can swing freely.

2 As this pendulum moves, gravity pulls it downward. When it reaches the bottom of its swing and starts going up again under its own momentum, gravity slows it down until it stops and swings back.

3 Swing the pendulum so that each swing is quite big. Time how long ten swings take. Then time ten smaller swings. Is there any difference between the times?

4 Add some more clay to make the weight heavier. Time the swings again. Can you see why pendulums are used to control the speed of some kinds of clock?

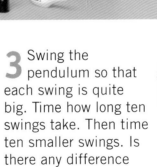

Conduct or insulate?

Materials that electricity can pass through are called electrical conductors. Materials it cannot pass through are electrical insulators. This is how you find out if a material is a conductor or not.

SEE: FLOWING ELECTRICITY PAGE 82

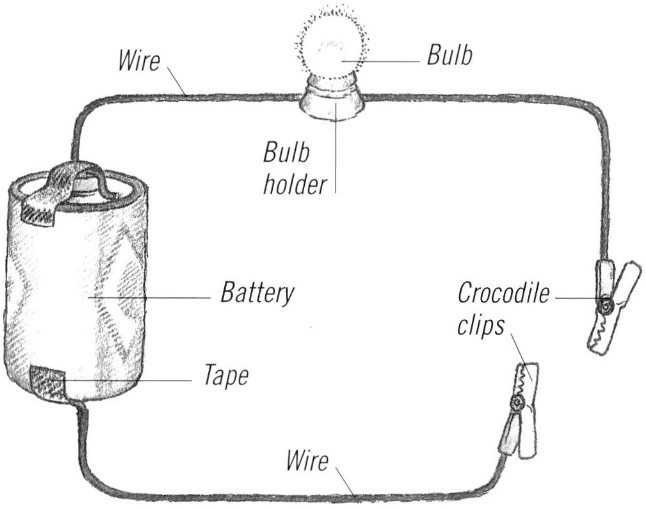

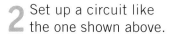

Wire — Bulb

Bulb holder

Battery

Crocodile clips

Tape

Wire

You will need

A battery (for a torch or a radio)
Bell wire (thin, insulated wire)
Scissors

Tape
A bulb and a bulb holder
Crocodile clips
Selection of objects and materials to test

1 Cut three pieces of wire about 50 centimetres long. Ask an adult to help you strip the plastic covering off the ends of each piece, so that the wires are bare. Put the bulb in the bulb holder.

2 Set up a circuit like the one shown above.

3 Put different objects or materials between the crocodile clips. What happens each time?

4 If the material is a conductor, it completes the circuit. The bulb lights up. If it's an insulator, the bulb stays out.

5 Try the "lead" or graphite in a pencil. Does the bulb light up, but only dimly?

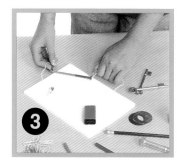
3

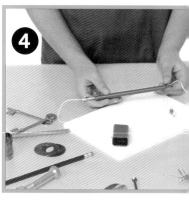
4

2

WARNING!
Take care! You need to use a sharp knife or the blade of a pair of scissors to cut the plastic coating away from the ends of the bell wire. Get an adult to help you.

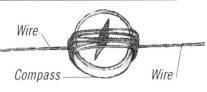

Wire

Compass   Wire

Static electricity

Rubbing two different insulating materials together may produce electrical charges on them—static electricity. This charge can pick up tiny items, almost like a magnet.

SEE: STATIC ELECTRICITY PAGE 80

You will need
A plastic rubbish bag
A soft cloth
Scrap paper, scissors

1 Tear a piece of scrap paper into tiny bits less than 5 millimetres across. Scatter the bits on a table.

2 Cut a piece of plastic dustbin bag about the size of this page. Lay it on the table and rub it hard, many times, with the cloth. This gives the plastic a static charge, which means it has tiny electrical charges on its surface.

3 Carefully lift the plastic and move it near to the scraps of paper. What happens?

Lightning flashes in the night sky. Lightning happens when static electricity, or electric charge, jumps from a cloud to the ground. The static is made when water droplets and ice crystals rub against each other inside the cloud.

Making a battery

Certain chemicals together produce electricity.

SEE: ELECTRICAL BATTERIES PAGE 84

You will need
Copper coins, zinc-coated nails, cooking foil
Crocodile clips
Bell wire (thin, insulated wire), scissors
Magnetic compass
Salt, water, jar

1 Cut a piece of bell wire about a metre long. With adult help, strip off the ends of the plastic coating on the wires.

2 Wrap the middle part of the wire around the compass about 12 times. Connect a crocodile clip to each end of the wire.

3 Fill a jar with warm water. Stir in salt until no more will dissolve.

4 Put a copper coin into one of the crocodile clips and a piece of aluminum foil or a zinc-coated (galvanized) nail into the other one.

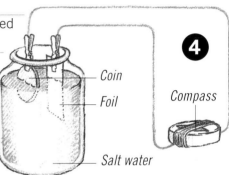

Coin

Foil

Compass

Salt water

5 Lower the clips into the salt water. If the needle twitches, your battery is making an electric current. It flows through the wire and makes a magnetic field.

Magnetic fields

A magnetic field is the area around a magnet where it pulls iron-containing objects toward itself. The pull spreads out all around the magnet. You can draw a picture of a magnetic field.

SEE: MYSTERIOUS MAGNETISM PAGE 92

You will need

A small magnetic compass
A selection of magnets
Sheets of paper
A pen or pencil

1 Put a magnet in the centre of a sheet of paper. Place the compass near the magnet.

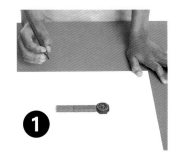

1

2 Draw an arrow showing the direction of the needle on the paper.

3 Keep moving the compass, and drawing lines. This way you will make a picture of the magnet's magnetic field.

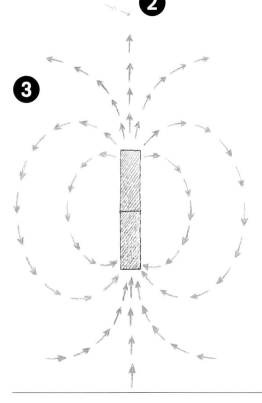

2

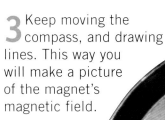

3

Making magnetism

Use a magnet to make another piece of metal magnetic. Remember that this only works for iron-containing objects.

SEE: MAGNETS PAGE 93

You will need

A magnet
Steel paperclips (steel is mostly iron)

1 Pick up a paperclip with the magnet, so the clip hangs down.

2 Can you pick up a second paperclip with the one on the magnet? The first paperclip has been turned into a magnet itself. This effect is called induced magnetism.

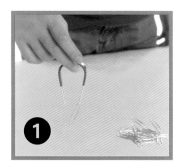

1

2

To set a compass, let the needle swing freely. Turn the compass base so that the needle lines up with North and South on the dial.

DID YOU KNOW?

A compass needle is itself a long, thin magnet. It lines up with the weak magnetic field of the Earth. But this is easily overcome by a nearby proper magnet.

A simple compass

A compass needle is a magnet that always points north-south.

SEE: MAGNETIC
EARTH PAGE 180

You will need

A shallow dish and water
Cork, craft knife
A steel needle
Magnet, magnetic compass
Tape

1 Ask an adult to cut a slice of cork about 5 millimetres thick. Tape the needle to the cork.

2 Stroke the needle many times lengthwise, in the same direction, with the same magnet end.

3 Float the cork on water. Does the needle turn to point north-south? Check using a real compass!

Radio waves

Radio waves are produced when an electric current changes strength or direction. Make your own weak radio waves.

SEE: BEYOND LIGHT PAGE 136

You will need

A radio that can receive AM
Bell wire (thin, insulated wire), scissors
A battery, up to 3 volts

1 Ask an adult to cut a piece of bell wire about a metre long and bare the ends. Turn on the radio and tune it until you cannot hear a radio station, just hiss or hum.

Lay the wire over the radio.

2 Hold one end of the wire on one terminal of the battery. Scratch the other end against the other terminal. Does the radio crackle? This is caused by the changing current in the wire creating very weak radio waves near the radio.

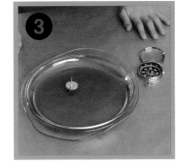

Mobile phones send out and receive very weak radio waves. These are beamed to and from a nearby transmitter, usually just a few miles away.

Make an electromagnet

You can make a magnet that you can switch on and off, using electricity.

SEE: ELECTRICITY AND MAGNETISM PAGE 90

You will need

2 metres of bell wire (thin, insulated wire)
Scissors or craft knife
A large steel nail or screw
Paperclips or other small metal objects
3 or 6 volt battery, tape

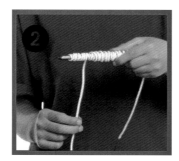

1 Ask an adult to strip about 2 centimetres of plastic covering from each end of the bell wire, to leave the metal wire bare underneath.

2 Starting about 20 centimetres from one end of the wire, wrap it round and round the large steel nail or screw, in a coil. Work up and down until you have about 20 centimetres of wire left.

3 Tape the ends of the wire to the terminals of the battery. Can you pick up paperclips with your electromagnet?

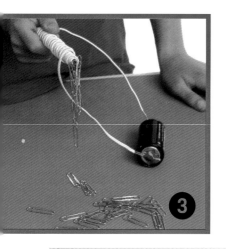

A monorail in Sydney, Australia, avoids the congested streets below to speed people across the city. The train is driven by electric motors.

An electric motor

You can use an electromagnet to make a simple electric motor.

SEE: ELECTRICITY TO MOVEMENT PAGE 96

You will need

Thin dowel
Thin and stiff cardboard
Paper clips, map pins
2 1.5 volt batteries
2 strong bar magnets
2 metres of bell wire (thin, insulated wire)
Kitchen foil
Scissors, glue, tape

2 Unbend two paperclips and tape them to the base, to make supports as shown in the picture below. The dowel should spin freely.

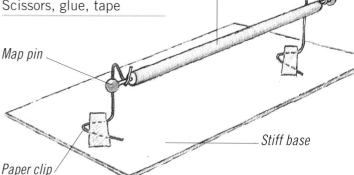

Dowel
Map pin
Paper clip
Stiff base

1 Cut a piece of stiff cardboard 30 x 20 centimetres, for the baseboard. Cut a piece of dowel about 20 centimetres long and push a map pin into each end, leaving about 5 millimetres of pin sticking out.

3 Cut a piece of stiff cardboard 8 x 1 centimetres. Fold it in half and tape it to the centre of the dowel to make a cross shape.

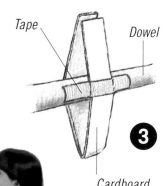

Tape
Dowel
Cardboard taped to dowel

DID YOU KNOW?

"Monorail" means one rail, rather than two, as in a normal train.

Some monorails ride on their single rails. Others hang below the rail.

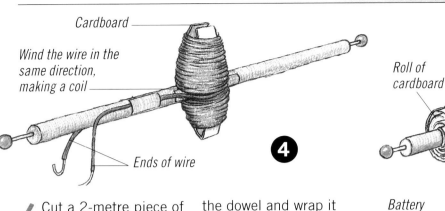

Cardboard

Wind the wire in the same direction, making a coil

Ends of wire

4

Gap lined up with armature

Foil

Roll of cardboard

Tape

6

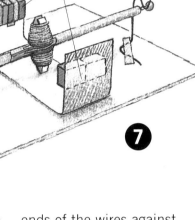

Battery goes here

Hold wires so one touches each piece of foil

Bar magnets

7

4 Cut a 2-metre piece of bell wire and ask an adult to bare about an 2 centimetres of wire at each end. Starting near one end of the wire, wrap it around the card until only a short length is left. Tape the loose ends to the dowel. This coil of wire is called the armature.

5 Cut a strip of thin cardboard 5 x 15 centimetres. Tape one end to

the dowel and wrap it round and round to make a roll or cylinder shape. Tape the end down.

6 Glue two pieces of kitchen foil to the cardboard roll. Leave gaps between them, in line with where the armature sticks out. Tape each wire end to a piece of foil.

7 Tape the magnets to a U-shaped piece of stiff cardboard, with the opposite poles facing each other. Fix this to the baseboard.

8 Cut two pieces of wire, each about 30 centimetres long. Ask an adult to bare about 2 centimetres at each end. Tape one end of each wire to one of the battery terminals. Hold the other

ends of the wires against the foil on opposite sides of the roll, as shown. Electricity flows, makes the wire coil into an electromagnet, and this turns in the magnetic field of the bar magnets

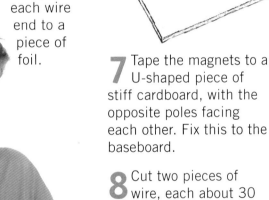

DID YOU KNOW?

Electric motors are very efficient at turning energy into movement. They convert 90 per cent of the electrical energy fed into them into useful movement.

Glossary

Atom
The smallest piece or particle of a chemical element (pure chemical substance) which still has the properties and features of that element.

Aompound
When two or more substances are combined chemically, so that their atoms are joined or bonded to each other.

Dissolving
When one substance, the solute, splits into its individual molecules or atoms and disperses in another substance, the solvent, to form a solution.

Electron
A negatively charged particle that goes around or orbits the nucleus of an atom. Movement of electrons constitutes a discharge or flow of electric current.

Electro-magnetic spectrum
The range of waves or rays which are electromagnetic in nature, being composed of electrical and magnetic forces. It includes radio waves, microwaves, infra-red, visible light, ultra-violet, X-rays and gamma rays.

Element
One of about 112 chemical substances, such as iron, silicon or carbon, that cannot be split chemically into simpler substances. Atoms of an element are all the same as each other, and different from the atoms of all other elements.

Energy
The capacity or ability to do work – to make events happen and cause changes. Energy exists in many forms, including light, heat, electricity, sound, motion and matter or chemicals. When energy is "used" it does not disappear, it is changed into other forms of energy.

Force
Any influence or action that tends to alter the motion of an object, making it slow down, speed up or change direction. It is measured in newtons.

Ion
An atom or group of atoms that has a positive charge (cation) or negative charge (anion).

Leptons
One of the main groups of fundamental or elementary particles. They include electrons and also muons and other particles. (See also quarks.)

Light-year
The distance that light travels in one year, which is 9,460,000 million kilometres.

Matter
Any type of substance, which has mass and can be detected. Most matter is made up of atoms.

Mixture
When two or more substances occur together and are mixed physically, but their atoms are not joined or combined chemically with each other.

Molecule
Two or more atoms linked or bonded together. They may be of the same chemical element, such as a molecule of oxygen gas which has two atoms of oxygen (O_2), or of different chemical elements, such as a molecule of common salt, which has one atom of sodium and one of chlorine (NaCl).

Neutron
A neutral or uncharged particle in the nucleus of an atom.

Pressure
The effect of a force pressing on an object or substance, measured in pascals (newtons per square metre).

Power
The rate of doing work or using energy.

Proton
A positively charged particle in the nucleus of an atom.

Quarks
One of the main groups of fundamental or elementary particles. Different types and combinations of quarks make up particles such as protons and neutrons. (See also leptons.)

Radiation
Energy or particles which are radiated, or beamed

or sent out, from a source.

Reflection

When rays, waves or other forms of energy meet a surface and bounce back again, such as when light rays bounce off a mirror.

Refraction

When rays, waves or other forms of energy bend at an angle as they pass from one substance or medium to another, such as light rays as they pass from air into water.

Solute

A substance (such as sugar) that dissolves in a solvent to form a solution.

Solution

A solute dissolved in a solvent.

Solvent

A substance (such as water) in which a solute dissolves, to form a solution.

Work

A measure of transferring energy which causes an object to move. If the object does not move, then technically, no work has been carried out.

BASIC SCIENTIFIC MEASUREMENTS AND CONVERSIONS

Length
metre *symbol* **m**
Other length units
1 inch (in) = 2.54 cm
1 foot (ft) = 12 in = 0.3048 m
1 yard (yd) = 3 ft = 0.9144 m
1 mile = 5280 ft = 1.61 km

Mass
gram *symbol* **g**
Other mass units
1 ounce (oz) = 28.35 g
1 pound (lb) = 16 oz = 0.45 kg
1 ton (imperial) = 2240 lb = 1016 kg = 1.016 tonnes (metric)

Amount of matter
mole *symbol* **mol**
1 mol contains the same number of atoms as 12 g of carbon-12

Time
second *symbol* **s**
Other time units
60 s = 1 minute
60 minutes = 1 hour
24 hours = 1 day
365.2422 days = 1 year

Temperature
kelvin *symbol* **K**
Other temperature units
°C = kelvin + 273.15
degrees Fahrenheit (°F) = 9/5 degrees Celsius (°C) + 32

Electric current
ampere *symbol* A

Light intensity
candela *symbol* cd

DERIVED MEASUREMENTS

Area
square metres *symbol* m^2
Other area units
1 hectare = 1,000 m^2
1 square foot = 1 sq ft = 144 sq in
1 square yard = 1 sq yd = 9 sq ft
1 acre = 4,840 sq yd

Volume
cubic centimetre
symbol **cc** or **cm^3**
litre *symbol* **l**
cubic metre *symbol* **m^3**
Other volume units
1 pint = 1 pt = 0.568 l
1 gallon = 1 gal = 8 pts = 4.55 l

Density (mass per unit volume)
grams per cubic centimetre
symbol **g/cm^3**

Speed or velocity
(distance moved with time)
kilometres per hour
symbol **km/h**
Other speed units
miles per hour *symbol* **mph**

Acceleration
(change in velocity with time)
metres per second per second
symbol **m/s^2**

Force or Weight
(mass times acceleration)
newtons *symbol* **N** or **kgm/s^2**

Momentum
(mass times speed)
kilograms *x* metres per second
symbol **kgm/s**

Pressure
(force per unit area)
newtons per square metre
symbol **N/m^2**
Other pressure units
1 mm Hg = 133.32 N/m^2
1 atmosphere = 760 mm Hg

Energy
(force times distance moved)
joule *symbol* **J**

Power
(energy used over time)
watt *symbol* **W**

Index

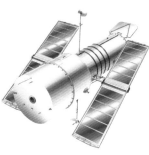
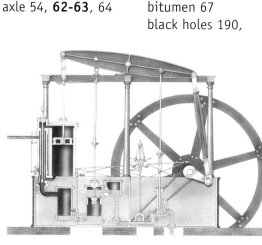

D

E

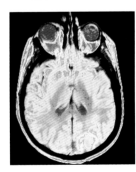

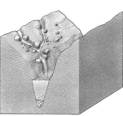

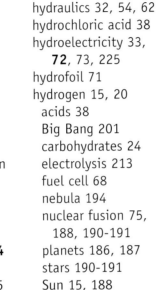

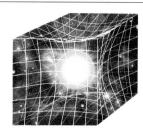

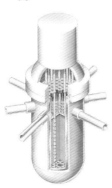
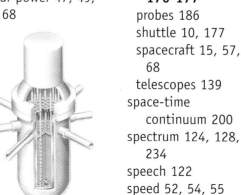

Acknowledgements

Artists
Mike Atkinson
Julian Baker
Julie Banyard
Andy Beckett
Kuo Kang Chen
Contour Publishing
Ron Dixon
Andrew Farmer
Mike Foster/Maltings Partnership
Jeremy Gower
Rob Jakeway
Roger Kent
Aziz Khan
Alan Male
Janos Marffy
Gillian Platt
Terry Riley
Peter Sarson
Mike Saunders
Guy Smith
Roger Smith
Roger Stewart
Techtype
Darrell Warner
Mike White
Alison Winfield

Model Photography
Mike Perry, David Lipson Photography Ltd

Models
Kate Birkett,
Alison Cobb,
Sam Connolly,
Alexander Green,
Jack, Robert and Sally Hutchinson,
Karen Jolly,
Sian Liddell,
April McGhee,
Alice McGhee,
Nicky Maynard,
Ned Miles,
Aaron Phipps,
Joshua Phipps,
Katie Reeve,
Nicholas Seels,
Naomi Tayler,
Chelsea Taylor.

Additional props
Vivienne Bolton and Peter Bull

The publishers would like to thank the following sources for the photographs used in this book:

Page 8 (B/L) Mary Evans Picture Library; Page 17 (T/L) David Parker/Science Photo Library; Page 23 (T/R) Dr. Jeremy Burgess/Science Photo Library; Page 31 (B/L) Pat Spillane at Creative Vision; Page 35 (T) The Stock Market; Page 41 (B/L) The Stock Market; Page 47 (R) Dan McCoy/The Stock Market; Page 50 (B/R) The Stock Market ; Page 51 (T/L) Martin Bond/Science Photo Library; Page 56 (B/R) The Stock Market; Page 60 (T/L) courtesy Capital Shopping Centres plc; Page 62 (T/R) The Stock Market; Page 69 (L) courtesy Honda; Page 73 (T/R) The Stock Market; Page 74 (B/L) courtesy Nuclear Electric plc; Page 75 (B/R) The Stock Market; Page 82 (T/C) courtesy BICC plc; (B/L) Science Photo Library; Page 85 (B/R) Dept. of Clinical Radiology, Salisbury District Hospital/ Science Photo Library; Page 91 (B/L) Taheshi Takahara/Science Photo Library; (B/R) The Stock Market; Page 95 (B/R) Dezo Hoffmann/Rex Features; Page 97 (T/L) James King-Holmes/Science Photo Library; Page 99 (T/R) courtesy National Power; Page 105 (B/R) Peter Menzel/Science Photo Library; Page 106 (T/L) David Parker/Science Photo Library; Page 112 (T/R) Leon Schadeberg/Rex Features; Page 113 (T/R) The Stock Market; Page 115 (B/L) The Stock Market; Page 119 (T/L) The Stock Market; Page 130 (B/L) Omikron/Science Photo Library; Page 131 (C) AKG, London; Page 135 (T/R) Nils Jorgensen/Rex Features; Page 136 (T/R) SIPA/Rex Features; Page 138 (C) The Stock Market; Page 139 (B) The Stock Market; Page 142 (T/L) NASA/Science Photo Library; Page 143 (B/L) Mary Evans Picture Library; Page 145 (B/R) courtesy Eurotunnel; Page 152 (B/L) NOAA/Science Photo Library; Page 153 (C/R) Chris Bonnington Picture Library; Page 155 (B/R) SIPA/Rex Features; Page 158 The Stock Market; Page 161 (T/L) The Stock Market; Page 163 (T/R) Rex Features; Page 167 (L/C) Rex Features; Page 171 (T/L) Rex Features; Page 198 (C) NASA/Rex Features; Page Nina Bermann/Rex Features; Page 185 (T/L) Rex Features, (C) The Stock Market; Page 194 (T/R) SIPA/Rex Features; Page 196 (T/R) NASA; Page 187 (T/C) Mary Evans Picture Library; Page 198 (B/L) Rex Features; Page 199 (T/R) SIPA/Rex Features Page 207 (T/R) Gary Lewis/Stock Market; Page 208/209 (C) The Stock Market; Page 214 (B/L) Stansted Airport Ltd; Page 215 (B/L) Justitz/The Stock Market; Page 218 (B/C) Mike Vines/Photolink; Page 224(T/L) Claude Nuridsany and Maria Perennou; Page 229 (T/R) Susanne Grant; Page 242 (B/R) B. Benjamin/The Stock Market.

All other photographs are from MKP Archives